End of track - Denver South Park & Hilltop

TRACKING

GHOST RAILROADS

IN COLORADO

A Five-part Guide to abandoned and scenic lines

by

Robert M. Ormes

CONTENTS

ISBN 0-937080-01-2

Published by

GREEN LIGHT GRAPHICS

(719) 633-5927
14 Beverly Place
Colorado Springs, Colorado 80903

TRACKING
GHOST RAILROADS
IN COLORADO

Two railroads circled mountain lakes to gain altitude — above, the Rio Grande Southern rounds Trout Lake; below the Denver and Salt Lake spirals Yankee Doodle.

Lake City's Caboose

Along the Animas Canyon to Silverton

A Rio Grande Southern tank near Dolores

INTRODUCTION

THIS BOOK IS A GUIDE for the motorist, jeeper, cyclist or hiker who wants to see what is left of the railroads that chuffed their way across the rising plains and then climbed over the mountain barriers. It is for the buff who when he drives through an old curving cut can still hear the screech of wheels on the rails and the long toot-toot of the train whistle echoing through the canyons.

THE MAPS are related to modern roads and jeep trails so the reader can use them to find and follow the grades. They also show such things as the gauge (standard if unspecified), the year of construction, of abandonment, and of any name changes that took place owing to reorganization. The script includes further guide information, brief historical summaries and a few other facts of interest.

THE EXPLORATIONS began in 1954 with a motor trip through the San Juan, mainly along the Rio Grande Southern, and ended in 1973 with a large but little known lumber railroad known as the Colorado & Southwestern. It has covered all of Colorado, crossed slightly into Wyoming and Utah, and dipped deeply into northern New Mexico. Some of the information is taken from an earlier book *Railroads and the Rockies*, which was put together too hastily and is long since out of print. Other sources are too numerous to mention. Coverage includes some live railroads, mainly of special scenic interest.

RECOMMENDED TRIPS include the following as starters:
1. Live railroads: The Silverton Branch and the Toltec Scenic Railroad - both all day rides behind narrow gauge steam locomotives. (Part V) Manitou and Pikes Peak Cog Railroad, Mount Manitou Incline (cable), and Cripple Creek & Victor Narrow Gauge (Part IV).
2. Grades converted to road without changing character: See Boreas Pass and the approaches to Alpine Tunnel of the Denver South Park & Pacific, the Argentine Central (both in Part III), Trout Lake to Lizard Head Pass on the Rio Grande Southern (Part V), and any combination of the Cripple Creek lines including the CS&CCD (Part IV).
3. Walking trips are many and varied, and most of them have some surprise or other. Notable among these are the north end of the Denver Pacifc and some of the ancient Arkansas Valley (Part I), Temple Canyon and above on the Grape Creek Branch (Part II), the Argentine Central and the two Floresta Branches (Part III) the Yule Creek and Treasure Mountain circle above Marble (Part IV), and Ophir to Vance Junction (Part V).
4. THE COLORADO RAILROAD MUSEUM at 17155 West 44th Avenue in Golden has a large sampling of retired rolling stock and many smaller items of interest. The first part of the collection there came in 1959 from an earlier museum south of Alamosa.

THE DEDICATION is to my family and friends and the many students in a series of Colorado College Railroad Seminars who have shared with me the pleasures of exploring, mapping and photographing, and thus contributed to this book. Thanks go also to those who have let me have photographs: Abby Kernochan, Frank Seely, and the Western History Libraries in Denver.

PART I
THE PRAIRIES

MAPS

The symbol Ⓥ is used ocassionally on the maps to indicate a satisfactory point on a road for finding or viewing grade.

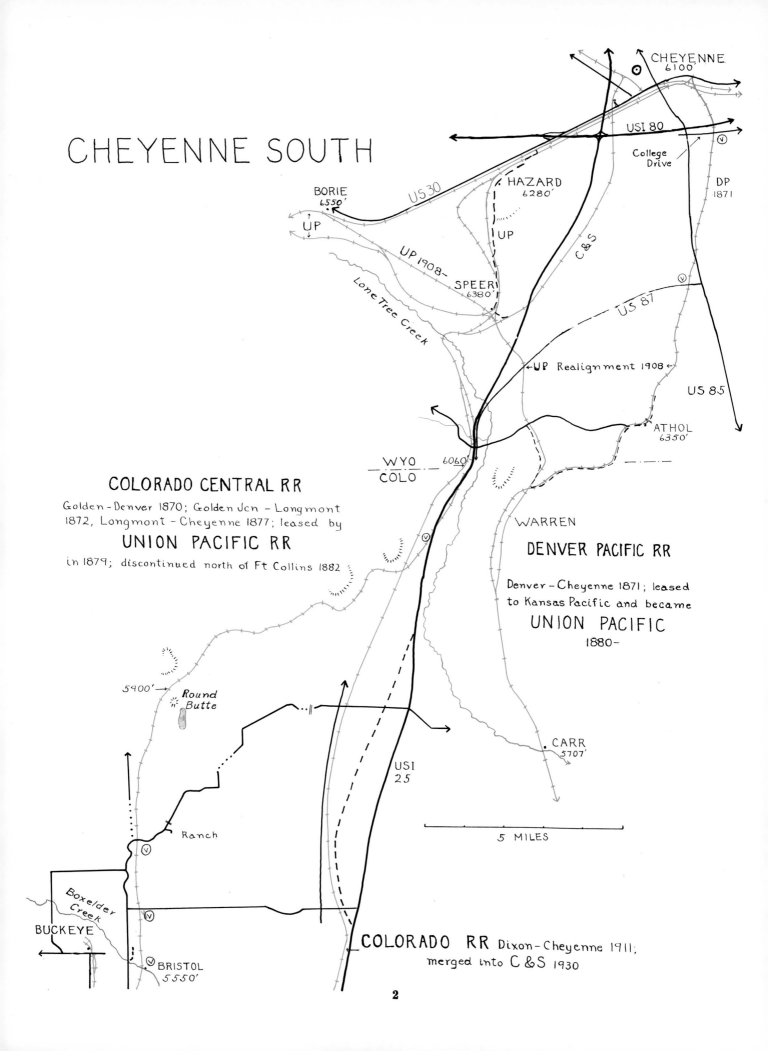

CHEYENNE SOUTH

CHEYENNE
6100

US| 80

College
Drive

DP
1871

HAZARD
6280'

BORIE
6550'

UP

UP

US 30

UP 1908-

SPEER
6380'

Lone Tree Creek

C & S

US 87

←UP Realignment 1908←

US 85

ATHOL
6350'

WYO   6060'
COLO

WARREN

COLORADO CENTRAL RR

Golden-Denver 1870; Golden Jcn – Longmont
1872, Longmont – Cheyenne 1877; leased by

UNION PACIFIC RR

in 1879; discontinued north of Ft Collins 1882

DENVER PACIFIC RR

Denver – Cheyenne 1871; leased
to Kansas Pacific and became

UNION PACIFIC

1880–

5900'

Round
Butte

CARR
5707'

USI
25

5 MILES

Ranch

Boxelder
Creek

BUCKEYE

BRISTOL
5550'

COLORADO RR Dixon-Cheyenne 1911;
merged into C & S 1930

2

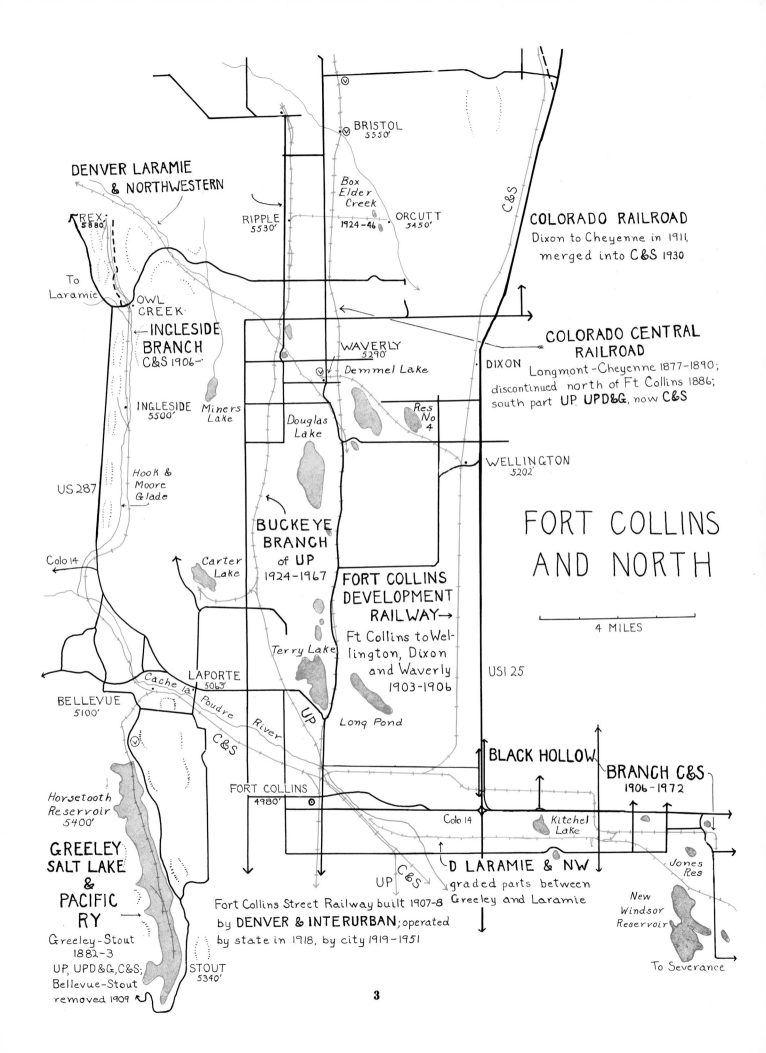

DENVER LARAMIE & NORTHWESTERN

REX 5880'

To Laramie

OWL CREEK

INGLESIDE BRANCH C&S 1906-

INGLESIDE 5500'

Miners Lake

US 287

Hook & Moore Glade

Colo 14

BUCKEYE BRANCH of UP 1924-1967

Carter Lake

LAPORTE 5063'

BELLEVUE 5100'

Cache la Poudre River

C&S

GREELEY SALT LAKE & PACIFIC RY

Horsetooth Reservoir 5400'

Greeley-Stout 1882-3
UP, UPD&G, C&S;
Bellevue-Stout
removed 1909

STOUT 5340'

RIPPLE 5530'

Box Elder Creek 1924-46

ORCUTT 5450'

BRISTOL 5550'

C&S

WAVERLY 5290'

Demmel Lake

Douglas Lake

Terry Lake

Long Pond

FORT COLLINS 4980'

COLORADO RAILROAD

Dixon to Cheyenne in 1911, merged into C&S 1930

COLORADO CENTRAL RAILROAD

Longmont-Cheyenne 1877-1890; discontinued north of Ft Collins 1886; south part UP, UPD&G, now C&S

DIXON

Res No 4

WELLINGTON 5202'

FORT COLLINS AND NORTH

4 MILES

FORT COLLINS DEVELOPMENT RAILWAY →

Ft Collins to Wellington, Dixon and Waverly 1903-1906

UP

US 25

BLACK HOLLOW

BRANCH C&S 1906-1972

Colo 14

Kitchel Lake

UP   C&S

D LARAMIE & NW

graded parts between Greeley and Laramie

Jones Res

New Windsor Reservoir

To Severance

Fort Collins Street Railway built 1907-8 by DENVER & INTERURBAN; operated by state in 1918, by city 1919-1951

NORTH AND EAST FROM DENVER, counting branches and subsidiaries of the major lines, and counting scenic and interurban lines and graded - only lines, there were some thirty ghost railroads. Those most attractive for exploring are the oldest, like the Colorado Central and the Denver Pacific; those least obliterated, such as the side roads from Longmont, Loveland, Lyons and Fort Collins; the scenics at Golden, and the curious Colorado Eastern.

Le Massena's series on *Colorado's Mountain Railroads* and *The Union Pacific in Colorado* by Le Massena and others provide trackage and coprorate histories of most of these lines and they also have illustrations and notes on the locomotives used in the age of steam. The 1913 Historical Railroad Map of the Rocky Mountain Railroad Club is valuable for a general location of the many lines, both operating and defunct.

The COLORADO CENTRAL, first of the state's railroads, has its genealogy explained in full in Overton's 1958 Gulf to the Rockies. It consisted of a narrow gauge line up Clear Creek, and the standard guage line represented in this set of maps - between Denver and Golden and thence north to Cheyenne - as well as a short cut connection between Julesburg, Colorado, on the UP main line, and LaSalle, close south of Greeley on the Denver Pacific. Overton's account of W.A.H. Loveland's activities and Le Massena's of Jay Gould's plays in Northern Colorado are the best way to an understanding of the why's of the main lines there. But to put it briefly Gould got control of the Union Pacific, built the Colorado Central as a main feeder to it at the expense of the Denver Pacific, bought the latter and the Kansas Pacific at depressed prices of which his rate arrangements were the cause, and then sold those two lines to his fellow directors of the UP at a handsome price under the threat of running them as a competitive road. After the UP owned this other route to Denver, there was little use for the northern part of the Colorado Central, or, as Denver grew in relative importance, for a connection between Golden and Cheyenne. Thus, the abandonments of both ends of the standard gauge Colorado Central.

The Colorado Central standard gauge has three segments of ghost railroad, the part from Colorado Central Junction near Broomfield via Boulder, Longmont and Loveland to Fort Collins having been absorbed into present day Colorado and Southern. One of the ghost segments goes north on each side of North Table Mountain, the west one from Golden and the east from Golden Junction or Wanamaker. The east line doesn't seem to be in evidence, but the west one can be followed north from near Golden to 60th Avenue, where it is wiped out by new housing developments. The third segment is very interesting - the one north to Cheyenne from Fort Collins. It is obliterated from Fort Collins to beyond Waverly by farming operations and in part perhaps by the highway, but at the crossing of Box Elder Creek, about 15.5 miles north of the wye north of Fort Collins where the Wellington road splits off from US 287, you can find it. Just beyond the Box Elder bridge there is a little dirt road running southeast along the creek. At .1 mile it turns left up a dry rock fork, which you can follow .3 mile north to lumpy rock outcropping. You can scramble up the east bank on foot and walk east on the flat .2 mile to the grade, which is distinct to both north and south. Some railroad seminar students walked south, crossed Box Elder Creek and found a couple of spikes in a ploughed up section beyond.

One can drive a mile farther north and take the road east, which crosses a less conspicuous part of grade .4 mile east of the N-S road (17.5 from the Wye north of Fort Collins). After a short wiggly section the road ends as a private road into a ranch about .2 mile east. If the rancher is in a happy mood you might

persuade him to let you poke along north on the grade, which lies just east of his house. The ranch runs north to about 4 miles south of the Wyoming line in a strip 4 miles wide - from 1 mile west of the N-S road line to 3 miles east of it. The grade leaves the ranch, and goes through the Meadow Springs Grazing Association land to the east and perhaps into the Soapstone Grazing Association land to the north of that before crossing the present C&S tracks and angling northeast into USI 25 at about mile-post 298, 5.5 miles north of the Carr exit.

CC grade used as a dam just south of Waverly School - 1962.

It appears 1/2 mile farther north on the east side of the highway before swinging back west into interdicted land. It seems doubtful that anyone will turn up grade more than a mile south of Box Elder Creek, although in 1962 I found a stretch serving as a dam to a pond. This was just east of the road north to Waverly at a point 3.6 miles north of where the Wellington road splits off north of Fort Collins. Two spikes just south of the dam line confirmed it as grade.

A crossroad runs west into the most heavily engineered section of the grade, which is near Round Butte, from I-25 at the Carr exit, but it is blocked west of the C&S track and you would need a key and permission to jeep in.

It is possible to find some of the northern end of the line by driving west from Cheyenne on the Otto Road toward Laramie. About 2 miles west of where the Otto underpasses US I-80, a dirt road crosses both tracks to the south and opens up the territory in which the CC made its last climb and curved east into the UP. Much of this pasture line from Bristol north is said to be visible from the air.

The DENVER PACIFIC RAILWAY was the road built north from Denver to the Union Pacific at Cheyenne when it became clear that the Union Pacific would not build the side line to Denver. The first 56 miles was put in operation January 1, 1871, and in October, 1873, the road leased, completed, and began to operate the 27-mile Denver and Boulder Valley, formed in 1870 to run to Boulder from the DP station of Hughes.

The DP went into receivership in April, 1878, and after purchasing control of both this line and the Kansas Pacific, Jay Gould sold both properties to the Union Pacific.

The Denver Pacific trackage in Colorado remains substantially the Union Pacific of today, through Brighton, Greeley and Carr. From about 1 mile south of the state boundary to Cheyenne, however, the present day route swings off to the west of the original, inviting explorers to prowl the old grade. You can find where it leaves the east part of Cheyenne running south by going east from US 85 on College Drive (just south of where 85 crosses USI 80). The DP crosses College Drive 1 mile east of 85: looking north you see where it dissolves into urban changes; to the south it is in fenced property. If you return west to 85 and go south on it about 3.6 miles, the grade comes into and crosses 85. You can follow 87 six miles west to I-25 and a mile south along the east side of the interstate to the Terry Ranch road. By going east here and obtaining permission at the ranch you can drive 4 miles east to the grade at Athol, and follow it. A locked gate prevents driving north on the railroad grade but you can walk it all the way back north to 87 and 85. It is possible to drive from Athol southwest on and beside the grade until it goes into the Union Pacific south of the Colorado line, and then to return northeast to the Athol crossroad on a road that parallels the grade just visited. Members of a 1971 Railroad Seminar group who investigated the DP reported that the grade south from Athol was most interesting, with good cuts and fills, one of the latter 30 feet high, and spikes to be picked up.

A story goes that the spike used by William Evans to celebrate completion of the Denver Pacific was a paper - wrapped iron one, the intended silver spike having disappeared because one Billy Barton who was to produce it had gotten drunk in Georgetown the night before and pawned it.

Walking the abandoned north portion of the Denver Pacific. (Photo by Mark Fox)

The BLACK HOLLOW BRANCH of the C&S taking off from the main line 3 miles east of north Fort Collins, was an agricultural feeder in sugar beet country. It was dismantled by the summer of 1971 except for the first mile or so of trackage at the west end, which was being used at that time for empty freight car space.

One can find the start rather easily and underpass USI-25 with the grade toward Ault and the side roads which cross the grade thereafter. It is quiet out at the terminus.

The BUCKEYE BRANCH of the Union Pacific served as an agricultural line. It was abandoned north of Carter Lake in 1967 and removed shortly afterward. The grade is still very much in evidence along the road to Buckeye and most of the east-west side roads that cross it. The north end, which had three or four terminal tracks angling off to the northwest from the

road corner, is pretty well smothered by current farming activity. I did not find the line east to Orcutt, perhaps because of ploughing.

The COLORADO RAILROAD COMPANY was a separate entity, incorporated in 1906, but was controlled from the start by the Colorado and Southern into which it was officially absorbed in 1930. It was in effect a holding company for three properties of the C&S: the Walsenburg and Western at Walsenburg, 1 1/2 miles, acquired in 1910; the Fort Collins Development Railroad, 19 miles, acquired in 1907; the Silica Branch of the Denver South Park and Pacific, 4 miles narrow gauge; and some other C&S trackage, mainly that connecting Dixon with Cheyenne.

The FORT COLLINS DEVELOPMENT RAILROAD was operated from the start by the C&S. The only abandonment is the piece from Wellington to Waverly. The grade at the Waverly end was visible a few years ago on the west side of the Fort Collins to Waverly highway.

The DENVER LONGMONT AND NORTHWESTERN was organized in 1881. It succeeded through a name change the Longmont and Erie company of 1878. The L&E had built no grade; the DL&Nw graded from Longmont to Mitchell in 1881. In a foreclosure of 1883 the property was acquired by the Colorado Northern Railway Company, which laid the near 10 miles of track, narrow gauge, in 1883. One Billy Boyles wrote the line up in 1952 as the pride of Longmont, where he described the little trains as puffing south over Empson Hill, crossing St. Vrain and later Boulder Creek and then ambling on to Canfield for a load of coal.

The COLORADO NORTHERN, successor of the DL&Nw, was consolidated in 1884 with the Denver Utah and Pacific Rail - Road Company of 1880 to form a new Denver Utah and Pacific Railroad Company, with plans to push west to the Utah line.

A hasty search for grade on this northern section of the DL&Nw - CN turned up nothing but a possibility in a ditch line curving east along the north side of a hill about 3 miles SSE of Longmont. Ploughing and irrigation have certainly done for most of it.

The DENVER UTAH AND PACIFIC, whose incorporators included David Moffat and friends of Denver, was the predecessor of the Denver and Salt Lake Railroad in its in-

The Denver Utah and Pacific cuts through a hill northeast of Broomfield.

5

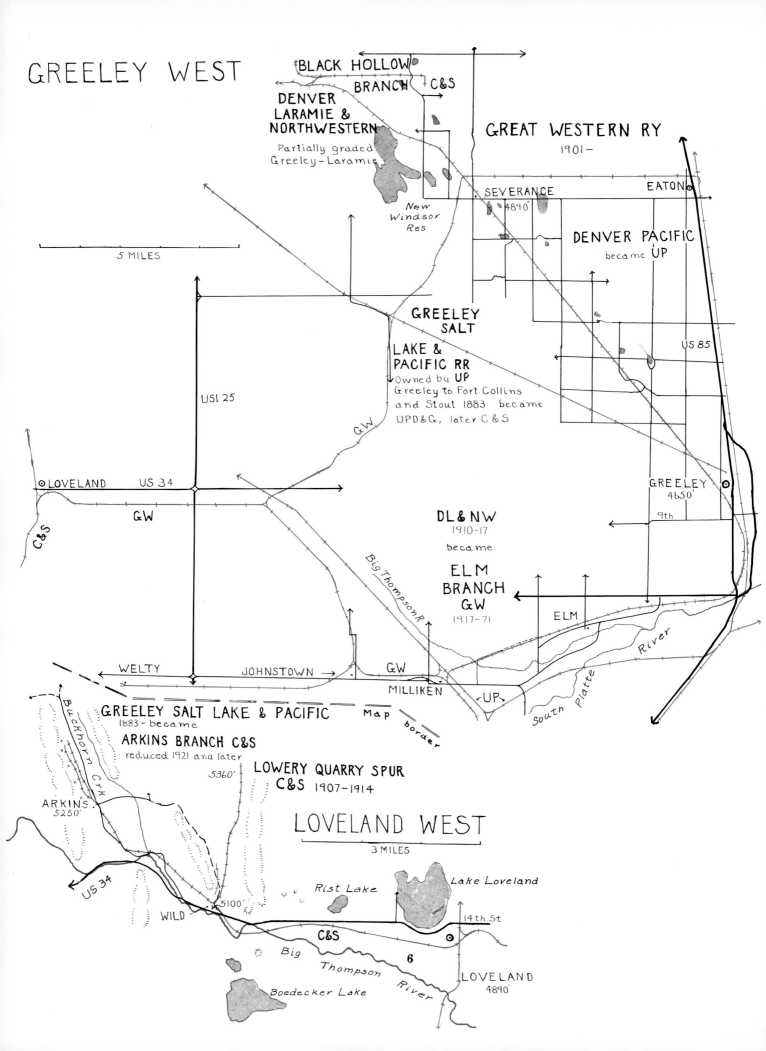

GREELEY WEST

BLACK HOLLOW BRANCH   C&S

DENVER LARAMIE & NORTHWESTERN
Partially graded Greeley–Laramie

New Windsor Res

GREAT WESTERN RY
1901–

SEVERANCE
4890'

EATON

DENVER PACIFIC
became UP

US 85

5 MILES

GREELEY SALT LAKE & PACIFIC RR
Owned by UP
Greeley to Fort Collins and Stout 1883 became UPD&G, later C&S

USI 25

GW

DL & NW
1910–17
became
ELM BRANCH GW
1917–71

GREELEY
4650

9th

LOVELAND   US 34

GW

C&S

Big Thompson R

ELM

WELTY

JOHNSTOWN

GW

MILLIKEN

–UP–

South Platte River

GREELEY SALT LAKE & PACIFIC
1883 – became
ARKINS BRANCH C&S
reduced 1921 and later

5360'

Map border

LOWERY QUARRY SPUR
C&S 1907–1914

ARKINS.
5250'

Buckhorn Crk

LOVELAND WEST

3 MILES

US 34

WILD

5100

Rist Lake

Lake Loveland

14th St

C&S

6

Big Thompson River

Boedecker Lake

LOVELAND
4890'

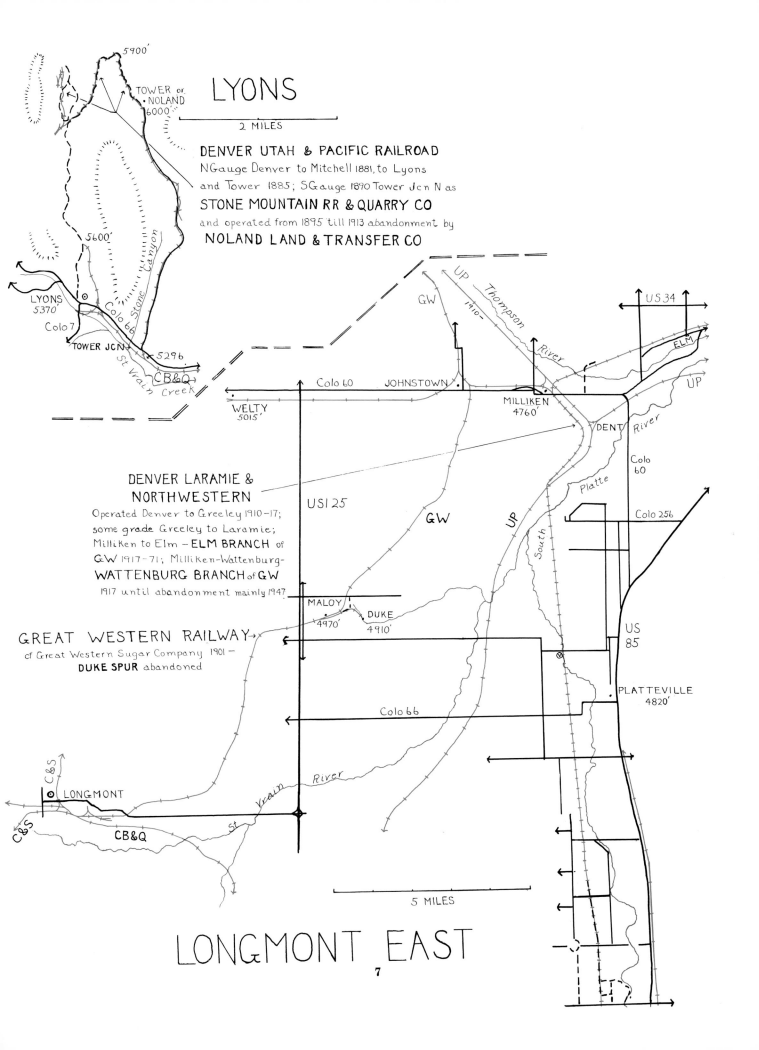

LYONS

2 MILES

DENVER UTAH & PACIFIC RAILROAD
N Gauge Denver to Mitchell 1881, to Lyons
and Tower 1885; S Gauge 1890 Tower Jcn N as
STONE MOUNTAIN RR & QUARRY CO
and operated from 1895 till 1913 abandonment by
NOLAND LAND & TRANSFER CO

5900'

TOWER or
• NOLAND
6000'

5600'

5370'

LYONS
5370'

Colo 7

Colo 66

TOWER JCN

5296

CB&Q

St Vrain Creek

Stone Canyon

UP Thompson River

GW

1910-

US 34

ELM

UP

Colo 60

JOHNSTOWN

MILLIKEN
4760'

DENT

River

WELTY
5015'

Colo 60

DENVER LARAMIE &
NORTHWESTERN
Operated Denver to Greeley 1910-17;
some grade Greeley to Laramie;
Milliken to Elm —**ELM BRANCH** of
GW 1917-71; Milliken-Wattenburg-
WATTENBURG BRANCH of GW
1917 until abandonment mainly 1947

Platte

Colo 256

US 1 25

GW

UP

South

MALOY
4970'

DUKE
4910'

GREAT WESTERN RAILWAY →
of Great Western Sugar Company 1901—
DUKE SPUR abandoned

US
85

PLATTEVILLE
4820'

Colo 66

C&S

C&S

LONGMONT

CB&Q

St Vrain River

5 MILES

C&S

LONGMONT EAST

7

tentions. The company graded main line from Denver west up into upper Boulder Creek drainage. They only railed this western ambition however as far as Hallack Junction and then continued north on a coal branch through old Broomfield to Mitchell. In a consolidation they acquired the Colorado Northern (earlier Denver Longmont and Northwestern) which made them a line to Longmont. This they extended to Lyons with a branch to Tower, to make a re - directed mainline. The Burlington and Missouri (in effect the Burlington) leased the line for the period 1889-1908 and then officially absorbed it. The Burlington standard gauged it in 1889-90, abandoning the narrow gauge route except north of Longmont: for the southern part they acquired trackage rights on the Denver Marshall and Boulder from Utah Junction to Burns Junction. Between Burns Junction and Erie they built their railroad on a Denver Western and Pacific grading purchased from the Union Pacific; from Erie to Longmont they laid track on a new course much farther east than the original.

Trackage north of Canfield is touched on under the Denver Longmont and Northwestern. To the south also this narrow gauge route is not always easy to follow. One presumably sees it on the north side of Colorado 36, 1.5 to 2 miles SSE of Broomfield's exit. Driving north from this exit on US 287 3 miles to Dillon Road, east 1 mile to 120th Street, and north 1/2 mile to a draw, you can walk .2 mile east up the east branch of the draw to the grade, and then follow it north, or south and east into the southeast branch of your same draw. The fill and cut there are worth a look. You can drive to a more northerly section of the grade by following Baseline Road east from Lafayette a mile to a gate just east of the crossing of Rock Creek and taking a road south there. You see evidence of the grade crossing of Rock Creek just west of you, and if you walk on south, it remains visible for a distance. A short spur leads around left (SE) to a mine there: the main line runs south along the stream before making a jog eastward. There is a second grade crossing about .3 mile to the east of Rock Creek, on higher ground. You can drive it north a little way from Baseline Road - until you are blocked by a stream crossing, and you can walk it to the south, starting in thick grass and weeds. Judging from the USGS Lafayette Quadrangle, the grade went down a little east of south from its Baseline Road crossing to a pants-shaped dry pond in the section 7 that is 2 1/2 miles ESE of Lafayette. It may have been a side line to a mine, or possibly an uncompleted through grade.

Ties help identify the Stone Mountain quarry line.

Most interesting of the DU&P is the unironed grading which took off from Hallack Junction for Utah. It is conspicuous a little west of the east entrance to Rocky Flats Plant. You drive on Colo. 128, either east on Colo. 93 or west from Broomfield, turning south on Indiana Avenue to the plant entrance. At about .3 miles west of Indiana, where the grade crosses the Flats road, you see a stretch coming up from the east and winding toward a cut a half mile north. The cut is also visible from 128 (120th Avenue). Some more of this grade can be seen from 93 as you drive north from the plant's west entrance and look west. The Denver Northwestern and Pacific (later Denver and Salt Lake) which fell heir to this ambition, used what is now the Denver and Rio Grande route, turning into the mountains three or four miles farther south.

The STONE MOUNTAIN RAILROAD AND QUARRY COMPANY was organized in 1890 to quarry and bring out the red sandstone north of Lyons. One can drive up to about where it U-bends to the south, the upper part on the old grade, and then proceed on foot to visit the quarry area to the west.

Great Western hauled sugar beets behind this curious saddle-tank locomotive. (Western History Collection - Denver Public Library)

The DENVER LARAMIE AND NORTHWESTERN was opened in 1910 with 56 miles of track - the first 3 miles from Denver to Utah Junction on the Denver and Salt Lake, a mile on the Greeley Terminal, and 52 miles of its own between these end segments, which ran by way of Wattenburg and Elm. Parts of it were graded from Greeley northwest through Severance and Fort Collins all the way to Laramie. There is said to be grade visible in places between Fort Collins and Laramie, but little if anything is left of the line between Greeley and Fort Collins, where reservoirs, irrigation and ploughing have taken over.

The finished part of the line north of Wattenburg became the property of the Great Western, the sugar company's railroad, but the tracks south of Wattenburg came out at the same time (1917). A little of this grade is visible along the west side of the South Platte both to the north and to the south of Colorado 7.

The GREAT WESTERN RAILROAD was incorporated by Great Western Sugar in 1901. In 1905 the company merged with several other sugar producers and by 1908 was operating 50 miles of railroad with five locomotives. Lines connected Johnstown with Longmont, Loveland and Milliken (Hillsboro), and

Windsor with Eaton. Though primarily a sugar beet railroad it registered over 125,000 passenger miles in 1919. In 1917 it acquired the Wattenburg - to - Greeley end of the Denver Laramie and Northwestern. The 28 miles south of Milliken became the Wattenburg Branch, abandoned some time after 1944; northeast of Milliken the first 5 miles became the Elm Branch, and the remainder from Elm to Greeley was removed.

One sees a nice bit of the Wattenburg Branch by taking a road west from the north end of Platteville which cuts across the grade close west of the river. Other sections of fill along the same side of the river look more like a flood levee, possibly super - imposed on the old grade. At little Wattenburg, 3 miles south of Fort Lupton and 2 north of the sugar factory at Brighton, you can see grade running north from the east side of town. Just south of Milliken you find the start of this Wattenburg Branch with an old car or two in an advanced state of decay.

In 1970 this bridge survived Great Westerns Elm Branch.

The half-mile spur to Duke began at the double - track and siding labeled Maloy. Going off I-25 at the Mead exit and north a mile on the frontage road, east on gravel 1 mile, then off right .1 mile, you come to Maloy. The Duke line, not here visible, ran off southeast into lower swampy ground where one can find some remnants on foot.

The Elm Branch ran ENE 4 1/2 miles along the Platte Valley. From a mile west of the UP track at Milliken you can drive north across the river to the grade and follow it on one side or the other pretty well to the end. There was a good trestle at mile 2.3 from Milliken in 1970. Rails were gone beyond mile 2.7 and were to be all taken out shortly.

The INGLESIDE BRANCH of the C&S was built to serve Great Western Sugar's Ingleside Quarry. The north end, Owl Creek to Rex, is accessible from US 287 at Owl Creek, about 18 miles north of Fort Collins. The little spur at Owl Creek is dead, but there seemed in 1971 to be intermittent activity on the line. The rails, which must bear heavy loads of stone, are spiked only minimally but are held in place mainly by rail anchors of heavy iron split at the top and bent around the rail base like a claw. These were driven vertically into the ground between ties. The side road which takes you north from Owl Creek to the end crosses some rough draw bottoms passable only by high-clearance cars.

The DENVER WESTERN AND PACIFIC RAILWAY

COMPANY was formed in 1880 by men from the East. Colorado and Southern records show that 6 segments of construction were started in 1881: 4 1/2 miles from Longmont toward Denver, 11 miles between Burns Junction and Erie, 1 mile in Left Hand Canon, 2 miles in St. Vrain Canon, 2 miles from Erie toward Longmont, and the 15 1/2 miles from Erie to Denver and Intermountain Junction. This last piece was placed in operation in 1886 by the Denver Marshall and Boulder. The DW&P went into receivership in 1882 and was purchased by the DM&B in 1885. The ambitious DW&P incorporation papers describe 5 plans, running all over the West and Southwest to the Pacific.

Very little of the grade north of Erie can be seen: there is probably a cut of it at the west side of Panama Reservoir No. 1, and a fill a mile south of there.

The CHICAGO BURLINGTON AND QUINCY RAILROAD came into Colorado as the Burlington and Missouri, reaching Denver in May of 1882. Five years later, mistaking Colorado for an agricultural paradise (or hoping others would do so) they developed the line from Midland to Cheyenne with stations at ten-mile intervals which is now in process of dissolution. Mr. C.L. Stanely of Keota remembers one well-filled passenger train in 61 years and a sheep train or two. Wheat has occasionally prospered the line even recently, but no mail and no passengers have gone over it in the last 20 years.

The ARKINS BRANCH of the C&S, originally Greeley Salt Lake and Pacific, was built to a red sandstone quarry area. To see it you drive 6 miles west on Loveland's Main Street on US 34; instead of crossing the Big Thompson you take a right up the side valley.

The LOWERY QUARRY SPUR, also C&S, turns off north from 34 a mile short of the Arkins Branch entrance. In February of 1971 there was a gate marked no trespassing but unlocked, and it was possible to see the lower end of the grade even under snow. Though the spur is supposed to have come out in 1914, there has been very recent operation of the lower end.

The GREELEY SALT LAKE AND PACIFIC was a Union Pacific controlled railroad in three segments: the long line from Greeley through Fort Collins to Stout, and the original of the

Looking north along Arkins Branch.

9

BROOMFIELD TO LONGMONT AND EAST

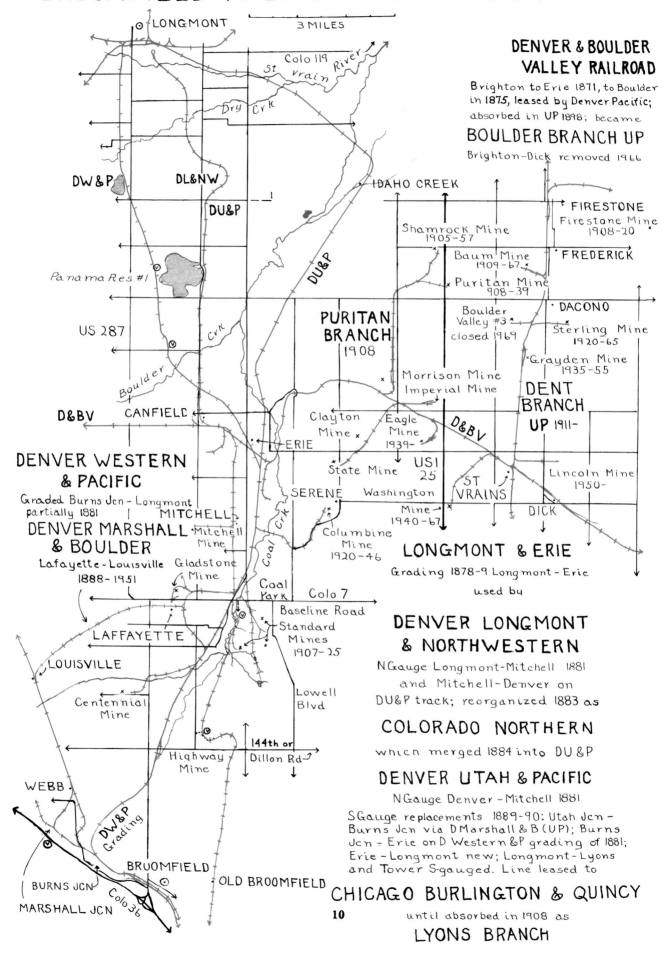

LONGMONT

3 MILES

Colo 119

St Vrain River

Dry Crk

DW&P

DL&NW

DU&P

IDAHO CREEK

Panama Res #1

US 287

Boulder Crk

PURITAN
BRANCH
1908

DU&P

Shamrock Mine
1905-57

Baum Mine
1909-67

Puritan Mine
908-39

Boulder
Valley #3
closed 1969

Morrison Mine
Imperial Mine

Clayton
Mine

Eagle
Mine
1939-

State Mine

Washington

D&BV

USI
25

D&BV   CANFIELD

ERIE

DENVER WESTERN
& PACIFIC

Graded Burns Jcn - Longmont
partially 1881

DENVER MARSHALL
& BOULDER

Lafayette - Louisville
1888-1951

MITCHELL

Mitchell
Mine

SERENE

Gladstone
Mine

Columbine
Mine
1920-46

Coal Crk

Coal
Park

Colo 7

Baseline Road

Standard
Mines
1907-25

LAFFAYETTE

LOUISVILLE

Centennial
Mine

Highway
Mine

144th or
Dillon Rd

Lowell
Blvd

WEBB

DW&P
Grading

BROOMFIELD

OLD BROOMFIELD

BURNS JCN

MARSHALL JCN

Colo 36

DENVER & BOULDER
VALLEY RAILROAD

Brighton to Erie 1871, to Boulder
in 1875, leased by Denver Pacific;
absorbed in UP 1898; became

BOULDER BRANCH UP

Brighton - Dick removed 1966

FIRESTONE
Firestone Mine
1908-20

FREDERICK

DACONO

Sterling Mine
1920-65

Grayden Mine
1935-55

DENT
BRANCH
UP 1911-

Lincoln Mine
1950-

ST
VRAINS

Mine
1940-67

DICK

LONGMONT & ERIE

Grading 1878-9 Longmont - Erie
used by

DENVER LONGMONT
& NORTHWESTERN

N Gauge Longmont - Mitchell 1881
and Mitchell - Denver on
DU&P track; reorganized 1883 as

COLORADO NORTHERN

which merged 1884 into DU&P

DENVER UTAH & PACIFIC

N Gauge Denver - Mitchell 1881

S Gauge replacements 1889-90: Utah Jcn -
Burns Jcn via D Marshall & B (UP); Burns
Jcn - Erie on D Western & P grading of 1881;
Erie - Longmont new; Longmont - Lyons
and Tower S-gauged. Line leased to

CHICAGO BURLINGTON & QUINCY

10

until absorbed in 1908 as

LYONS BRANCH

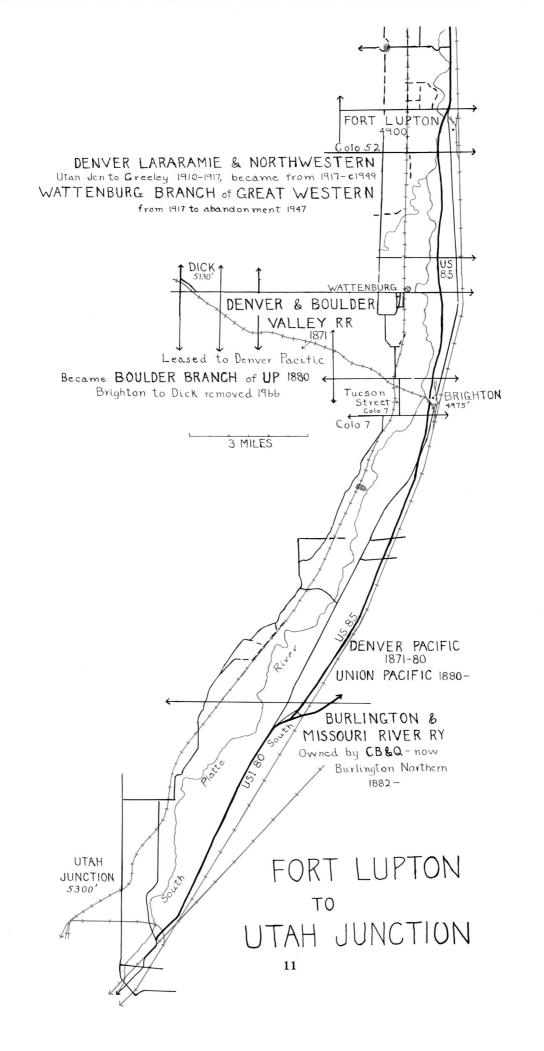

FORT LUPTON
4900

Colo 52

DENVER LARARAMIE & NORTHWESTERN
Utah Jcn to Greeley 1910-1917, became from 1917-c.1949
WATTENBURG BRANCH of GREAT WESTERN
from 1917 to abandonment 1947

US
85

DICK
5130'

WATTENBURG

DENVER & BOULDER
VALLEY RR
1871

Leased to Denver Pacific

Became BOULDER BRANCH of UP 1880
Brighton to Dick removed 1966

Tucson
Street
Colo 7

Colo 7

BRIGHTON
4975'

3 MILES

River

US 85

DENVER PACIFIC
1871-80
UNION PACIFIC 1880-

Platte

US 80 South

BURLINGTON &
MISSOURI RIVER RY
Owned by CB&Q - now
Burlington Northern
1882 -

South

UTAH
JUNCTION
5300'

FORT LUPTON
TO
UTAH JUNCTION

11

A Greeley Salt Lake and Pacific train reflects Union Pacific ownership: the cars are Colorado Central, the locomotive South Park (Denver Public Library).

Arkins Branch out of Loveland, both standard gauge, and the narrow gauge Boulder west to Sunset with its 66 bridges. All were connected by Union Pacific trackage. The first is in use from Greeley through Fort Collins to Bellevue on the Ingleside Branch. The second, the Arkins Branch, was continued into the late ..0's under C&S. The third was replaced after an 1894 flood had washed it out, by the Colorado and Northwestern, which constructed a higher and safer roadbed and continued the line beyond Sunset in two directions - to Ward and to Eldora.

The line to Stout ends beneath the surface of Horsetooth Reservoir, but beginning 1/2 mile north of the dam and continuing north for .2 mile there is a stretch of grade parallel to the road and 50 yards west of it. A mile north of the dam the grade reappears immediately west of the road and angles off through a deep cut in a northerly direction farther west. You can climb the fence and walk through the cut and along the grade in the field beyond. If you find a spike you are lucky. I spent nearly an hour extracting one from a pitch pine fence post with the help of the car jack and some soft rocks which broke up when used as hammers.

The UNION PACIFIC has operated on its own and through subsidiary companies since the beginning of railroading in the state. Robert Le Massena's *Union Pacific in Colorado* gives the best brief account of these lines. In addition to those covered here under the Colorado Central, Greeley Salt Lake and Pacific, etc., there was considerable trackage in the northern Colorado coal spurs off both the main north-south line and the old Denver and Boulder Valley. Most of these have been excepted from the coverage of this book.

The DENVER MARSHALL AND BOULDER RAILWAY COMPANY was formed in May of 1885 to acquire the Denver Western and Pacific Railway, a five - year - old corporation with little more than some franchises. The DM&Boulder ran the line from Argo Junction, just north of Denver, to Boulder by way of Marshall, which opened in 1886 under Union Pacific and supplanted the older route to Boulder and northward which the Colorado Central had built. Besides this 27-mile line the road built in 1888 from Louisville to Lafayette, a 3-mile track. The railroad's purpose on incorporation was to continue to Longmont and Greeley and from a point on this line over the Rocky Mountains to the west line of the state. As a Union Pacific road it offered a more direct route to Boulder from Denver than did the Colorado Central. In the 1890 consolidation it became part of the UPD&Gulf. The CB&Q branch line to Lyons from Denver made use of 11 miles of this railroad north from Argo Junction to Burns Junction.

Some of the Louisville - Lafayette grade can be seen from roads that cross it, and the other abandoned part, between Boulder and Coalton, is visible both as you drive along Colo. 36 and if you drive from Boulder south on 93 to Marshall and there turn east.

The DENVER AND BOULDER VALLEY RAILROAD, running west from the old Denver Pacific line at Brighton (then called Hughes) made it to coal mines in 1873 and the next year to Boulder. It came into the UP province through being leased to the Denver Pacific, the latter having been organized by about the same Denver group - John Evans, W.N. Byers, Cheesman and others.

The abandoned east end can be traced if you drive west from Fort Lupton on Colorado 7 and take the first road north after crossing the Platte (Tucson Street), after a mile turn east on 128th Avenue, north on 21 Road; west on 4 Road, north on 15 Road, etc., so as to catch the railroad as it angles WNW. Lines to the various mines are not fully covered here. One that interested me was the old State Mine, for which one goes west on 8 Road and south from it on 5 Road. Railroad is not visible in the mine area but can be found a mile or so to the northwest. It rates as one of the longest of the area's coal spurs and perhaps one of the first abandoned.

The GOLDEN BOULDER AND CARIBOU was incorporated and built late in 1877 from Boulder to the Marshall Coal Bank. The corporate intention was a railroad from Golden to Boulder to Caribou, with branches to coal banks. David Moffat, the original owner, sold the road to the Kansas Pacific, and when that road came to the Union Pacific by 1880, the latter operated the railroad in connection with the Colorado Central. The UP reports the trackage in 1887 as 3.22 miles.

A map of the grade indicates it went through a little pond north of Marshall. Any fragments remaining would be on the coal banks, which are high and dry.

The DENVER AND INTERURBAN RAILROAD, which was owned by the C&S, ran NNE from Denver and then west to Argo, paralleled the C&S (earlier Denver Marshall and Boulder) to Burns Junction. It continued into Boulder on a loop route which was electrified for the purpose, using both that line and the present C&S line into Boulder from Burns Junction through Louisville. This line also included the side road in to Eldorado Springs, known as the Eldorado Springs Railway, and the street car system in Fort Collins which was to have been connected to the rest of the Interurban.

Some evidence of the grade remained three years ago on the line to Eldorado Springs as well as on the Denver Marshall and Boulder route.

The LOOKOUT MOUNTAIN FUNICULAR begins near the first left elbow of the Lookout Mountain Road, which leaves Golden as 19th Street and crosses US 6. West of US 6 you keep left. There are two stone pillars to mark the side road to the terminus, but as the ground is posted the visitor should either obtain permission, find a route in to the upper part of the grade, or wait for a foggy day. The top of the mountain belonged to Rees Vidler. The Vidler name appears on various clear Creek mining projects and his incline railway was probably built from ore earnings. It was very profitable, but only until a road permitted the influx of automobiles to get up Lookout Mountain an easier way. This line — like the Mount Manitou Incline at Manitou Springs, had two cars hung on the ends of a cable so that one goes up while the other comes down. There were three rails except for a passing stretch in the middle. Cars carried 100 passengers each.

The CASTLE ROCK SCENIC RAILWAY, on the west corner of South Table Mountain at Golden remains a conspicuous scar as seen from the start of Jefferson County Road 93, in the northwest part of town. You drive the two - block diagonal road from the corner of East and 13th Streets, and park with permission at the end. It makes a short steep trail climb. This line was built by one Charles Quaintance, who "owned the mountain" and sold burrow rides to the top. When Lookout Mountain Funicular proved a success, he put in his cable line and added a dance hall at the upper end.

The DENVER AND MIDDLE PARK RAILROAD COMPANY was incorporated in the spring of 1883 and became along with the Greeley Salt Lake and Pacific and the Georgetown Breckenridge and Leadville a part of the Union Pacific owned system in Colorado, on which McMechen says the Union Pacific spent over $2 million. This company surveyed for a railroad over Berthoud Pass in its first year, and in 1884 built the 4 1/2 miles between Ralston and Glencoe. It was a 3 - foot - gauge line. The original purpose was to build from Denver via Ralston Creek (no further route details) to Hot Sulphur Springs in Middle Park.

Coal from Leyden on the Denver & Northwestern (Colorado State Historical Society).

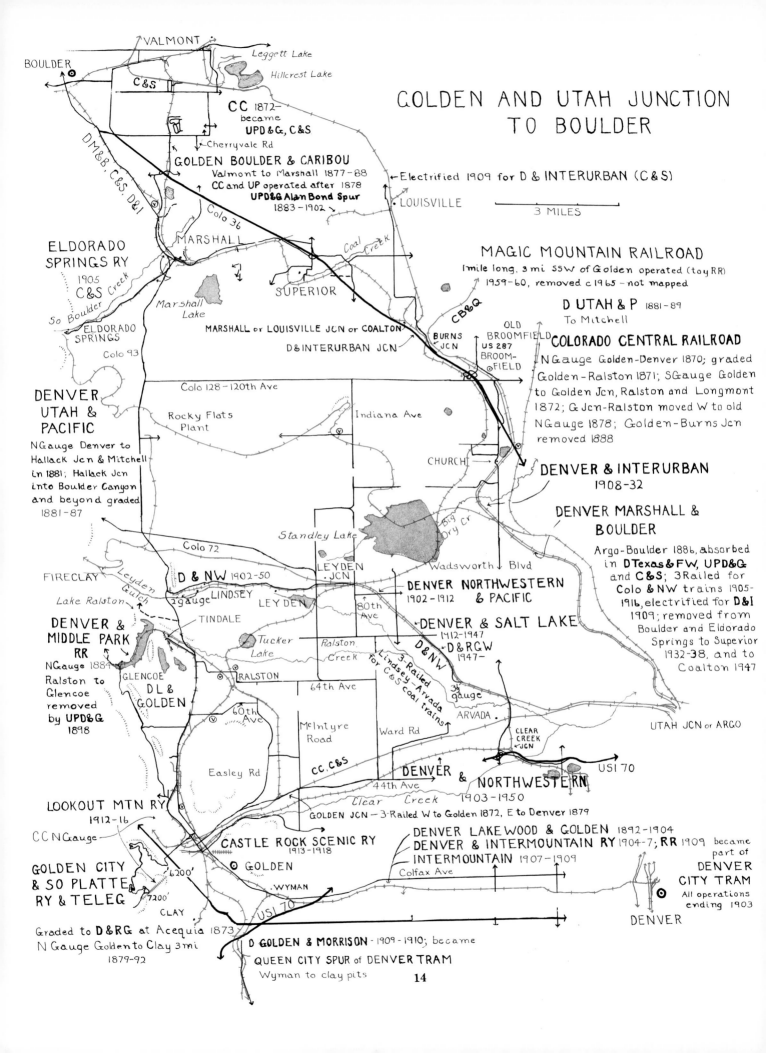

GOLDEN AND UTAH JUNCTION TO BOULDER

VALMONT

BOULDER

C&S

Leggett Lake

Hillcrest Lake

CC 1872—became
UPD&G, C&S

← Cherryvale Rd

GOLDEN BOULDER & CARIBOU
Valmont to Marshall 1877-88
CC and UP operated after 1878
UPD&G Alan Bond Spur
1883-1902 →

←Electrified 1909 for D & INTERURBAN (C&S)

· LOUISVILLE

3 MILES

DM&B, C&S, D&I

Colo 36

MARSHALL

Coal Creek

SUPERIOR

MAGIC MOUNTAIN RAILROAD
1mile long, 3 mi SSW of Golden operated (toy RR)
1959-60, removed c 1965 - not mapped

ELDORADO
SPRINGS RY
1905
C&S

So Boulder Creek

Marshall Lake

ELDORADO
SPRINGS

Colo 93

MARSHALL or LOUISVILLE JCN or COALTON
D&INTERURBAN JCN

CB&Q

BURNS JCN

OLD
BROOMFIELD
US 287
BROOM-FIELD

D UTAH & P 1881-89
To Mitchell

COLORADO CENTRAL RAILROAD
N Gauge Golden-Denver 1870; graded
Golden-Ralston 1871; S Gauge Golden
to Golden Jcn, Ralston and Longmont
1872; G Jcn-Ralston moved W to old
N Gauge 1878; Golden-Burns Jcn
removed 1888

DENVER
UTAH &
PACIFIC
N Gauge Denver to
Hallack Jcn & Mitchell
in 1881; Hallack Jcn
into Boulder Canyon
and beyond graded
1881-87

Colo 128 - 120th Ave

Rocky Flats
Plant

Indiana Ave

CHURCH

DENVER & INTERURBAN
1908-32

DENVER MARSHALL &
BOULDER

Argo-Boulder 1886, absorbed
in D Texas & FW, UPD&G
and C&S; 3Railed for
Colo & NW trains 1905-
1916, electrified for D&I
1909; removed from
Boulder and Eldorado
Springs to Superior
1932-38, and to
Coalton 1947

Colo 72

FIRECLAY

Leyden Gulch

Lake Ralston

D & NW 1902-50
2 gauge LINDSEY

LINDALE

DENVER &
MIDDLE PARK
RR
N Gauge 1884
Ralston to
Glencoe
removed
by UPD&G
1898

GLENCOE

DL &
GOLDEN

60th Ave

Easley Rd

Standley Lake

LEYDEN
JCN

LEYDEN

80th Ave

Tucker
Lake

RALSTON

64th Ave

Ralston
Creek

McIntyre
Road

CC, C&S

Big Dry Cr

Wadsworth Blvd

DENVER NORTHWESTERN
& PACIFIC
1902-1912

DENVER & SALT LAKE
1912-1947
D&RGW
1947-

3-Railed
for C&S coal trains

D&NW

3½ gauge

ARVADA ·

UTAH JCN or ARGO

CLEAR
CREEK
JCN

US I 70

Ward Rd

LOOKOUT MTN RY
1912-16

CC N Gauge

GOLDEN CITY
& SO PLATTE
RY & TELEG

Graded to D&RG at Acequia 1873
N Gauge Golden to Clay 3mi
1879-92

44th Ave

Clear   Creek

GOLDEN JCN — 3-Railed W to Golden 1872, E to Denver 1879

CASTLE ROCK SCENIC RY
1913-1918

6200'

⊙ GOLDEN

7200'

CLAY

· WYMAN

US I 70

D GOLDEN & MORRISON - 1909-1910; became
QUEEN CITY SPUR of DENVER TRAM
Wyman to clay pits

DENVER &
NORTHWESTERN
1903-1950

DENVER LAKEWOOD & GOLDEN 1892-1904
DENVER & INTERMOUNTAIN RY 1904-7; RR 1909 became
INTERMOUNTAIN 1907-1909   part of

Colfax Ave

DENVER
CITY TRAM
All operations
ending 1903

DENVER

14

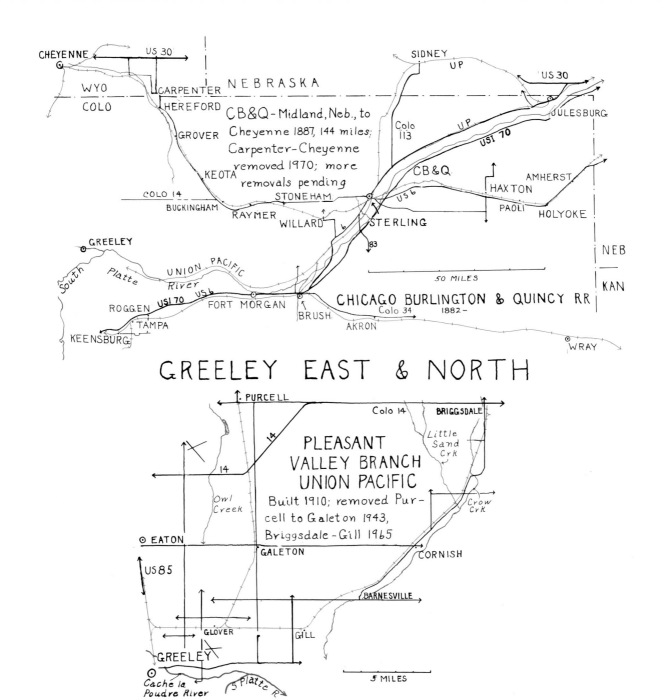

CHEYENNE

US 30

WYO
COLO

CARPENTER

HEREFORD

GROVER

KEOTA

COLO 14

BUCKINGHAM

RAYMER

NEBRASKA

SIDNEY

UP

US 30

JULESBURG

Colo 113

UP

USI 70

CB&Q

AMHERST

HAXTON

PAOLI

HOLYOKE

NEB

KAN

CB&Q - Midland, Neb., to Cheyenne 1887, 144 miles; Carpenter-Cheyenne removed 1970; more removals pending

STONEHAM

WILLARD

STERLING

US6

6

83

GREELEY

South Platte

UNION PACIFIC River

USI 70   US6

ROGGEN

FORT MORGAN

BRUSH

Colo 34

AKRON

50 MILES

CHICAGO BURLINGTON & QUINCY RR   1882-

TAMPA

KEENSBURG

WRAY

GREELEY EAST & NORTH

PURCELL

Colo 14

BRIGGSDALE

14

Little Sand Crk

14

Owl Creek

Crow Crk

PLEASANT VALLEY BRANCH UNION PACIFIC

Built 1910; removed Purcell to Galeton 1943, Briggsdale-Gill 1965

EATON

GALETON

CORNISH

US 85

BARNESVILLE

GLOVER

GILL

GREELEY

Cache la Poudre River

S Platte R

5 MILES

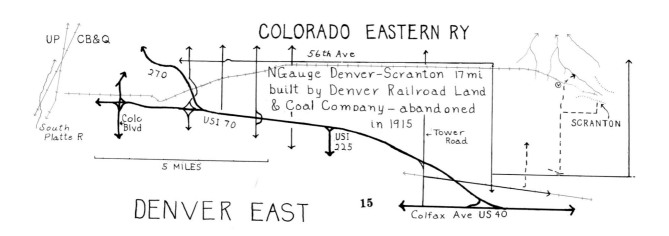

UP   CB&Q

COLORADO EASTERN RY

56th Ave

270

South Platte R

Colo Blvd

USI 70

N Gauge Denver-Scranton 17 mi built by Denver Railroad Land & Coal Company - abandoned in 1915

USI 225

Tower Road

SCRANTON

5 MILES

DENVER EAST

15

Colfax Ave US 40

It affected a connection between Ralston and a coal mine at Glencoe, 4 miles west. Some seminar students found a little of the line in 1970, and though the upper end is submerged there was evidence above water of the works for which it was built.

The DENVER AND NORTHWESTERN was a curious mixture of a coal railroad and an interurban, organized by Moffat, Evans, and others. The primary line ran from the Denver Tramway's coal-fed electric power plant on the Platte River in Denver to the coal mines at Leyden, with a branch added to Golden. The west end, consisting of a mile of 2-foot gauge track west of Leyden, comes into Colorado 93 about 8 miles north of Golden, and you can find a good deal of the rest by taking the road east from there down Leyden Gulch.

Denver's spacious Union Station. (Harold Seely collection)

The GOLDEN CITY AND SOUTH PLATTE RAILWAY AND TELEGRAPH COMPANY was set up for incorporation on December 30, 1871, but not filed until the next April. It was part of the Loveland plan for leaving Denver in the center of a railroad vacuum. The main line was to be the 16 miles from Golden to the D&RG tracks at Littleton, and a branch to and up Bear Creek to its headwaters in the main range. A considerable part of the grade was built before a realignment of forces and the 1873 panic caused shelving of the project.

The company ironed the northernmost mile of their planned railroad six years later and extended it 2 more miles to some clay pits to the SSW. One might find some evidence down there of this going end of the affair.

The DENVER LAKEWOOD AND GOLDEN, which built and operated a steam railroad from Denver to Barnum in 1893, was the first of the interurbans of the Denver area. The main line, which subsequently became Intermountain, and then as electric railroad the Denver and Intermountain, soon afterward went west from Denver to Golden and north from there to coal mining west of Ralston. It became part of the Denver Tram system, and since 1953, when electric service was discontinued, has become the Associated Railroad, in service from Denver yards to the Federal Center, which it reaches by a south extension. The history of this and other interurbans is told succinctly in Volume I of Le Massena's series on *Colorado's Mountain Railroads.*

The grade line west from the Federal Center is generally traceable south of Colfax Avenue.

The COLORADO EASTERN RAILROAD went out from Denver to a low-grade coal mine, reportedly on 18 and 21 pound rails, but it achieved importance as a property because of valuable land holdings in Denver. For a report on it, including some merriment, see Charles S. Ryland's *The Colorado Eastern.*

While there may be traces of it left closely paralleling 56th Avenue, the coal terminus is the part to see. Take USI 70 east from Denver to Tower Road, exit south .2 mile, turn east and go under I-70 (and the Union Pacific tracks). Then take the first road north for 2 miles, go east along a fence. When stopped by another fence turn north and drive and walk about .3 mile to the grade. You can walk WNW along it, but to the east, where Scranton was, there seems to be nothing left. The only evidence even of coal was a little pile a badger had brought up out of his hole. On our walk west we were startled to see a herd of some 30 antelope that wheeled back and forth in a mixture of fear and curiosity. There were three gates involved, the first of which was marked "No trespassing." One should seek permission for this tour from the farmhouse half a mile east of the first north turn. It is on the north side of the east-west road.

The LEHIGH BRANCH of the D&RG was unknown to me until I noticed it among abandonments in a D&RG Profile Book given me by Mr. Jackson Thode of that company. I found then that it was shown on the Colorado Railroad Club's Hotchkiss map. After an abortive try from Louviers and then from farther north which ended with a trip along the Silica Branch of the C&S, I found Lehigh Gulch on the Kassler Quadrangle. This showed the way in, which was to drive to Sedalia and south across both railroad tracks, and then straight west. The road turns north to a farmhouse to end. There you should ask permission to walk over the hill west about a mile. The grade, which follows Lehigh Gulch, appears in part as two separate lines, the older having been washed out and replaced. After visiting the mine area, which was less littered than most of them are, we took a shortcut down the draw bottom, in which recent washing has produced a deep steep-sided gully. We saw there some exposed skeletal parts of animals which were too high to reach from the bottom. These call for investigation too.

The CASTLE ROCK QUARRY SPURS and the quarries they served are covered historically in an article by Mr. and Mrs. James R. Harvey in the May 1946 *Colorado Magazine.* Quarrying began, we learn, when Silas Madge, whose farm was 2 miles south of Castle Rock, sent some of the light colored stone which caps several mesas in the vicinity to be assayed in Denver. He was told there was no precious metal in the rock, a rhyolite from a lava flow, but that it had excellent qualities for building. He took some stone out as early as 1872, and by 1881 a 2.6 mile spur went in to his quarry from Douglas on the D&RG. Shortly afterwards 1000 carloads of his stone went to Colorado Springs to build Palmer's Antlers Hotel.

The O'Brien Quarry soon attracted another D&RG line up Sellar's Creek. The Santa Fe Quarry was the last on the scene and the last to wind up operations, which were most of the time managed by a powerful Swede named Gus Nelson. The Harvey story includes a list of the major buildings from Castle Rock stone.

To visit the O'Brien and Madge you turn south in Castle Rock .3 mile east of the town's central traffic light. Some remnants of grade are visible along the road, and you can see about where the first camp was at Hathaway and where the steeper grade of the tramline left the railroad. There is a no-trespassing sign to stop you from going up the mesa on the west side, but I heard that permission to go up the grade could be had for the asking. A little short of this point, at 3.5 miles from where you turned south in town, a road runs off to the west and climbs Madge Mesa. You can see signs of the work done up there and then at the bottom of the hill walk off down the grade for a mile or so. The Santa Fe Quarry shows little of its mile of railroad except the curve where it left the main line, but the mesa top is a curious place to visit and takes no great length of time.

The COLORADO-KANSAS RAILWAY COMPANY was chartered in April, 1911, as successor to the Kansas-Colorado Railroad. Credited in the 1920 Poor's Manual with 1 locomotive, 1 passenger car, and 16 freight cars, it ran between Pueblo and Stone City 22 miles to the northwest. The corportion was dissolved in 1934, but the Colorado Railroad, Inc., was formed to reopen it. The name Kansas belongs to the venture because in its earlier incorporation in 1908 as the Kansas-Colorado the line is described as running through several Kansas counties and into Colorado as far west as Canon City. Dismantling took place in the summer of 1958.

The BP&N tank was the town standpipe for many years after its railroad duties ended.

A visit to Castle Rock's Madge Quarry.

The railroad served to bring out both stone and fireclay from the Stone City area, much of it to go farther than Pueblo on Santa Fe and Missouri Pacific tracks. There are remains of a processing plant on the north side of Booth Creek. In 1971 you could find beginnings of the railroad on both sides of US 50 a mile west of where 50 crosses the AT&SF tracks, but Pueblo West has obliterated most of that end of the line not fenced off from access. By driving 19 miles farther west on 50 and then north, you can explore things at the Stone City end, either by entering the Fort Carson property - the gate is sometimes open - or by driving around the to the Beaver Creek Ranch. From the latter you can walk to the west end of the track, and with permission from the ranch owners you can also see the unironed grade that was built on the east side of Turkey Creek. According to old timers who were associated with the road, this grade represented an early intention to go farther north on the line of the Lytle Road, east of Booth Mountain - perhaps all the way to Cripple Creek. There is a very impressive fill where a spur from this line went across Beaver Creek into Stone City.

The PUEBLO AND ARKANSAS VALLEY was the Santa Fe subsidiary which built the 148 mile line from Granada to Pueblo in 1876 and the 98 miles from La Junta through Trinidad to the New Mexico line in 1878, acing out through the latter move the D&RG's plan and effort to cross Raton Pass

from Trinidad. The P&AV also built the extension from Pueblo to Florence and later Canon City, and together with the Canon City and San Juan which is absorbed, the grade and trackage through the Royal Gorge constructed there during the Royal Gorge War of 1877-80. The same instrument of the Santa Fe was used through a restatement of purpose in 1878 that included the building of railroad within Colorado that paralleled all existing lines of the Denver and Rio Grande.

The grade of this abandonment, Pueblo to Canon City, is not everywhere very accessible and is perhaps less interesting to pursue than is its place in paper railroad history.

The BEAVER PENROSE AND NORTHERN RAILWAY was incorporated in January of 1909 and built from Beaver on the D&RG east of Florence to Penrose by the first of June. The papers express an intention to go on to Oro Junta, junction point for Canon City on the Florence and Cripple Creek, but track ended three - or four-tenths of a mile beyond the Penrose water tank, making it a 6½ mile road with 1½ miles in sidings. Poor's of 1914 shows it as operating with one locomotive and one combination car. It was almost totally owned by the Beaver Land and Irrigation Company. The Poor's report shows 1365 passengers carried for 8190 passenger miles and 676,031 ton miles of freight for 1914, with the result of a small operating deficit. Mr. Charles Tutt, who succeeded Spencer Penrose as its president, informed me that it never ran profitably.

Few people remember the railroad, but the water tower supplied the town of Penrose into the 60's. Much of the grade can be traced: the least molested parts are those reached by driving the little side road west from S Road, and by following the grade from US 50 south to near Beaver.

The PORTLAND CEMENT COMPANY RAILROAD was not separately incorporated or dignified by any official name I know of. In the process of trying to check out the Beaver Penrose and Northern I found a piece of grade parallel and very close north of US 50 about .2 to .4 mile west of the access road to Colo. 120 from the eastern end of the Penrose streets and roads. I thought this was part of the BP&N till I found it crossed that at right angles. I then decided it must be part of the Santa Fe's abandoned line to Canon City, but found it had strayed much too far from the river. Then I knew it must be the projected west extenson of the Colorado Kansas Railroad to Stone City - a most interesting discovery since no one seemed to know the in-

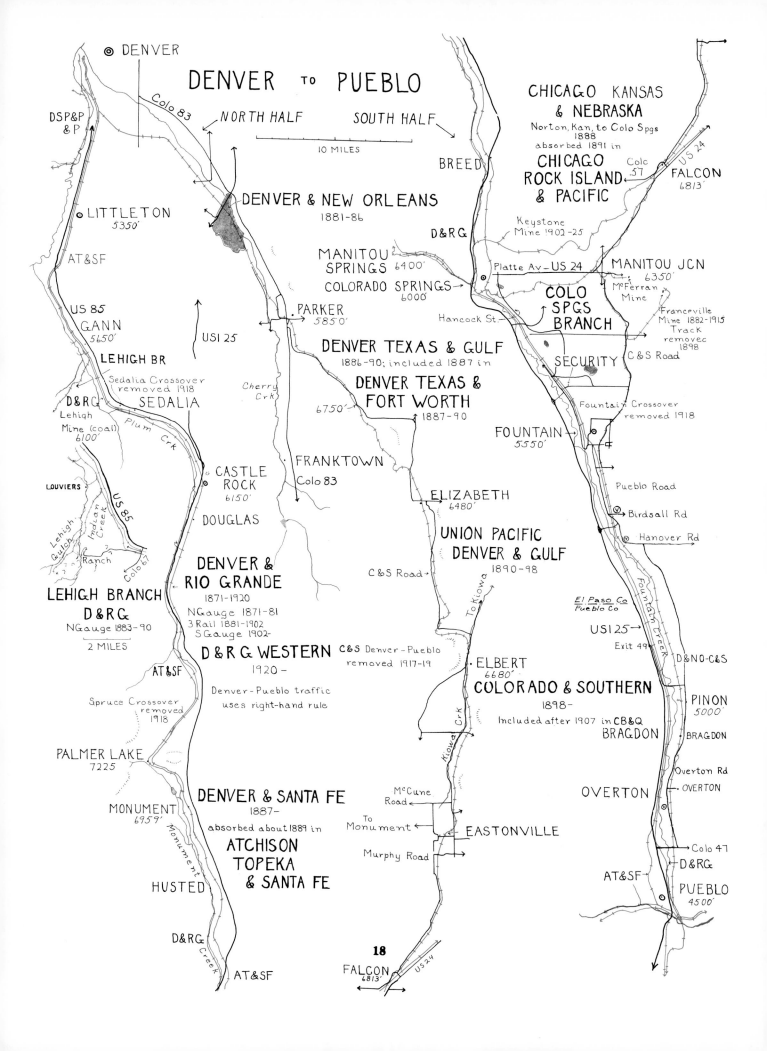

DENVER TO PUEBLO

NORTH HALF   SOUTH HALF

10 MILES

DENVER

DSP&P&P

Colo 83

LITTLETON
5350'

AT&SF

US 85

GANN
5650'

LEHIGH BR

Sedalia Crossover
removed 1918

D&RG   SEDALIA

Lehigh
Mine (coal)
6100'

Plum Crk

LOUVIERS

US 85

Lehigh Gulch

Indian Creek

Ranch   Colo 67

LEHIGH BRANCH
D&RG
N Gauge 1883-90
2 MILES

CASTLE
ROCK
6150'

DOUGLAS

DENVER &
RIO GRANDE
1871-1920
N Gauge 1871-81
3 Rail 1881-1902
S Gauge 1902-

D&RG WESTERN
1920-

Denver-Pueblo traffic
uses right-hand rule

AT&SF

Spruce Crossover
removed 1918

PALMER LAKE
7225

MONUMENT
6959'

Monument

DENVER & SANTA FE
1887-

absorbed about 1889 in

ATCHISON
TOPEKA
& SANTA FE

HUSTED

Monument Creek

D&RG

AT&SF

DENVER & NEW ORLEANS
1881-86

USI 25

Cherry Crk

PARKER
5850'

DENVER TEXAS & GULF
1886-90; included 1887 in

DENVER TEXAS &
FORT WORTH
6750'   1887-90

FRANKTOWN
Colo 83

ELIZABETH
6480'

UNION PACIFIC
DENVER & GULF
1890-98

C&S Road

C&S Denver-Pueblo
removed 1917-19

ELBERT
6680'

COLORADO & SOUTHERN
1898-

Included after 1907 in CB&Q

To Kiowa

Kiowa Crk

McCune
Road

To
Monument

Murphy Road

EASTONVILLE

18

FALCON
6813'   US 24

BREED

CHICAGO KANSAS
& NEBRASKA
Norton, Kan, to Colo Spgs
1888
absorbed 1891 in

CHICAGO
ROCK ISLAND
& PACIFIC

D&RG

Keystone
Mine 1902-25

Colo 57

FALCON
6813'

US 24

MANITOU
SPRINGS 6400'

COLORADO SPRINGS
6000'

Platte Av - US 24

MANITOU JCN
6350'

McFerran
Mine

Hancock St

COLO
SPGS
BRANCH

Franceville
Mine 1882-1915
Track
removed
1898

SECURITY

C&S Road

Fountain Crossover
removed 1918

FOUNTAIN
5550'

Pueblo Road

Birdsall Rd

Hanover Rd

El Paso Co
Pueblo Co

Fountain Creek

US 25

Exit 49

D&NO-C&S

PINON
5000'

BRAGDON

BRAGDON

Overton Rd

OVERTON

OVERTON

Colo 47

D&RG

AT&SF

PUEBLO
4500'

CASTLE ROCK QUARRIES

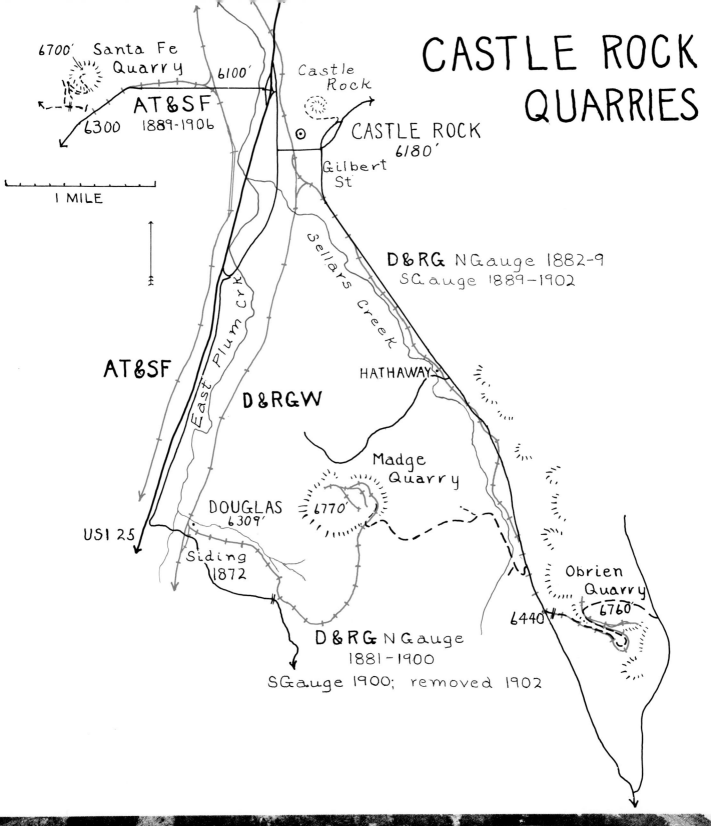

6700' Santa Fe Quarry

6100'

AT&SF 1889-1906

6300

Castle Rock

⊙

CASTLE ROCK 6180'

Gilbert St

D&RG N Gauge 1882-9
S Gauge 1889-1902

1 MILE

AT&SF

East Plum Crk

Sellars Creek

D&RGW

HATHAWAY

Madge Quarry

6770'

DOUGLAS 6309'

Siding 1872

Obrien Quarry

6760'

6440'

D&RG N Gauge 1881-1900
S Gauge 1900; removed 1902

US 25

Ties and substation ready for the Canon City & Royal Gorge at mile 6½   (Courtesy Fred Merriam, Sr.)

19

B P & N Trains came north through Penrose, then west to the tank

Pinons in the background indicate this Colorado Kansas train was near its Stone City terminus

The little 0-4-0 that hauled limestone from a Beaver Creek Quarry to Portland; the car is labeled Nebraska Cement Company (Photo courtesy Henry Cozad).

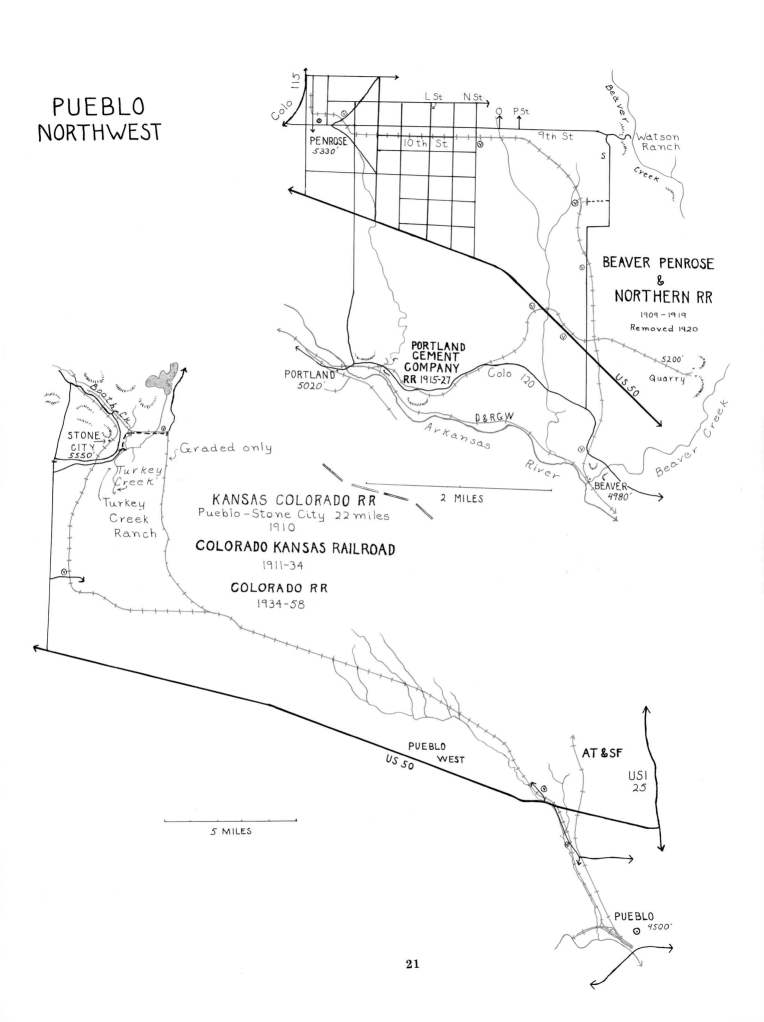

PUEBLO
NORTHWEST

Colo 115

L St   N St

O   P St

PENROSE
5330'

10th St

9th St

S

Beaver

Watson
Ranch

Creek

BEAVER PENROSE
&
NORTHERN RR
1909-1919
Removed 1920

5200'
Quarry

PORTLAND
CEMENT
COMPANY
RR 1915-27

PORTLAND
5020'

Colo 120

US 50

D&RGW

Arkansas

River

Beaver Creek

BEAVER
4980'

Booth Ck

STONE
CITY
5550'

Graded only

Turkey
Creek

Turkey
Creek
Ranch

KANSAS COLORADO RR
Pueblo-Stone City 22 miles
1910

COLORADO KANSAS RAILROAD
1911-34

COLORADO RR
1934-58

2 MILES

PUEBLO
US 50   WEST

AT & SF

US I
25

5 MILES

PUEBLO
4500'

21

tention to extend had been carried out. Finally I walked it out, ended up at Portland, and afterward inquired by mail.

Mr. Springman of the Ideal Cement Company confirmed that it had been their line to a limestone quarry in Beaver Creek. With his help I learned through Mr. Henry Cozad of Wetmore that the railroad began operations about 1915 with a small saddle tank 0-4-0. As this locomotive could only push 4 cars up the heavy grades, the company changed in a couple of years to a 2-6-0 obtained from the D&RG. At the time of the closing in 1927 they were operating with a 600 class Rio Grande engine.

The first cement was made along the Arkansas here in 1898. 1908 saw two companies - the Colorado Portland at Concrete, and the Portland. With Boettcher president of both, the Colorado Portland disappeared. The Ideal Cement Company, active by 1910, bought the Portland and the US Portland (another company in the area) and in 1948 built the ten million dollar plant at Portland.

Except for a section in the field south of US 50, all the grade is conspicuously easy to find, starting at the stretch beside 50 and working both ways. Since this is low country with heat and rattlers, a winter excursion is recommended.

The FLORENCE AND CRIPPLE CREEK RAILROAD COMPANY built the first railroad into Cripple Creek, the narrow - gauge line up Phantom Canon from Florence. The 40-mile main line had a life of 18 years-from 1894 until 1912-with the roadbed inside the gold district used a good deal longer by the surviving interests. Cafky finds that David Moffat, though not an incorporator, was the main push behind this project, which was launched on April 17, 1893, after successful negotiations for the road up Eight-mile Creek in Phantom Canon. James A. McCandless, Florence citizen who had helped to push through the Florence and Cripple Creek Free Road the year before, was one whose name appeared on the charter document; others were from Leadville and Denver. The narrow-gauge plan was a natural one since the D&RG running through Florence was still double-gauged and could take F&CC cars on to Pueblo.

This plan followed an abortive one drawn up by Florence men in 1892 under the name of the Florence Cripple Creek and State Line.

This wreck took place in 1894 - the crowd is from nearby Victor. (State Historical Society)

High dry air keeps this stretch of F&CC grade in good condition.

The first line in the canon was laid without due regard for flash floods — much of it on the earlier road, with low bridges substituted for the fords. Cafky believes the two tunnels bored through were intended as part of a permanent alignment which was planned from the start to replace the first one. In the second summer of operation, an August flood washed out much of the stretch of track between the "Narrows," where confining cliffs forced the road to round one of the bends on a trestle built over the watercourse, and the lower end of Phantom Canon, where Eight-mile Creek debouched on to the plain. The lower 3 miles of this stretch was lifted higher above the water to a second grading that was only slightly less temporary than the first. The upper 6 miles was slanted up the sidewall at a steady 4 percent, which made it relatively flood-proof. The initial cost of $800,000 was increased to about $1,000,000 with this reconstruction.

The road enjoyed the prosperity of increasing traffic up through 1899 and built in that year a 2-mile branch just north of Florence to some new reduction mills there, and the separately incorporated Canon City and Cripple Creek Railroad from Canon City to Oro Junta on the main line. Along with its former rival, the Midland, the F&CC and this Canon City line were taken over at the end of 1899 by the Denver and Southwestern Railway Company. After the competition with the new and shorter standard-gauge CS&CCD brought about the rate war of 1902, this holding company lost out to a successor one, the Cripple Creek Central, whose management was local.

After 1900, Colorado Springs gradually replaced Florence as a milling capital, and by 1910 the lucrative downhill ore traffic dwindled, and with it the varnish service fell off from three passenger trains a day to one mixed. There were coal shipments into the camp through most of the period since coal was used for local ore processing as well as heating. But by 1911 the main source of revenue was from moving ore within the camp. Loads from the mines on the narrow-gauge line were shoveled into standard-gauge cars at Walker Transfer and Bull Hill. This traffic went down to Colorado Springs on the Short Line, now owned and operated in harmony with the older Cripple Creek roads by the C&S. In 1911, the F&CC leased the Short Line so that all three properties could be managed in complete coordination.

In the summer of 1912 a second flood, more devastating than the first, gathered up a 30-foot wall of water, roared down Pahntom Canon and left the lower 5 miles of that sector three-fourths extensively damaged and one-fourth entirely missing. The Carlton interests did not have $150,000 worth of use for this line south out of the district, and when Canon City sued to force them to rebuild it, they first offered to give it away for a motor road, and then when Canon City pressed the suit, dissolved the F&CC company. This move took place three years after the flood, and the dismantling of all the line south of Victor was begun. Trackage within the district was conveyed to the Golden Circle, a leased subsidiary also owned by the Carltons' holding company. The Golden Circle was succeeded in name by the Cripple Creek and Colorado Springs. In 1917 the last named company dismantled the remaining F&CC track from Victor to Cripple Creek, broadened the old Golden Circle track from Victor up to Vista Grande, and sold the narrow-gauge rolling stock remaining from the F&CC.

The F&CC was called the String Line because its windings resemble those of a dropped string.

The above information is largely from Morris Cafky's *Rails Around Gold Hill*, printed in 1955 for the Rocky Mountain Railroad Club by World Press of Denver. The script is good reading and well illustrated, and though now a rare book it is available in the major Colorado libraries. As the map shows, one drives the grade almost all the way from 1.5 miles north of US 50 to Cripple Creek on the very scenic but sometimes rough and dusty Phantom Canyon Road and the blacktop of Colorado 67.

The CANON CITY AND CRIPPLE CREEK RAILROAD COMPANY was formed in 1898 when Denver men injected a little capital as well as some restraint into the several plans to connect the two towns. The company let a contract in August for a 7-mile track from Canon City northeast across Fourmile Creek to Oro Junction, at mile-post 7 on the Florence and Cripple Creek.

The Canon City & Cripple Creek Railroad was raising sizeable trees in 1962.

The plans included a line to Westcliffe which was never started. Considerable passenger traffic and some freight went over this line to Florence's rival town. The east end of it, skirting the mountain base among gray rocks and pinon trees, makes a pleasant cool weather walk, starting with a scramble across the ravine of the creek.

The COAL SPURS OF CANON CITY AND FLORENCE played a heavy role in early railroad history. General Palmer's success as a railroad man came from his investments in advance of the railroad in townsite and coal lands, from Colorado Springs to Alamosa and Durango, and from the Colorado piedmont and western slope to the great coal holdings in Utah. Labran or Florence was an early asset of the highest importance, supplying large tonnage to his Colorado Coal and Iron Company, predecessor of the CF&I at Pueblo, to Denver and the other railroads there, and to the Cripple Creek District and Colorado Springs, to Westcliffe and to Leadville. This strength had its accompanying weakness, which seemed, particularly during the Royal Gorge War, to be more important and was at least more spectacular. In putting his station in South Pueblo, where he had the land that was to be used for his iron works, instead of in Pueblo; in refusing to take the railroad into Canon City from Florence and in to Trinidad from El Moro, he created the enemies who helped the rival Santa Fe to get ahead of him on Raton Pass and in the "Grand Canyon" of the Arkansas.

Like the D&RG the Santa Fe built their railroad first to Florence and later to Canon City. *The Canon City Record* under Doc Little's editing has published numerous articles about the region's railroads and coal camps, but a full story of the coal camps there has yet to be written. It would certainly start with the fact that Florence contained the seeds of what destroyed steam railroading: the second oldest oil well in the United States, and the oldest well still producing, the latter having been sunk 1205 feet in 1882.

The earliest important mine was one in Coal Creek, goal of the D&RG's Labran Branch. One Jesse Frazer had hauled coal from there to Canon City in 1860. Coal Creek was already large when it was incorporated in 1889. Opera stars and stock company casts had registered in its hotel. There was a bad fire in 1907, but the branch was not abandoned until 1913 nor removed until 1924.

I am indebted to the *Canon City Record,* to Rosemae Campbell's 1972 history of Fremont County, *From Trappers to Tourists;* and to two students from Florence - Dean and Dani MacBeth, for most of the statements about the area. Mrs. Campbell for example tells how Florence became a conventions town for burros that were pensioned from the mines.

Williamsburg, platted by Henry and Willard Teller, was the center for a dozen or so of mines, an important one that of the Rocky Mountain Fuel Company. Rockvale was platted by Benjamin Rockafellow and friends who organized the Canon City Coal Company in 1880. C.C. Osgood of the CF&I and Victor American Fuel Companies bought the mines there in 1896 and held them until 1903, when the Rockafeller interests stepped into the area. (Their absentee ownership was reflected in the mine labor troubles of 1904). Mines stretched out in this region: one could walk underground from the Coal Creek Mine to Rockvale to the Fremont Mine in Bear Gulch. Rockvale still has its railroad line but the Fremont was damaged by fire and flood in 1921 and the machinery came out in 1927.

The Victor American set up the Radiant Mine - later the Pyrolite - which produced 500 tons daily in its active period. This camp was closed until the depression, when it became a CCC camp known as Kenwood. W.D. Corley of Colorado Springs bought coal land farther south up the hill and in 1945 extended track from the Santa Fe Branch to Kenwood. When he had asked the Santa Fe people to haul some equipment up to him they replied that they had permission to abandon the line. Because they were required to offer it for sale to any interested party on the route, he was able to buy it in. His extension to the Corley Mine was built with rails from the Pueblo street car system and operated with a war surplus Union Pacific switch

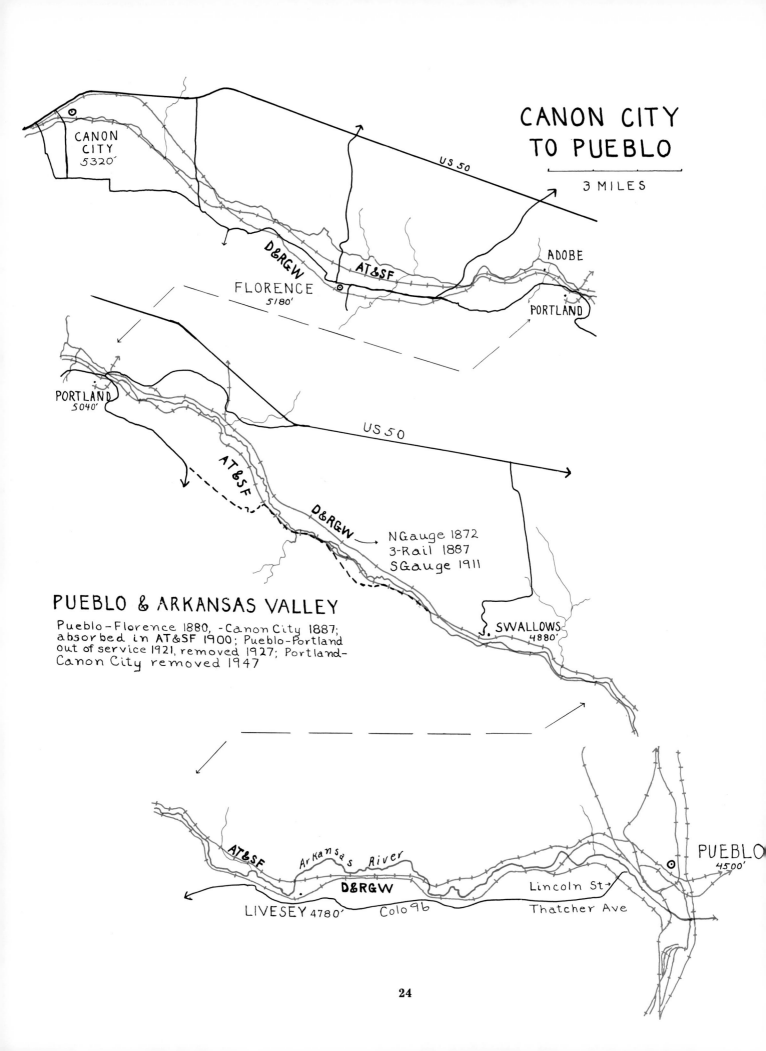

CANON CITY
TO PUEBLO

3 MILES

CANON
CITY
5320'

US 50

D&RGW

AT&SF

FLORENCE
5180'

ADOBE

PORTLAND

PORTLAND
5040'

US 50

AT&SF

D&RGW

N Gauge 1872
3-Rail 1887
S Gauge 1911

SWALLOWS
4880'

PUEBLO & ARKANSAS VALLEY

Pueblo-Florence 1880, -Canon City 1887;
absorbed in AT&SF 1900; Pueblo-Portland
out of service 1921, removed 1927; Portland-
Canon City removed 1947

AT&SF

Arkansas River

D&RGW

LIVESEY 4780'

Colo 96

Lincoln St→

Thatcher Ave

PUEBLO
4500'

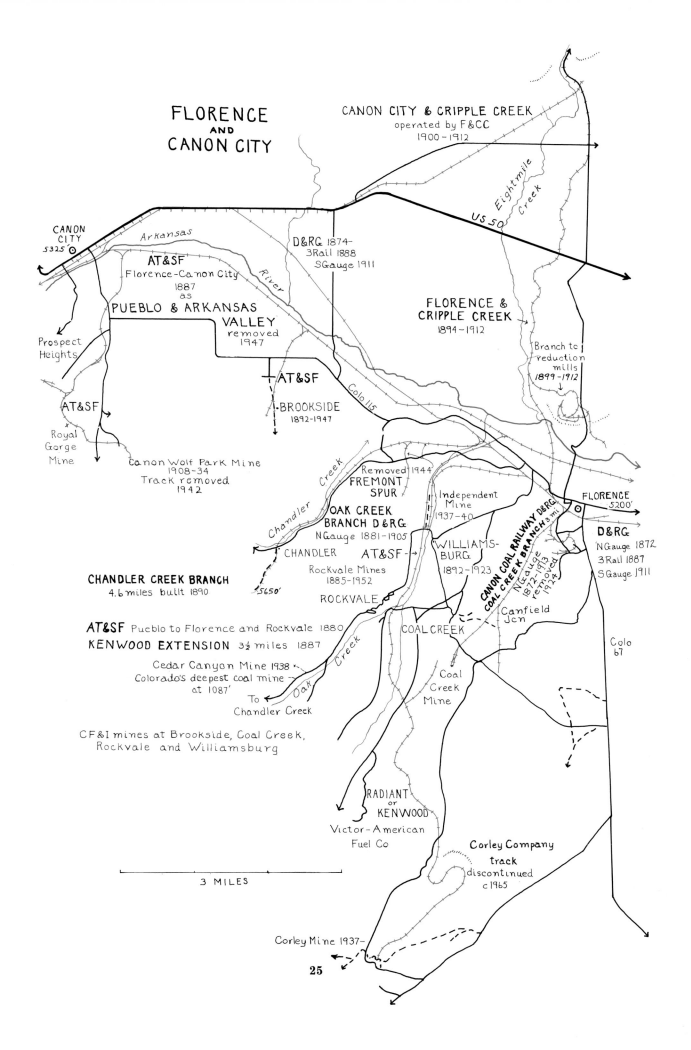

FLORENCE
AND
CANON CITY

CANON CITY & CRIPPLE CREEK
operated by F&CC
1900-1912

Arkansas

CANON CITY
5325'

AT&SF
Florence-Canon City
1887
as
PUEBLO & ARKANSAS
VALLEY
removed
1947

D&RG 1874-
3 Rail 1888
S Gauge 1911

River

US 50

Eightmile Creek

FLORENCE &
CRIPPLE CREEK
1894-1912

Prospect
Heights

Branch to
reduction
mills
1899-1912

AT&SF

AT&SF
BROOKSIDE
1892-1947

Colo 115

Royal
Gorge
Mine

Canon Wolf Park Mine
1908-34
Track removed
1942

Creek

Removed 1944
FREMONT
SPUR

OAK CREEK
BRANCH D&RG
N Gauge 1881-1905

Chandler

Independent
Mine
1937-40

FLORENCE
5200'

CANON COAL RAILWAY D&RG
COAL CREEK BRANCH 3 mi.

D&RG
N Gauge 1872
3 Rail 1887
S Gauge 1911

CHANDLER

AT&SF
Rockvale Mines
1885-1952

WILLIAMS-
BURG
1892-1923

N Gauge
1872-1913
removed
1924

CHANDLER CREEK BRANCH
4.6 miles built 1890

5650'

ROCKVALE

Canfield
Jcn

Colo
67

AT&SF Pueblo to Florence and Rockvale 1880
KENWOOD EXTENSION 3½ miles 1887

COAL CREEK

Creek

Cedar Canyon Mine 1938
Colorado's deepest coal mine
at 1087'

To
Chandler Creek

Oak

Coal
Creek
Mine

CF&I mines at Brookside, Coal Creek,
Rockvale and Williamsburg

3 MILES

RADIANT
or
KENWOOD

Victor-American
Fuel Co

Corley Company
track
discontinued
c 1965

Corley Mine 1937-

engine. With Corley's S-bend at the top, this was the longest coal branch in the area.

Brookside was an 1888 project of the Canon City Coal Company. Water closed the mine in 1911, but coal continued to be trucked out until a 1940 fire.

At Canon City, the Santa Fe still have the lower end of the track south from town in service. Like their Oak Creek Branch, it is tied into the D&RGW main line. Prospect Heights, incorporated in 1905, was a tiny open town which local option filled with saloons and the like. This had been the site of a CF&I mine since 1888. Mr. Sidney Adams tells me the Royal Gorge Mine was a coal source and perhaps a property of the New Jersey Zinc Company, whose smelter was nearby. The 1885 Wolf Park Mine was a near rival to the Cedar Canon, being 1029 feet deep. The Cotter Corporation occupies the old campsite of Wolf Park. The Nonac (Canon reversed) was the largest of the Fremont County mines. It ended a fifty-odd year operation in 1949.

It is not hard, given time, to find sections of most old grades with a car, but it would take a dogged interest in coal chips to cover the lines - there are over 20 miles of them well separated.

The DENVER AND NEW ORLEANS RAILROAD was the northern link in what became the Panhandle system, connecting Denver with the Gulf at Galveston. Overton's *Gulf to the Rockies* tells the story of how this child of John Evans and the southern cousin sired by Grenville Dodge — the Fort Worth and Denver City — were connected through a third company, the Denver Texas and Fort Worth, which built in the gap between Trinidad and the Texas State line and also served as the owning company for the other two.

The D&NO Railroad Company was set up in January, 1881, by Evans, David Moffat, S.H. Elbert, C.B. Kountze, and others of Denver, who raised $1,500,000, and the construction company, headed by W.S. Cheesman, built the first 52 miles by May of 1882. The railroad then mortgaged this trackage to get on into Pueblo, a total of 125 miles. The route went wide to the east of the D&RG — up to South Denver along Cherry Creek and out to Parker, Elizabeth, and Elbert, then south through Eastonville to Falcon, where the Rock Island later crossed it, and southwest to Manitou Junction and back to parallel the D&RG from Fountain on to Southern Junction, south of Bessemer. The road bought Franceville Coal Mine 14 miles east of Colorado Springs in the spring of 1882 and ran a 4 1/2 mile spur northeast to it from Franceville Junction, a little south of Manitou Junction. From the latter point a spur went in to Colorado Springs.

This side line into the stronghold of the D&RG was put down in a curious furtive operation. It seems the management had secured from the city council a right of way through town along Moreno Street from the east, and north along Sawatch Street to a depot area on Huerfano (now Colorado Avenue). The newspaper story, told in the *Daily Gazette* of October 6, 1882, indicates the D&NO people had been spooked a day or so earlier by the appearance of a transit man, a rod man, and a peg driver who were marking out lots for the Colorado Springs Company — General Palmer's real estate organization — and so to avoid trouble came in at 2:30 in the morning with 100 wagons full of rails and ties and quickly set them down on the designated streets. The railroad would have had a hard time operating. Ties were first strewn along the streets, then arranged so that there were four or five to a rail length. Some loose spiking was done and then at the intersections piles of dirt were heaped on top to make it possible for wagons and carriages to drive across them.

This was the only dirt moved in the operation. The line was not put into proper operation until a month or so later, when the grade between the town and the railroad was finished. In the meanime what passenger business there was came in from Jimmie's Camp on Tally-ho coaches.

The windswept grade was built as Denver & New Orleans; it came out as C&S.

In the information furnished *Poor's Manual* for 1884, the D&NO claimed 4,000,000 passenger miles and 5,000,000 ton miles of freight business, with 200 freight cars, 13 passenger cars, and 10 locomotives to haul them. No dollar signs are to be found in the report, however, and by 1886 the reported rolling stock had changed to 8 locomotives, 4 passenger cars and 248 freight cars. Bonds necessary to build the segment in to Pueblo were defaulted and in March, 1886, the railroad became the Denver Texas and Gulf.

The DENVER AND NEW ORLEANS RAILWAY COMPANY, formed in 1885 as successor to the railroad company of the same name, lived only five days before it became the Denver Texas and Gulf, the Colorado Segment of the Denver Texas and Fort Worth. Its incorporators included Evans and some of the same associates as the Rail Road Company. Two additional branches are mentioned — one from Easton to the east line of Colorado where the north fork of the Smoky Hill and the south fork of the Republican Rivers cross the line; to Horseshoe in the Mosquito Range — reached by way of the South Platte — and thence to Aspen by way of Leadville. The Coal Field Branch was described as running from where the main line crosses "Frejole" Creek southwest to the coal fields of Las Animas County.

D&NO trackage from Denver to Pueblo, 134 miles, remained in the Denver Texas and Gulf and its owner company the Denver Texas and Fort Worth, in the Union Pacific Denver and Gulf, and continued into the C&S organization until 1913, when the part south of the Rock Island was little used. It was pulled out in various segments between 1917 and 1919 and so left only the line from Denver to Falcon. With the dismantling process, passenger service between Denver and Colorado Springs, which had always been too slow to amount to anything, was declared discontinued by the company. Residents along this so-called Elizabeth line got the schedule resumed, and for a time you could go out 18 miles to Falcon on the Rock Island train leaving Colorado Springs at 1:15 and then ride north to Denver. If the train was on time you got there at 5:45. In 1936 65 miles of track north of Falcon came out, and in 1938 another mile. This left only the 8 1/2 miles out to Connors, east of Englewood.

The Denver Texas and Gulf period was followed by one of Union Pacific ownership in which the road was joined with the other UP railroads in northern Colorado - mainly the Colorado Central and the Denver South Park and Pacific to make the Union Pacific Denver and Gulf Railway. This era was followed by a receivership in which the UP was separated from the UPD&G and the latter reassembled with some changes as the Colorado and Southern, the Burlington-owned subsidiary which operates the north-south railroad today.

By taking Colorado 83 from about First Avenue at Colorado Boulevard you are guided into the grade of the line out of Denver. You can follow it to the vicinity of Cherry Creek Dam. As of 1971 there was a little stretch to be found just west and north of Parker, but there is far livelier evidence after you cross the high ground between there and Elizabeth, and continue south along near the grade to Manitou Junction. You are clearly on the railroad line on C&S road most of the way on to Fountain - you may see some antelope along there too - and you can find stretches near the old Pueblo road and the Overton Road, particularly where the Hanover Road starts east from Fountain Creek, and for a few miles north from Colorado 47 - the road between Pueblo and the Southern Colorado State College campus.

Between Pueblo and Walsenburg a joint-use agreement obtains between the D&RGW and the C&S like that between the D&RGW and the AT&SF between Denver and Pueblo, but in the latter case, where there were two separated lines, the crossovers were eliminated so as to make two parallel tracks, whereas in the former the two companies laid a double-width grade in a joint-construction agreement. A search by car for stretches of the grade which this doubletrack superceded will take you into country that seems very big and very quiet con-trasted with the traffic of arterial I-25. One sees placid prairie canyons, cow pastures & occasional deserted barns and farmhouses. The old grade has the air of wandering off in a no-man's land. It has been pretty well cleaned up but there are some artifacts still to be found. Long stretches can be walked but not often driven, for bridges are missing and there are deep washes and fences. The easiest way to explore is to make intermittent sallies from the highway. By going off I-25 at Exit 32 and driving out East to Lime you can find the old line close to the new and running off from it spurs to the quarry and to the north. The quarry branch and the main line south are in posted ground. The latter shows an interesting interruption where it crossed a creek but it is not very tempting country to walk in, especially when hot. From Exit 29 you can reach a stretch for walking to the north of the little P51 Ranch and can see grade to the south on the Verde Road. The whole Verde Road detour is about 12 miles long. From the Graneros Road you can drive a stretch both north and south, and a much longer stretch is possible for you from about 6 miles east of Walsenburg on Colorado 10. The Cuchara Junction to Walsenburg line is close north of Highway 10.

The ARKANSAS VALLEY RAILWAY COMPANY, fathered by Kansas Pacific officials and Pueblo men, was incorporated twice with the same expression of intentions — in September of both 1871 and 1872. The scheme was to extend the KP to Pueblo. The plan represents a revision of the earlier Colorado and New Mexico Railway Company's intention of 1870 to build two lines in extension of the KP track westward from Kit Carson. One line was to go via Fort Lyon and Animas City (Las Animas) in Bent County to Albuquerque; the other, a branch called the Arkansas Valley Railway, was to run to Pueblo from Fort Lyon. The Arkansas Valley Railway which had descended from these intentions was completed from Kit Carson (called Carson City for a time) to Las Animas and the 76.5 miles put in operation by the leasing KP. Newspaper stories indicate there was at least some grading and perhaps rails were laid beyond Las Animas to or toward La Junta. Both the KP and the Santa Fe were voted bond subsidies by the enthusiastic Pueblans, but the offer to the KP was apparently withdrawn in a second round of voting. The extension saw only a year or two of service and the rails were taken up in an abandonment that is remembered as Colorado's first, now 95 years old.

Some of the grade is dust-bowled, some has been ploughed, some is just plain lost, and there may be some covered by an old wagon road that shows on the early USGS quadrangles, but there are stretches in the short grass of pasture land where you know you are on the line. On a tangent near the north end I walked more than a mile on what could have been just a straight road without finding the least tie chip or cut or fill, and on the return found a spike within 30 yards of my car.

Employees of Colorado Interstate Gas Company were of help on the north end of the line and in the south I obtained permission from a kindly rancher whose pasture road crosses the ditch north of Mulberry Road a mile east of the Las Animas to Haswell Highway. There are some fringe benefits to this expedition - the Interstate Gas operation, a multitude of high-jumping jack rabbits near Pumpkin Center on Colorado 94, some long distance views of the mountains (likelier in winter time), and various stopping spots along the Arkansas River.

This road had a particularly hard struggle for existence before it got lengthened out into a full-grown Burlington north-south system. There were early boasts of a pact with the Midland, there was Evans' Denver New Orleans and Missouri Pacific,

A well-preserved white oak tie - the nearest thing to finding some of the Arkansas Valley Railroad's ill-fated grade.

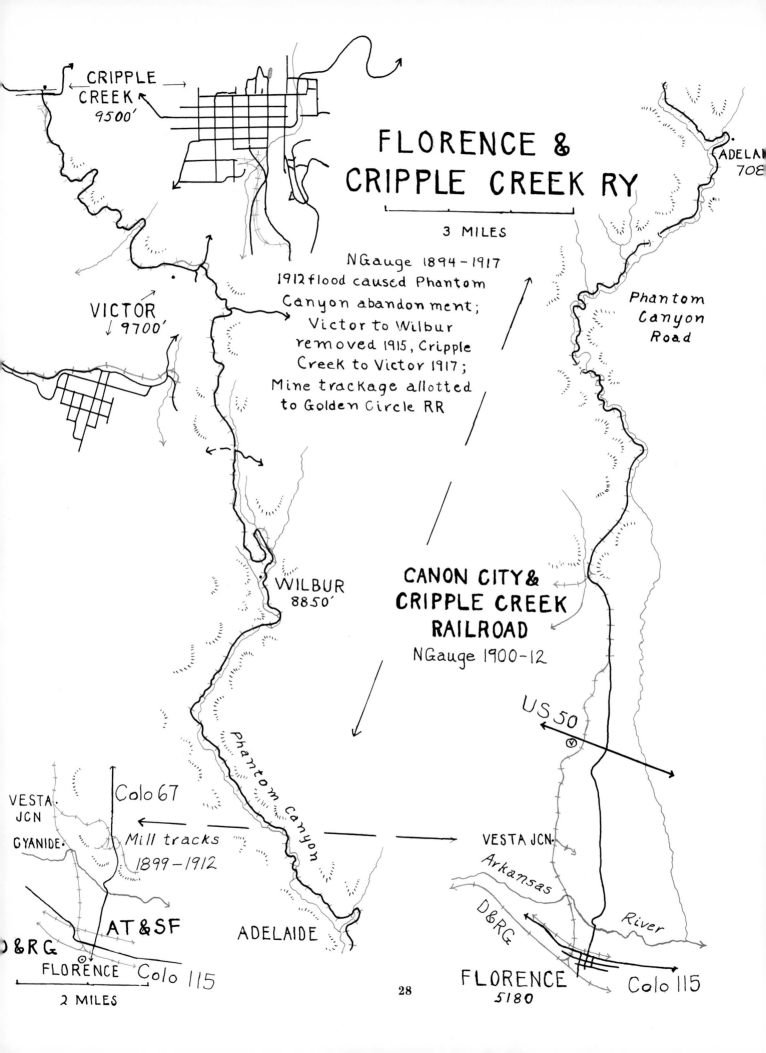

FLORENCE & CRIPPLE CREEK RY

CRIPPLE CREEK 9500'

VICTOR ↓9700'

ADELAI 708

Phantom Canyon Road

3 MILES

NGauge 1894-1917
1912 flood caused Phantom Canyon abandonment;
Victor to Wilbur removed 1915, Cripple Creek to Victor 1917;
Mine trackage allotted to Golden Circle RR

WILBUR 8850'

CANON CITY & CRIPPLE CREEK RAILROAD

NGauge 1900-12

US 50

VESTA JCN

CYANIDE

Colo 67

Mill tracks 1899-1912

AT & SF

D&RG

FLORENCE   Colo 115

2 MILES

Phantom Canyon

ADELAIDE

VESTA JCN

Arkansas

D&RG

River

FLORENCE 5180

Colo 115

28

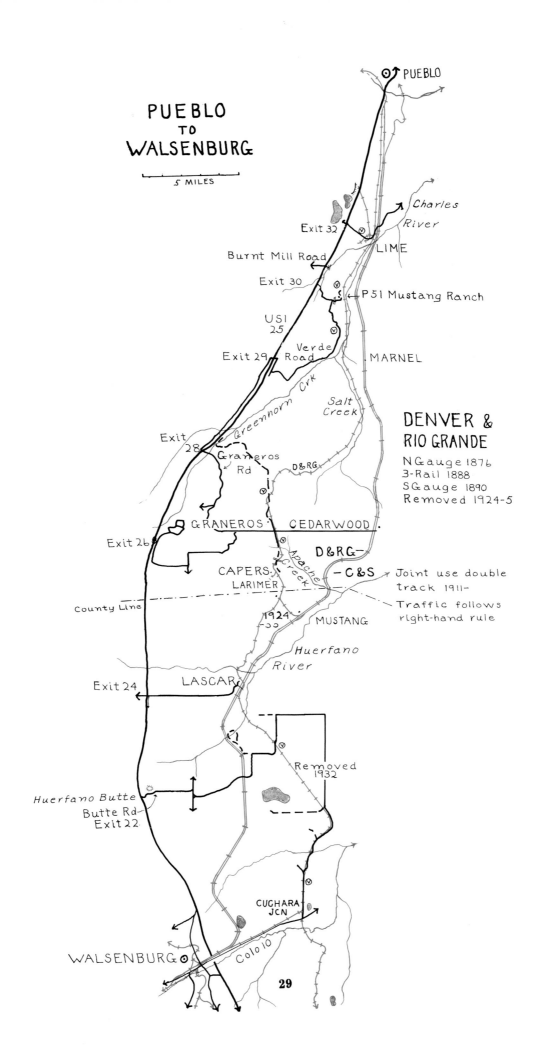

PUEBLO
TO
WALSENBURG

5 MILES

O→ PUEBLO

Charles River

Exit 32

Burnt Mill Road

LIME

Exit 30

← P 51 Mustang Ranch

USI 25

Verde Road

MARNEL

Exit 29

Greenhorn Crk

Salt Creek

DENVER &
RIO GRANDE
N Gauge 1876
3-Rail 1888
S Gauge 1890
Removed 1924-5

Exit 28

Graneros Rd

D&RG

GRANEROS

CEDARWOOD

Exit 26

D&RG—

Apache Creek

CAPERS

LARIMER

— C&S → Joint use double track 1911 -

County Line

1924

MUSTANG

Traffic follows right-hand rule

Huerfano River

Exit 24

LASCAR

Removed 1932

Huerfano Butte
Butte Rd
Exit 22

CUGHARA JCN

WALSENBURG ⊙

Colo 10

29

with which he got the bona fide offer from the MoPac to buy the line and helped induce Grenville Dodge to bring fresh strength into the venture. To counter the Colorado Pool, which arranged traffic reciprocation among the D&RG, the Santa Fe, and the Union Pacific, and later the CB&Q, Evans got a court order to force the Santa Fe to do business with D&NO and sued the CB&Q with a similar intention. The road was a disappointment up through its UPD&Gulf period, when Evans fought to get it into local control with a separate receivership from the UP.

Beginnings of the D&NO however were characterized by the usual confidence and gaiety of railroad incorporations. It was heralded as the Peak and Crescent line, in honor of the terminal cities. McMechen calls it the second spoke in John Evans' intention to make Denver a great rail hub. The plan written into the papers of incorporation was to build from Denver by way of Cherry Creek and south to La Junta and to connect with the Texas Pacific, the Houston and Texas Central and the Rio Grande extention of the Missouri Kansas and Texas in the state of Texas. Colorado Springs was to be reached by a branch. Another branch was to run down the Big Sandy to the KP at River Bend, and on to the east line of the state. This would be on the line taken by the Rock Island later in its line east from Colorado Springs through Falcon.

In the amended articles of the following January, the proposed line was to go to near the head of the Purgatoire (east of Trinidad), and thence to Emory's Gap and across New Mexico to the Canadian River in Texas, and thence to New Orleans. Branches were to go to Silver Cliff (supposedly from the Walsenburg end), to Canon City, and the head of the Arkansas River, and to Gunnison and the southwestern corner of Colorado by way of the Dolores mines.

In a second amendment of a year and a half later, they really rolled up their sleeves and put in the branches. To begin with, the route south from Denver was more specifically described as following Cherry Creek, Running Creek (which runs north through Elizabeth), and Kiowa Creek (which runs north through Ebert) to Manitou Junction and Franceville, then to Pueblo, Emroy's Gap, and the Canadian River. Lines were to include (1) one along Cherry Creek from Parkers to the lava beds, with an extension to Summit Park in El Paso County (an euphemism for Palmer Lake), and (by no specified route) through Park County to Buena Vista, (2) to Colorado Springs and Manitou and by way of Ute Pass and the South Platte to Fairplay, Hoosier Pass, and Breckenridge, branching off at Hartsell's Ranch to Buena Vista, Leadville, Tennessee Pass, and Redcliff, (3) a branch to Franceville (which was actually built), (4) from Little Buttes southwest up the Arkansas and Hardscrabble to Rosita, through Music Pass to Saguache and through Cochetopa Pass and down to Gunnison, called the Rosita Branch, (5) to Alamosa from somewhere along San Luis Creek on the Rosita Branch, (6) to Canon City from the Hardscrabble on the Rosita Branch, (7) from Bessemer west to the Rosita Branch near the forking point of the Hardscrabble, (8) from Rattle Snake Buttes west through Walsenburg and by way of Mosca or Sand Pass to Saguache — called the Huerfano Branch, (9) south to Trinidad, and by running west up Longs Creek to and along the state line, into New Mexico (10) from this Trinidad Branch at the mouth of Longs Creek (5 miles southwest of Trinidad) west up the Animas (Rio de las Animas Perditas) to and over San Francisco Pass to the Conejos, (11) to the coal in the Raton Mountains, by way of San Francisco Creek, called the Coal Field Branch, and (12) to Colfax, Mora, San Miguel, Las Vegas, and Albuquerque in an extension of the Trinidad branch southward.

A rail - mounted shovel at the quarry (Courtesy Ideal Cement Company).

From this break in the D&RG's longest tangent one sees the bumpy crest of the Sangre de Cristo Range.

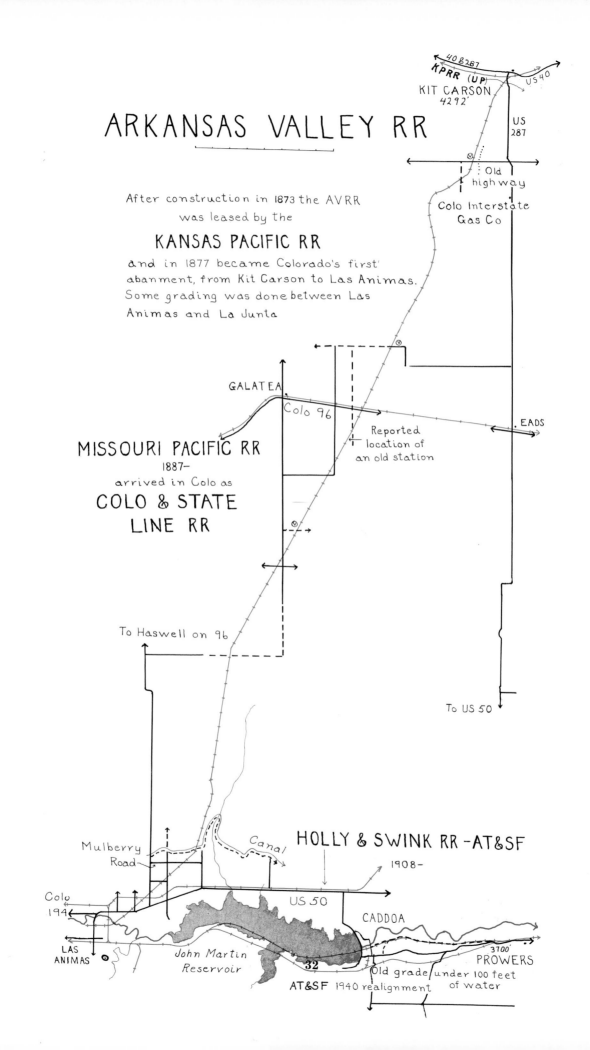

ARKANSAS VALLEY RR

After construction in 1873 the AVRR
was leased by the

KANSAS PACIFIC RR

and in 1877 became Colorado's first
abanment, from Kit Carson to Las Animas.
Some grading was done between Las
Animas and La Junta

KPRR (UP)
40 & 287
US 40
KIT CARSON
4292'

US 287

Old highway

Colo Interstate Gas Co

GALATEA

Colo 96

MISSOURI PACIFIC RR
1887—
arrived in Colo as
COLO & STATE LINE RR

Reported location of an old station

EADS

To Haswell on 96

To US 50

Mulberry Road

Canal

HOLLY & SWINK RR - AT&SF
1908—

US 50

Colo 194

CADDOA

LAS ANIMAS

John Martin Reservoir

32

3700'
PROWERS

Old grade under 100 feet of water

AT&SF 1940 realignment

PART II
SOUTH CENTRAL COLORADO

MAPS

The Canon City & Royal Gorge, seen from US 50 east of the Gorge

The DENVER AND RIO GRANDE has a complete line of abandonment from Pueblo to Trinidad. General Palmer's railroad was built south to El Moro in the Trinidad region, and west from Walsenburg on this line to La Veta, in 1878. Both termini were in coal land and both had possibilities of extension to the Rio Grande of his railroad's intended destiny. In 1877 the south line went on to Engleville though under a separate name because of the mother road's financial problems, and in that year and the next the west line went over La Veta Pass and reached the Rio Grande at Palmer's town of Alamosa. When the war with the Santa Fe deflected the D&RG westward, the south line became a coal branch, serving mines to the west of it with spurs and branches.

Palmer had in a sense started what became the Colorado Fuel and Iron Company in Pueblo by merging coal and land companies and then setting up the Colorado Coal and Iron Company. This corporation was in turn merged with some other holdings of D. C. Osgood to become the CF&I in 1884, about the time Palmer was losing his influence in the Rio Grande and developing a new coal and railroad empire in Utah.

Much of the abandoned D&RG is generally well to the east of I-25 and only accessible here and there by car. One can leave 25 at the Lime exit, No. 32, and find both the main line and branch trackage at what was first San Carlos, a settlement by 1897, then Lime from 1900 on. The limestone quarry there was a handy source for the CF&I, starting in 1888. Exits 30 and 29, and 28 and 26 make possible loop routes, the latter pair giving an opportunity to drive the grade a modest distance north and south. A longer loop is possible in very uncrowded country between the Butte Road exit and Colorado 10 outside of Walsenburg. On the latter you are just south of the track that came in from Cuchara Junction to go over La Veta Pass.

South of Walsenburg you may make it out to Rouse Junction on the grade line and perhaps also from Exit 15, but the only good road accesses are those from Exit 14 and the loop route passing El Moro, Hoene Road and Exit 9.

Except for the line to the flourishing Allen Mine on the Purgatoire, all of the coal branches from Walsenburg to Trinidad and west have been abandoned. Ghost camps, ghost mines and ghost railroads are less exciting to most explorers in these dry foothills than in the multi-colored mountains with their shelf roads - loops, tunnels and grand vistas, but once you are bitten by the bug of railroad esthetics you can find in the cool months much that is entertaining in the blackened fills, the buff colored sandstone and the gray cement foundations that you see there.

The LOMA BRANCH of the D&RG, when this project was begun in 1961, was something one ducked under to get into the north end of Walsenburg. You could drive out 7 1/2 miles from the town on Colorado 69 to a tipple and live tracks at the Belcarbon Mine of the Calument Fuel Company, and three miles more past other coal hills. Now, you can make a loop, starting west from the first right turn inside the town and keeping right through the hog-back to the first mines, cutting across west from Gordon to Alamo and the Major Ranch, and then returning by a route northeast to 69, with whatever detours you have time for and the side roads will allow. Alamo itself is as strangely peaceful as a sunny ruin in Greece, and despite the difference it struck me with almost the same sort of surprise. This Alamo Coal Company town was named in Spanish for its cottonwood trees.

The D&RG did not build all of this branch: the Victor Coal

The Loma Branch heads northwest

and Coke Company built and sold to them the stretch between Pictou and Maitland. Pictou and Kebler No. 1 (and perhaps others of the mines) were CF&I coal sources.

The WALSENBURG AND WESTERN RAILWAY COMPANY was formed in February of 1907 by a Denver group whose plan was to build from Walsenburg northwest to Talpa, along the Huerfano River through Gardiner to Malachite, and from there to Westcliff. Two branches were proposed: from some point on the line north to St. Mary's, and from Malachite west through Mosca Pass into the San Luis Valley. St. Mary's is on the Huerfano about 10 or 12 miles northwest of Walsenburg. When constructed, the railroad was actually 1.35 miles long, running from Walsenburg to the McNally Mine. The C&S operated it within the framework of another subsidiary, the Colorado Railroad, from 1910 until 1912.

The extreme brevity of this railroad made me want to see it, and perhaps your curiosity will also be aroused. It left the C&S track at Main and 4th Street, went west up 4th 2 blocks, made two half-right turns to cross the Loma Branch route about Marten and Montana, then turned WSW to the McNally Mine, a CF&I operation, in 1913-14. The railroad was C&S by that time.

COAL SPURS SOUTH OF WALSENBURG include one to the Globe Mine. To reach this you drive a mile west of Main Street on US 160, turn south on the Bear Creek Road, cross the river and round the hill, where you will see first a ghost town, and afterward a road on which you can double back east (at mile 2.7 from 7th Street). It is also easy to drive 1.8 miles south from 160 on Main Street and the Ideal Road, and walk west up the live C&S track past the Cameron to the Globe. The Cameron was mined by the CF&I from 1917 to 1946.

There is more to see and in pleasanter country if you continue south on the Ideal Road. After it crosses the C&S live track, the grade to the Ideal Mine is first on your right and then on your left. Depending on road conditions you can drive or walk east to the mine, which is visible from the road. It supplied CF&I from 1910 to 1929.

Old Rouse has some puzzling grade lines to work on and so is well worth a visit. You have to use the frontage road from north or south, in the latter case underpassing to the east and back to get into the DL Ranch, where you ask for permission and instructions.

The landmark and permission point for the Colorado and Wyoming's branch up to the CF&I camp and mine at Hezron is an improved trailer house just west of where the frontage road underpasses I-25 a mile or so north of the Rouse exit - No. 16. I found the road sketchy and high-centered west of the live C&S and old D&RG lines, and some of the grade was washed out.

The later Rouse, reached by going south from the same Rouse exit, takes you into what seems like an almost continuous coal mine area. On my first visit, Harry Capps, an 85-year old rancher, told me of wagoning out the instruments of a John Philip Sousa band from a derailed train at Rouse to the main line junction in 1929. Life couldn't have always been as drab there as it looks now.

The Rapson Mine was one of many under the horizontal sandstone strata west of the plains

Walking toward Pryor the visitor looks at the Spanish Peaks

The old US 85-87 serves as a frontage road south from exit 15. Just back (west) of a desultory little farm 1.4 miles south of the exit you find the remnants of a spur coming in from the south to the Black Diamond Mine. The whole place when I was there seemed to be in possession of an exhausted horse.

Driving another two miles or so on the old highway or Rugby Road brings you to the Rapson and Rugby spurs. The Rapson track was still in place on my first visit, and the Rugby removal seemed fresh, but the lack of any good road on the Rugby Branch caused me to drop from the agenda Primrose, the camp for the mining there.

The Jewel and the Southwestern Mines were both served by a spur from Higgins. Only the terminal area can be reached by car. A little north of the road in and near the mine you may find a knowledgeable rancher to talk to. Lynn, near Higgins, is said to have got its fame from an explosion in a Du Pont facility there.

The railroad spur to Aguilar went up Green Canyon, which is closed by a padlocked gate and would require permission for prowling. The Brodhead is perhaps the best known of the mines, but there were also the Empire, the Royal, the Gem and the Green Canyon. Aguilar, named for Jose Ramon Aguilar, is old, having served as an Indian trading post.

From exit No. 12 one can drive quite passable roads up the two long mine canyons. For Canon del Agua head west from the Ludlow Monument. There is evidence of a big operation including beehive coking at Hastings, and a good deal more above on the way to and at Delagua, which like Hastings, and like the

railroad at the beginning, was a Victor-American Fuel Company property. Hastings had a disastrous methane gas explosion which was researched by Francis Rizzari for a *Brand Book* article of 1968, entitled "When Hastings Counted Their Dead." The Victor-American Fuel Company, which became defunct in 1951, had been in turn the Victor Coal Company, the Victor Coal and Coke Company, and the Victor Fuel Company. The Denver Times of December 31, 1898 reported it was then operating mines and / or making coke in eight camps within 20 miles of Trinidad. There were 716 coke ovens with an output of 1000 tons a day.

The ROAD CANON RAILROAD COMPANY was set up in August of 1889 by C.F. Meek, William G. Evans, and others connected with the Denver Texas road to put a coal railroad up the Road Canon and its tributaries. The railroad was graded by this company in 1889 and included in the 1890 Union Pacific Denver and Gulf Consolidation which put the 2.82-mile track in by March of 1891 and added a half-mile to it in 1898. The C&S extended it to Bear Canon Mine in 1915 - 17, though the name of Road Canon was defunct before that time, and in 1955 it was taken out.

Looking east on the Rugby line

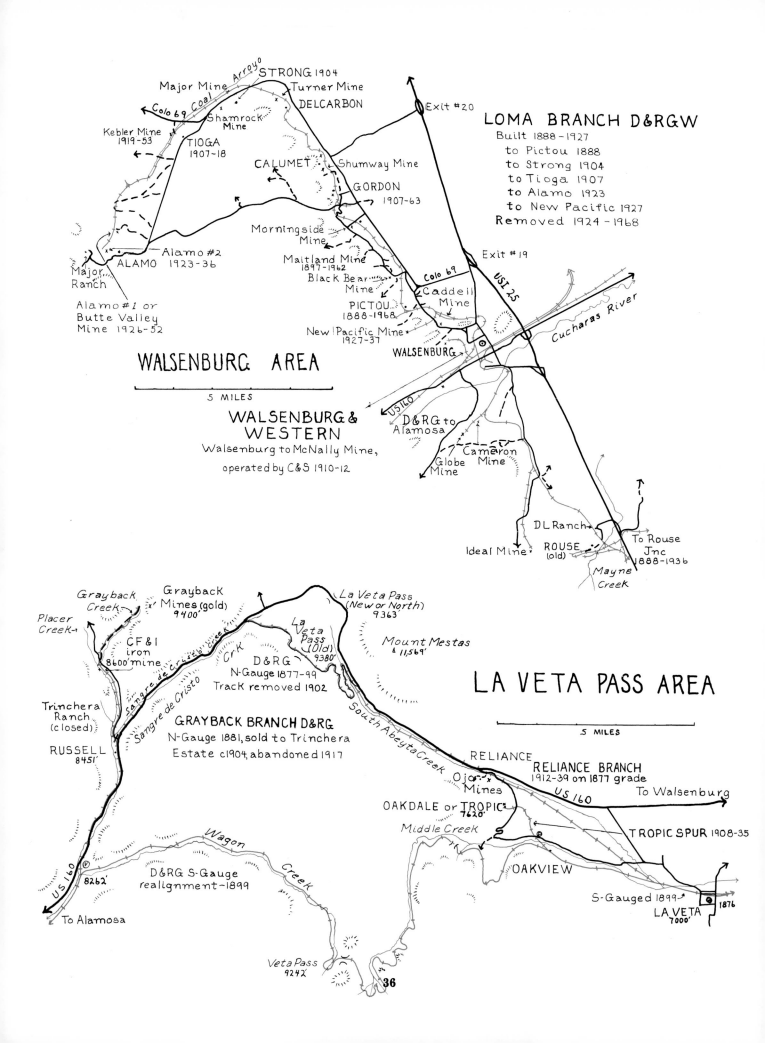

WALSENBURG AREA

Major Mine   STRONG 1904
Colo 69   Coal   Arroyo   Turner Mine
   Shamrock   DELCARBON
   Mine
Kebler Mine
1919-53
   TIOGA
   1907-18
            CALUMET   Shumway Mine
                         GORDON
                         1907-63
            Morningside
            Mine
Alamo #2   Maitland Mine
ALAMO 1923-36   1897-1962
Major   Black Bear
Ranch   Mine   Caddell
Alamo #1 or   Colo 69   Mine
Butte Valley   PICTOU
Mine 1926-52   1888-1968
            New Pacific Mine   WALSENBURG
            1927-37

Exit #20

LOMA BRANCH D&RGW
Built 1888-1927
   to Pictou 1888
   to Strong 1904
   to Tioga 1907
   to Alamo 1923
   to New Pacific 1927
Removed 1924-1968

Exit #19

USI 25

Cucharas River

US160

D&RG to
Alamosa
            Cameron
            Mine
   Globe
   Mine

5 MILES

WALSENBURG &
WESTERN
Walsenburg to McNally Mine,
operated by C&S 1910-12

DL Ranch
         ROUSE   To Rouse
Ideal Mine (old)   Jnc
                      1888-1936
            Mayne
            Creek

LA VETA PASS AREA

Grayback
Creek   Grayback
          Mines (gold)   La Veta Pass
Placer   9400'   (New or North)
Creek→   9363'
          CF&I   La
          iron   Veta   Mount Mestas
          8600' mine   Pass   △ 11,569'
                       (Old)
                       9380'
Trinchera   Crk   D&RG
Ranch   N-Gauge 1877-99
(closed)   Track removed 1902
RUSSELL   GRAYBACK BRANCH D&RG
8451'   N-Gauge 1881, sold to Trinchera
          Estate c1904, abandoned 1917

5 MILES

                                 RELIANCE
                                          RELIANCE BRANCH
                         Ojo   1912-39 on 1877 grade
                         Mines   US160   To Walsenburg
          Wagon   OAKDALE or TROPIC
US 160   7620'
8262'   Middle Creek   TROPIC SPUR 1908-35
          D&RG S-Gauge
          realignment-1899   OAKVIEW
To Alamosa
                                       S-Gauged 1899   LA VETA
                                                           7000'   1876
                    Veta Pass
                    9242'

Cane cactus decorates the Jewel Mine grade

Road Canon, for which you head south and then west from the monument, is somewhat narrow and tortuous at the upper end, and as one drives up, he has to wonder what it must have looked like filled with smoke and activity.

The Ludlow Monument reminds you more than anything else in Colorado of the struggles and the grief of the men who dug the coal and of their families. The major tragedy took place when two women and eleven children were suffocated in a fire that swept through a temporary tent camp the families were occupying instead of the company houses. The most readable story about the strike is Barron B. Beshoar's book *Out of the Depths*.

To reach the Ludlow Mine, head south from the Monument and instead of taking the Road Canon road stay on the east side of the C&S until a road U-turns across the tracks to a small farm and walk up the grade (on high fill) from there.

Slag hills and coke ovens at Hastings

The CHICOSA CANON RAILROAD COMPANY was organized by C.F. Meek and others connected with the Denver Texas and Gulf, allowing Forbes coal to ride on D&RG rails where the DT&G had trackage rights. This line was connected to the tracks of the UPD&G when they came through in 1895.

Exit 11 is superimposed on the Rio Grande's Chicosa Junction. A frontage road runs south along the west side of I-25 and then right turns into the two mine canyons I enjoyed most between Walsenburg and Trinidad. In the north one you can climb up a grade of a cable railroad with a tunnel in it, connecting the mine, high on the south hillside, to the railroad tracks below. The south canyon leads to Forbes and the Cox and Wood Mine. When I went in 1969 it was drivable up to the end of the first heavily mined area and the rest was a walk on the grade somewhat shaded by the chicosa or brushwood from which the line perhaps got its name. Part way up a spur crossed the creek bed and went on a little way to a stone quarry.

The short spur to Thor and the Union Mine there is visible from the highway just north of where it overpasses the C&S tracks. You can climb a fence or two and go in to investigate a two-pronged terminus and a stretch of grade to the north toward what was Bowen.

Tipple track in Berwind Canyon

The TRINIDAD GAS AND ELECTRIC COMPANY RAILROAD operated on standard gauge track with two miles of track in the town and a line via Sopris to Starkville. It was combined with the Trinidad Light and Power Company to make the Southern Colorado Power and Railway Company in 1908, and extended that year to Cokedale. Another company, the Colorado Light and Power, took over in 1909; this was succeeded in 1910 by the Trinidad Electric Transmission Railway and Gas Company, which operated the line until it died in 1923. It doesn't seem likely you would find much to identify there now unless perhaps on the line south to Starkville.

An April 28, 1904 article of the *Trinidad Chronicle-News* describes the line as 12 miles long, beginning on East Main, turning south on Commercial to Pine, on Pine to the power plant just west of Day's Lake and west of the Santa Fe tracks; thence west along the Santa Fe right of way for a mile and then bearing right following the Stonewall Wagon Road past Jansen to the Colorado and Wyoming Rock Quarry, south from there to the new town of Piedmont (built 1903) by the Rocky Mountain Fuel Company, from where one line goes in to Sopris (temporarily over the C&S tracks) and another to the Colorado Supply Company's store at Starkville.

WALSENBURG
TO
RUGBY

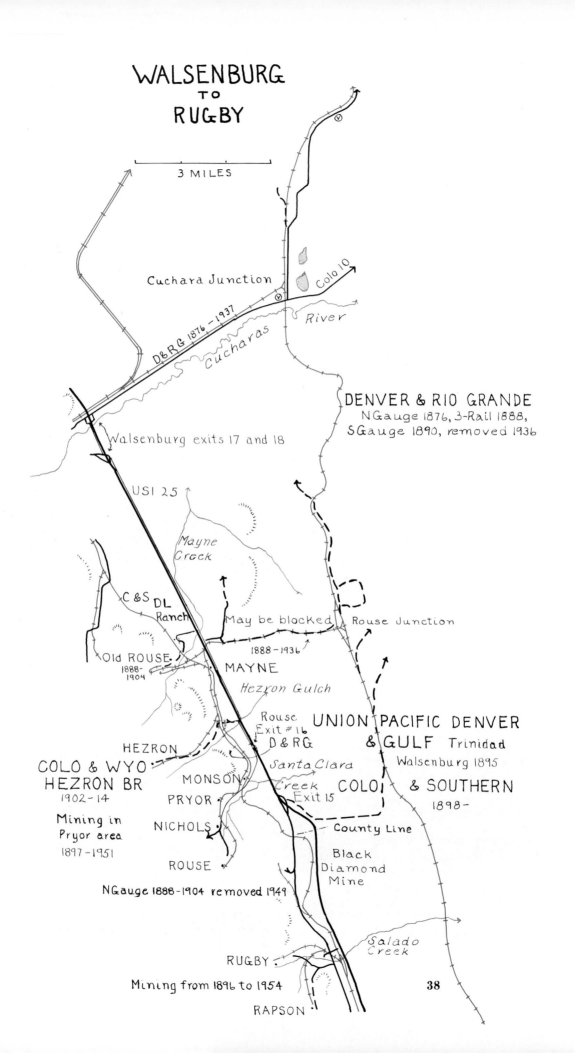

3 MILES

Cuchara Junction

Colo 10

River

Cucharas

D&RG 1876-1937

DENVER & RIO GRANDE
N Gauge 1876, 3-Rail 1888,
S Gauge 1890, removed 1936

Walsenburg exits 17 and 18

US I 25

Mayne
Creek

C & S   DL
         Ranch

May be blocked   Rouse Junction

1888-1936

Old ROUSE
1888-
1904

MAYNE

Hezron Gulch

Rouse
Exit #16   UNION PACIFIC DENVER
D&RG   & GULF   Trinidad

HEZRON   Walsenburg 1895

COLO & WYO   *Santa Clara*   COLO   & SOUTHERN
HEZRON BR MONSON   *Creek*   Exit 15   1898-
1902-14
           PRYOR
Mining in   County Line
Pryor area   NICHOLS
1897-1951   Black
                          Diamond
           ROUSE   Mine

N Gauge 1888-1904 removed 1949

                          Salado
                          Creek

RUGBY

Mining from 1896 to 1954   38

RAPSON

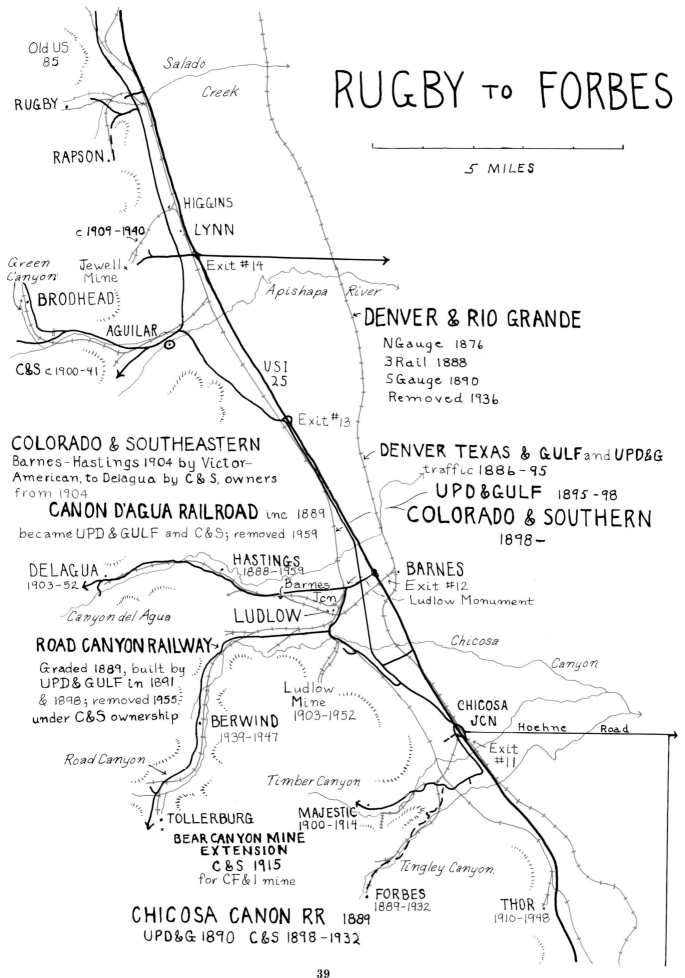

RUGBY TO FORBES

5 MILES

Old US 85

RUGBY .

RAPSON .

Salado Creek

HIGGINS

c 1909-1940

LYNN

Jewell Mine

Exit #14

Green Canyon

BRODHEAD

AGUILAR

Apishapa River

C&S c 1900-41

USI 25

Exit #13

DENVER & RIO GRANDE

NGauge 1876
3 Rail 1888
S Gauge 1890
Removed 1936

COLORADO & SOUTHEASTERN
Barnes-Hastings 1904 by Victor-
American, to Delagua by C&S, owners
from 1904

DENVER TEXAS & GULF and UPD&G
traffic 1886-95

UPD&GULF 1895-98
COLORADO & SOUTHERN
1898-

CANON D'AGUA RAILROAD inc 1889
became UPD&GULF and C&S; removed 1959

HASTINGS
1888-1959

DELAGUA .
1903-52

Barnes
Jcn

Canyon del Agua

LUDLOW

. BARNES
Exit #12
Ludlow Monument

Chicosa

Canyon

ROAD CANYON RAILWAY →
Graded 1889, built by
UPD&GULF in 1891
& 1898; removed 1955
under C&S ownership

Road Canyon

BERWIND
1939-1947

Ludlow Mine
1903-1952

CHICOSA JCN

Hoehne Road

Exit #11

Timber Canyon

. TOLLERBURG

MAJESTIC
1900-1914

BEAR CANYON MINE EXTENSION
C&S 1915
for CF&I mine

Tingley Canyon

. FORBES
1889-1932

THOR
1910-1948

CHICOSA CANON RR 1889
UPD&G 1890   C&S 1898-1932

The EL MORO RAILWAY COMPANY was a Palmer line organized when D&RG credit was weak, to run the two or three miles between El Moro and the mines of the Southern Colorado Town and Coal Company. The agreement by which the capital was secured was signed in October, 1877, a few days after the incorporation by Palmer associates. The description indicates this is the line shown on the El Moro Quadrangle to Engle.

El Moro and Engleville both supplied the CF&I with coal. To reach the line from Trinidad drive east on Main Street to one block past Porter Street (Engle Street), where either a right turn or a half right can be made. Take the full right up Engle Street till it T's into Obregon, where you turn left or east. Distance from Main Street to Engleville is 2¹/₂ miles. From near the end of the road you can see the grade north along the farther or east hillside of the Engleville draw. You can walk down this grade from Engleville or can retrace car road to where it splits on the mesa, a mile below Engleville, and take the right hand branch down 1 mile to where it T's into the E—W road, and turn right. As you drive east you look south and see the Engleville grade running parallel to you along the north side of a butte, then turning south into a draw. When you are 1¹/₂ miles east of the T, take the ¹/₂ mile farm road running south from your main road. The first part of this is on the Engleville Branch cinder track, and you can see and walk to much of the grade from this farm, with permission of its owners.

Engleville itself is not pretty, but when you have passed through the live litter of cans and shacks, the grade itself has a kind of aloof dignity.

The GREY CREEK BRANCH went through the Denver Texas and Gulf and UP Denver and Gulf ownerships to become a C&S branch. With a little persistence you can find some of the north end from west of where it started at Beshoar Junction, but the upper part has more attraction. For that you go east from Trinidad on Main Street to 2¹/₂ miles from Exit No. 8 of I-25, turn south on a gravel road, east after ¹/₂ miles, etc., (this is the same road used to find the lower part of the Engleville Branch described above) and at a point 5 miles from Trinidad you make a right turn on a mesa. You have just crossed the Grey Creek grade line at this turn, and can follow it on foot either way, and perhaps find a spike or two. The land to the south is posted, and a car gets you very little distance anyway. So if you want the works, come with a jeep and get yourself permission and a key from James Cummings, the owner, in Trinidad.

This tie stockade, photographed on the way to Forbes in 1961, is no longer standing

The Santa Fe's route over Raton Pass, used briefly, still preserves the cut at the top

The ATCHISON TOPEKA AND SANTA FE started mining coal at Starkville in 1878, presumably at first for their own locomotives. American Smelting and Refining also coked there. The Santa Fe shoefly track over Raton Pass, in use from November 10, 1878 to September 7, 1879, is in posted land, but no one seems likely to give you trouble if you cut down the hill from the highway pass and explore this area reminiscent of the war with the D&RG. There is a little cut at the pass top, and you can work either way from there to find the switchbacks. Be prepared for some heavy bushwhacking in the undergrowth.

Chicken Creek, or Gallinas Canon, to which the D&RG crews were deflected when they found Morley's AT&SF crews on the Dick Wooten toll road over Raton Pass, has a separate exit (No. 2), about a mile below the start of the canyon itself. I was able some years ago to drive up in the canyon about 6 miles, some of it on what must have been grade, to a more definite section of grading which was distinct from the road on the hillside, and found some more stretches above that. To get in now would require permission and a key from James Cummings in Trinidad.

The LONG CANYON BRANCH of the C&S is one of the most remote railroad lines you can find to visit in Colorado. It was an extension of the short DT&Gulf line west from Trinidad to Sopris. The major product was lumber from the ponderosa forests. You can see some of the Sopris line and the branch east from it to Piedmont - both coal sources for the CF&I - if you

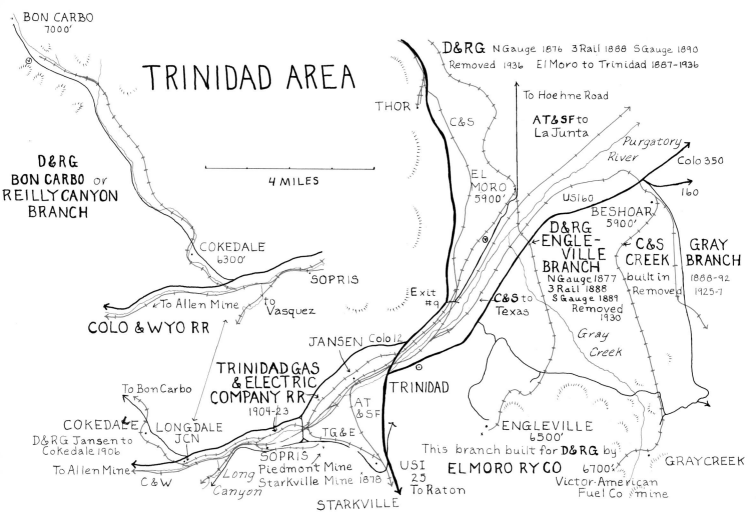

TRINIDAD AREA

BON CARBO
7000'

D&RG
BON CARBO or
REILLY CANYON
BRANCH

|• • • • • •|
4 MILES

COKEDALE
6300'

SOPRIS

←To Allen Mine   to Vasquez

COLO & WYO RR

THOR

D&RG N Gauge 1876 3 Rail 1888 S Gauge 1890
Removed 1936   El Moro to Trinidad 1887-1936

To Hoehne Road

C&S

AT&SF to
La Junta

Purgatory
River

EL
MORO
5900'

US160

Colo 350

160

BESHOAR
5900'

D&RG.
ENGLE-
VILLE
BRANCH
N Gauge 1877
3 Rail 1888
S Gauge 1889
Removed
1930

C&S
CREEK
built in
Removed

GRAY
BRANCH
1888-92
1925-7

Exit
#9

←C&S to
Texas

Gray
Creek

JANSEN Colo 12

TRINIDAD GAS
& ELECTRIC
COMPANY RR
1904-23

To Bon Carbo

COKEDALE
D&RG Jansen to
Cokedale 1906

LONGDALE
JCN

TG&E

AT
&SF

TRINIDAD

To Allen Mine

C&W

SOPRIS
Piedmont Mine
Starkville Mine 1878

Long
Canyon

USI
25
To Raton

STARKVILLE

ENGLEVILLE
6500'

This branch built for D&RG by
ELMORO RY CO   6700'
Victor-American
Fuel Co mine

GRAYCREEK

A Rio Grande train comes down old La Veta Pass - more grade shows on the hilltop above. (State Historical Society)

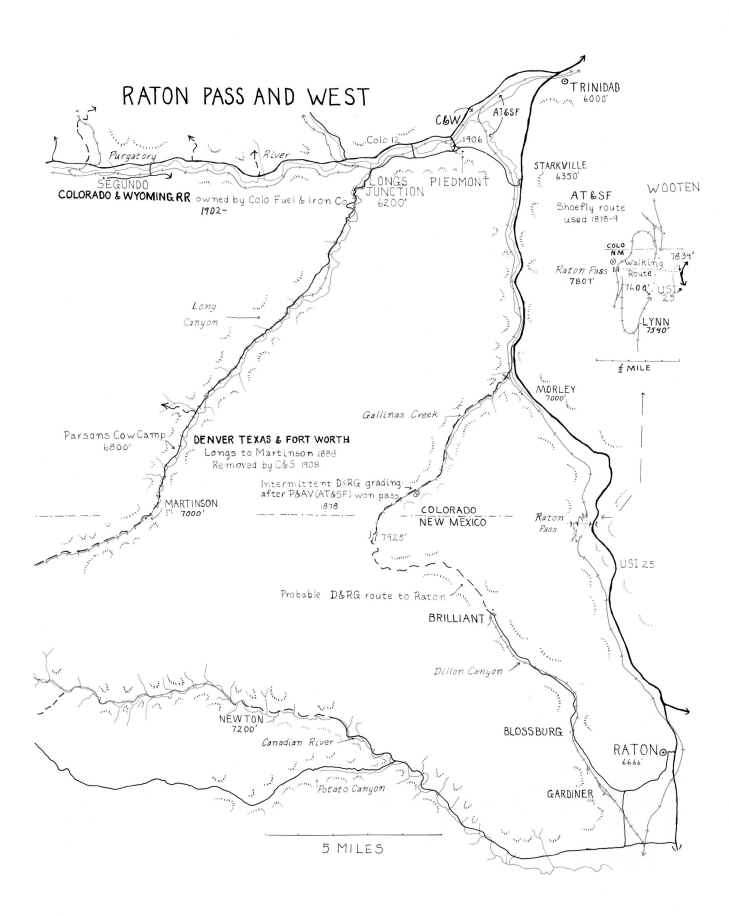

RATON PASS AND WEST

Purgatory River

SEGUNDO
COLORADO & WYOMING RR owned by Colo Fuel & Iron Co.
1902-

Colo 12

C&W

AT&SF
1906

PIEDMONT

LONGS
JUNCTION
6200'

STARKVILLE
6350'

TRINIDAD
6000'

WOOTEN

AT&SF
Shoefly route
used 1878-9

COLO
NM
Raton Pass
7807'

Walking
Route

7834'

7600' USI
25

LYNN
7540'

½ MILE

Long
Canyon

Parsons Cow Camp
6800'

DENVER TEXAS & FORT WORTH
Longs to Martinson 1888
Removed by C&S 1908

Gallinas Creek

MORLEY
7000'

Intermittent D&RG grading
after P&AV (AT&SF) won pass
1878

MARTINSON
7000'

COLORADO
NEW MEXICO

7925'

Raton
Pass

USI 25

Probable D&RG route to Raton

BRILLIANT

Dillon Canyon

NEWTON
7200'

Canadian River

BLOSSBURG

RATON
6666'

Potato Canyon

GARDINER

5 MILES

No spikes here, but a wooden replacement to keep the tie from rotting

head west from Starkville, and you can follow the Long Canyon road for a good many miles, seeing here and there pieces of grade and at times driving on it on the road. In 1961 I went up 15 miles to about 3 miles short of the state line in an old Ford I had. It began to be rough there, so I picked up a few ties, which were shrunk by that time to round pitchy cores that made a fine blaze in my fireplace at home. I re-drove the northern 10 miles of this road in 1971 and found little changed. You might be able to jeep all the way over the hill to Catskill provided the Parsons Ranch people do not keep it locked, but there is a better way to go in from Raton. First inquire by telephone of the Kayser Steel Company to see if their gates are open. Drive west in Raton to 7th Street, and south out of town on that road, taking a left or south fork at the foot of a hill just beyond town. This soon T's into a road west from I-25 which takes you up the Canadian River and its tributary Potato Creek and over a lot of hill country where you are as likely to see a wild turkey as a human. Suddenly you arrive at a piece of live Santa Fe trackage with coal cars and big tipple, this about 37 miles from Raton.

The best route down to the Canadian River is little more than a track in the grass. It leaves this road 7.2 miles east of the Santa Fe track crossing, or 26.9 miles west of the road split just

This sketchy bit of grading along Gallinas Canyon is a reminder of the Santa Fe's conquest of Raton Pass

south of Raton (swe above). You drive 2 miles down north past a little pond and then at the Canadian River turn right. It is a mile or so east to Catskill, where the action was.

From a little short of the Kayser Steel area - the coal mine - a road leads up to the Casa Grande area at Vermejo Park. It might be possible by making arrangements with the ranch there in advance to use their side road going north in Springs Canyon. It has a little side branch east into Vasquez, the west end of the old railroad. The Ash Mountain and Casa Grande 15' Quadrangles would be helpful in understanding the terrain. At this time closed gates will prevent you from completing a loop that would take you back to Trinidad via Tercio and Stonewall.

It is hard to believe that quiet Long Canyon ever reverberated with the busy noises of lumber trains from New Mexico

The REILLY CANYON BRANCH of the D&RG makes an excursion of about 18 miles round trip from Colorado 12 west of Trinidad. The coke ovens, most of the grade, and the ghost town of Bon Carbo at the mine are all easily accessible by car. The D&RG used trackage agreement to reach Longdale Junction when they were operating the branch.

THE COLORADO AND WYOMING RAILWAY COMPANY is a property of the Colorado Fuel and Iron Company owned through its subsidiary the Colorado Industrial Company, which also owned the Crystal River Railroad. It has a north segment which brings iron ore west to Guernsey from the mines at Sunrise, Wyoming, 6½ miles.

There is a middle section at Minnequa consisting of over 100 miles of yard switching tracks at the CF&I plant. This would be hard to map. There are also 4½ miles of side tracks at the Sunrise end and 13½ miles in the southern division.

The southern segment, separated from the northern one by 400 miles of the track of other railroads, runs from 2 miles west of Trinidad on the Santa Fe. This railroad, built in 1902 and 1903, went 32 miles west along the Purgatory and its south fork to Cuatro with a 1½ mile branch to Hezron and a 3-mile branch to Primero. By 1904 there were 42 locomotives and over 400 cars in operation, and the number increased for several years. In 1906 a spur to Piedmont was added, a little under a mile long. The Hezron Branch came out soon after 1914.

A 1957 letter from W.D. Cool, General Auditor, indicates that original construction went to Tercio, and in 1951-52 was reduced 11 miles to terminate at Weston, with a new track being built to serve the Allen Mine.

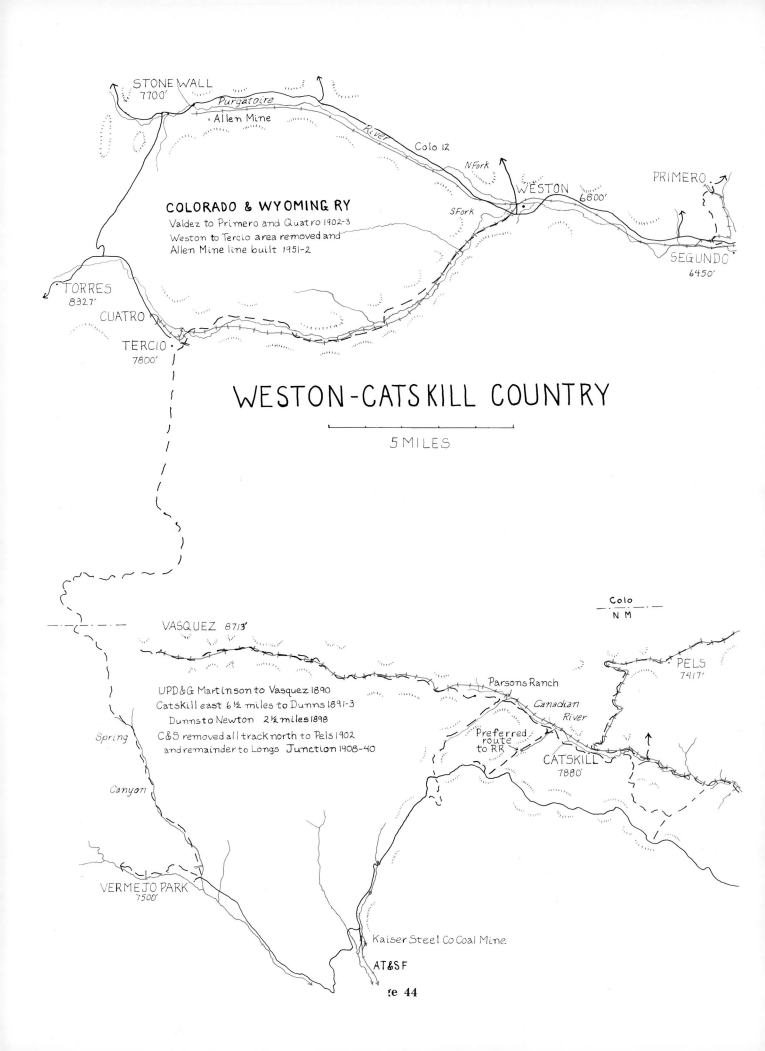

STONE WALL
7700'

Purgatoire

× Allen Mine

River

Colo 12

N Fork

WESTON
6800'

PRIMERO

S Fork

COLORADO & WYOMING RY

Valdez to Primero and Quatro 1902-3

Weston to Tercio area removed and
Allen Mine line built 1951-2

SEGUNDO
6450'

TORRES
8327'

CUATRO

TERCIO
7800'

WESTON-CATSKILL COUNTRY

5 MILES

Colo
___
N M

VASQUEZ 8713'

PELS
7417'

Parsons Ranch

UPD&G Martinson to Vasquez 1890

Catskill east 6½ miles to Dunns 1891-3

Dunns to Newton 2½ miles 1898

C&S removed all track north to Pels 1902

and remainder to Longs Junction 1908-40

*Canadian
River*

Spring

Preferred
route
to RR

CATSKILL
7880'

Canyon

VERMEJO PARK
7500'

Kaiser Steel Co Coal Mine

AT&SF

re 44

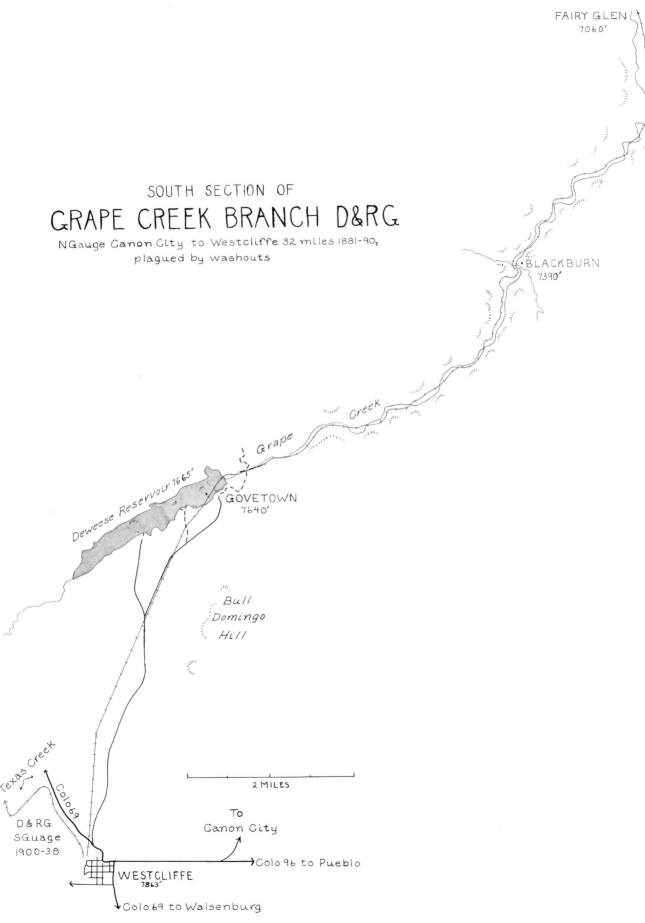

FAIRY GLEN
7060'

SOUTH SECTION OF
GRAPE CREEK BRANCH D&RG
N Gauge Canon City to Westcliffe 32 miles 1881-90,
plagued by washouts

•BLACKBURN
7390'

Grape Creek

Deweese Reservoir 7665'

GOVETOWN
7640'

Bull
Domingo
Hill

2 MILES

To Texas Creek

Colo 69

To
Canon City

D&RG
S Guage
1900-38

Colo 96 to Pueblo

WESTCLIFFE
7863'

Colo 69 to Walsenburg

45

The Allen works the same coal vein as the Tercio mine and presently supplies the full needs of the CF&I Company. The middle section at Pueblo now has about 100 miles of trackage within the plant. Tom Cone and Randy Serna, two boys from a railroad seminar of mine, found the gate at Tercio unlocked and jeeped the full 1.5 miles from there to Weston on and off the grade. Generally, this is not possible. I have only walked a little of it from the Weston end. The same pair found their way to the Primero Mine with a three-mile walk starting north up a canyon from BeBee's Goat Ranch. The grade came into the canyon after about a mile and at the end were foundations of buildings, the mine and the ruins of Primero School.

All the numbered mines from Primero to Quinto, and Valdez, near Segundo, were CF&I workings and were attached or close to the C&W.

The TROPIC SPUR of the D&RG, first of two coal lines west of La Veta, is on a road running west and northwest from the north part of the town. At a junction about 2.5 miles from town you keep west on a valley road rather than WNW over the mesa, and are soon aware of a broken grade which crossed the road from south to north. You can see the rest of it as you go on into Oakdale and the terminus. There is a curious lot of concrete structure around the end to invite your skill at reconstructing.

Remains of the Tercio line of the Colorado & Wyoming

The PLACER SPUR of the D&RG, sometimes referred to as the Grayback Branch, is the prize piece of the area. It is in closed land of the Trinchera Estate, so to see it legally you should seek permission in advance from their office. Having made no arrangements, two of us slipped over the hill and took the long walk up the Placer Creek and tributary Grayback Creek Roads to the mines there. Placer Creek has some quite high fill overgrown with healthy sage bushes and some signs of an old loading area but we saw nothing of the iron mine which supplied CF&I and perhaps some of its ancestors. The steeper trail-road up to the Grayback Mines seems in part to have covered the old grade, and in part to have run to its left up grades that must have run to 6% in places. A trailer-house and some tools gave evidence of recent work on the level of the stream, some of it possibly sluicing for free gold. This was one of those cases of taking a mountain walk and a railroad excursion all in one.

The CC&RG was well on the way to being built when this photo was taken (Courtesy of Fred Merriam)

The GRAPE CREEK BRANCH was a part of the great surge of D&RG construction after the Royal Gorge War. Silver mining had already gotten a good start in the Wet Mountain Valley, and Iron Mountain was developed into an ore source for the Colorado Fuel and Iron Company. The creek was particularly susceptible to floods, and in its second year the line was washed out. The track was put in shape in 1884 but 1889 saw an even greater destruction and brought about the abandonment.

The RELIANCE BRANCH of the D&RG has interest as a recent one on an old bed. The terminus is visible from US 160 about 6 miles west of the west exit for La Veta.

US 160 has buried much of the old D&RG narrow gauge main line after Reliance, where it crossed to the highway side of the road, but the earlier 160 route over La Veta Pass proper lets you drive the muleshoe section on what is now secondary road and rejoin the highway on the west side. Once in a while on the west slope you can see suggestions of fill where the road digressed from the grade, and at the mouth of Railroad Canyon, where the new grade comes into view, the bridge on the old one is still in place and worth a look.

Sangre de Cristo Pass, which is approximately the North La Veta Pass of US 160, was Captain Gunnison's route though he approached it on the east side from farther north than we do. He speaks of exploring there while his men cut a roadway through the aspens and instead of gouging out the hillside tied the wagons to successive trees to prevent their capsizing.

Colorado College Seminar groups helped in the exploration of old railroads.

46

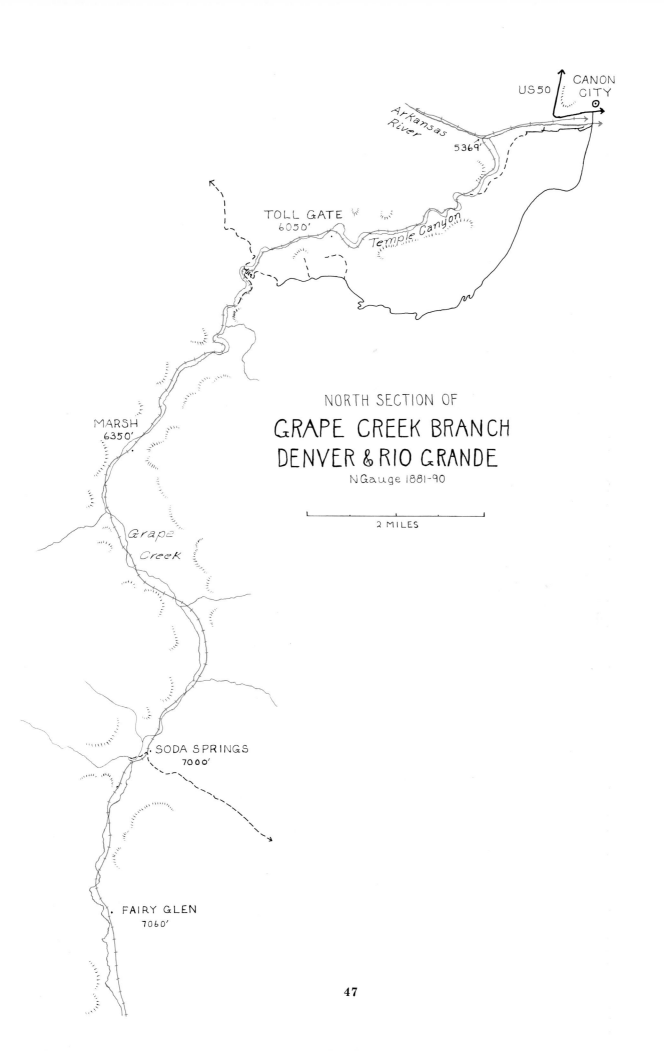

US 50

CANON
CITY

Arkansas
River

5369'

TOLL GATE
6050'

Temple Canyon

NORTH SECTION OF

GRAPE CREEK BRANCH
DENVER & RIO GRANDE

N Gauge 1881-90

2 MILES

MARSH
6350'

Grape
Creek

SODA SPRINGS
7000'

FAIRY GLEN
7060'

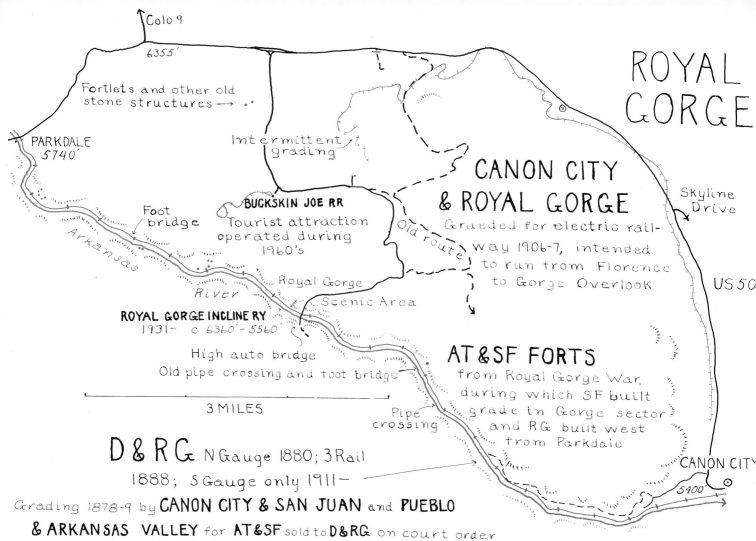

ROYAL GORGE

Colo 9
6355'

Fortlets and other old
stone structures → .•

PARKDALE
5740'

Intermittent
grading

L

CANON CITY
& ROYAL GORGE

Graded for electric rail-
way 1906-7, intended
to run from Florence
to Gorge Overlook

Skyline
Drive

US 50

Foot
bridge

BUCKSKIN JOE RR

Tourist attraction
operated during
1960's

Old route

Arkansas

River

Royal Gorge

Scenic Area

ROYAL GORGE INCLINE RY
1931- c 6360'- 5560'

High auto bridge
Old pipe crossing and foot bridge →

3 MILES

AT & SF FORTS

from Royal Gorge War,
during which SF built
grade in Gorge sector
and RG built west
from Parkdale

Pipe
crossing

CANON CITY

5400'

D & RG N Gauge 1880; 3 Rail
1888; S Gauge only 1911—
Grading 1878-9 by CANON CITY & SAN JUAN and PUEBLO
& ARKANSAS VALLEY for AT&SF sold to D&RG on court order

A Major Fortification in the Royal Gorge War. (Courtesy Canon City Museum)

48

By heading south from First and Main in Canon City you come after 8 miles on a passable dirt road to Grape Creek and can follow the grade in a car for 1/2 mile along the canyon. You can make a long walk up the canyon by only crossing once: the grade is up on the hillside and is sometimes so washed off that you have to scramble along a few feet of cliff to continue. There is also a heavy growth of cane cactus, sometimes thick enough to drive you up the hill for a detour. To make it all the way up to DeWeese Reservoir you would probably have to have a sleeping bag.

The walk down the canyon from the same road crossing takes you through Temple Canyon, where there is a lot of handsome granite on the sides - enough in fact to make you wade the creek, usually in water about a foot deep, about 25 or 30 times. The railroad made only 5 of its total of 35 crossings in this stretch, but except for a few short stretches and a bent rail or two that's all gone and the cliffs drive you relentlessly from side to side.

It is easy to spot the 5 miles of grade at the top end as you drive from Westcliffe out to the reservoir - that is until it dips into the water.

The flat roadbed produces the best trees and cactus plants on these dry hillsides

The CANON CITY AND ROYAL GORGE RAILROAD was incorporated early in 1907 to operate a railroad and a plant to supply power for the Canon City area. The railroad would run a line to the top of the gorge. This company succeeded to the franchises of the Canon City Florence and Royal Gorge Interurban Railway Company, chartered a year earlier. Roadbed built by this company can be seen as a motorist approaches the gorge mesa from Canon City.

Mr. Elwood G. White of Canon City writes that his grandfather had the contract to build the grade from Florence to the top of the Gorge and did the work now visible in 1906-07. Mr. White states that his grandfather and a partner were not paid, which suggests that some of the capital subscribed did not materialize. Mr. White tells me that the total project involved three companies: the Gorge one, the Florence Electric to link Florence with Canon City, and a Canon City and Cripple Creek District as well.

A Second Street bridge in Florence has two plate girders visible from underneath to show where the railroad was to cross, but grade is not evident until you get north of Canon City on US 50 close to where that highway starts to turn west and climb. It

is very distinct on the left side of the road till near the top of the hill on a section remembered as a predecessor of highway 50. You can walk into it from 1.25 miles east of the Gorge exit. In one place it runs square into a ridge and suggests a short tunnel was planned.

A picture in the February 3, 1971 Canon City Record shows a stretch with poles erected for the intended trolley and ties laid. The story indicates there was a try in 1912 at reviving the project. Mr. Fred Merriam, whose plumbing store basement at 404 Main Street yielded up a prospectus and directors' meeting minutes will probably sell you some of the $1.5 million in stock certificates at a favorable discount.

The ROYAL GORGE INCLINE RAILWAY runs on a 37% grade on 3-foot track for a distance of 1550 feet as part of the tourist attraction complex, permitting visitors to descend the bridge area to the Gorge and the hanging bridge section constructed by the Pueblo and Arkansas Valley.

The first trains through the defile were Rio Grande. This one has just passed the Santa Fe - built hanging bridge (Jackson Collection - Colorado State Historical Society)

The ROYAL GORGE WAR was not restricted to the Gorge. There the Santa Fe seized the advantage from the D&RG with the help of crews recruited from Canon City's citizenry, who remembered with anger that the D&RG railroad had approached their town from Pueblo and then stopped short at the coal mines of Florence. When D&RG men found the mouth of the Gorge pre-empted by the enemy road, they leap-frogged beyond them to choke them off in a cold wading operation that proved a failure because they couldn't get supplies through. They gave this up in favor of other flanking moves. One of these was to go toward the southern San Juan by way of La Veta Pass (from which they could have come north over Poncha Pass into the Arkansas above the Gorge); the other was to take possession of the advantageous positions in the Arkansas Valley above the Gorge stretch. Thus the forts within the Gorge section can be assumed those of the Santa Fe and those above Parkdale those of the D&RG.

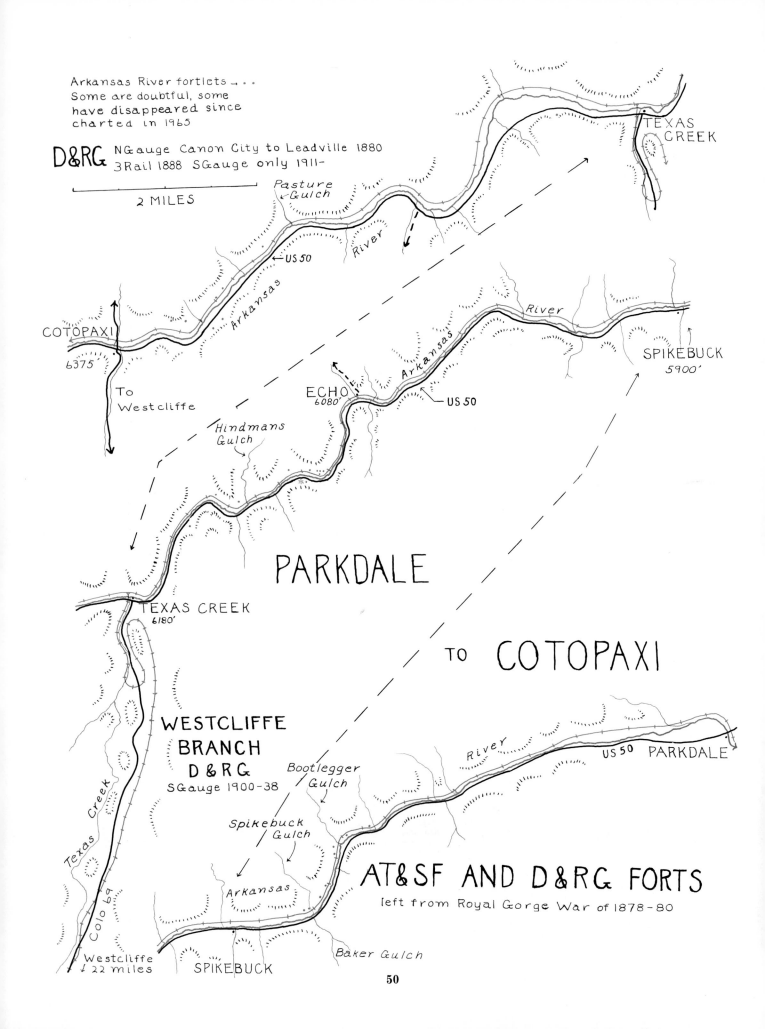

Arkansas River fortlets …
Some are doubtful, some
have disappeared since
charted in 1965

D&RG N Gauge Canon City to Leadville 1880
3 Rail 1888 S Gauge only 1911–

2 MILES

TEXAS
CREEK

Pasture
Gulch

←US 50

Arkansas   River

River

COTOPAXI

6375

To
Westcliffe

ECHO
6080'

Arkansas

←US 50

SPIKEBUCK
5900'

Hindmans
Gulch

PARKDALE

TO COTOPAXI

TEXAS CREEK
6180'

WESTCLIFFE
BRANCH
D&RG
S Gauge 1900–38

Bootlegger
Gulch

River

US 50   PARKDALE

Texas Creek

Colo 69

Spikebuck
Gulch

Arkansas

AT&SF AND D&RG FORTS
left from Royal Gorge War of 1878–80

Westcliffe
↓ 22 miles

SPIKEBUCK

Baker Gulch

50

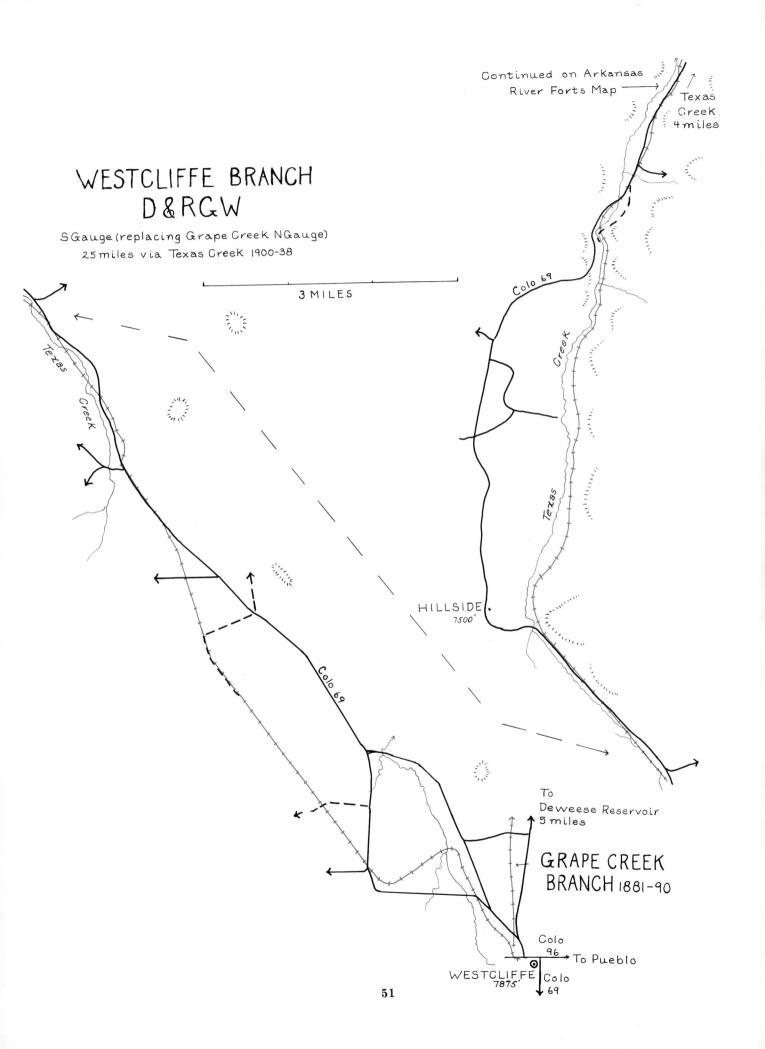

WESTCLIFFE BRANCH
D&RGW

S Gauge (replacing Grape Creek N Gauge)
25 miles via Texas Creek 1900-38

3 MILES

Continued on Arkansas
River Forts Map →

Texas
Creek
4 miles

Texas Creek

Colo 69

Creek

Texas

HILLSIDE
7500'

Colo 69

To
Deweese Reservoir
5 miles

GRAPE CREEK
BRANCH 1881-90

Colo
96 → To Pueblo

WESTCLIFFE
7875'

Colo
69

51

A Santa Fe fort east of the old wooden pipe crossing in the gorge

A two-man Rio Grande fort above Parkdale

Spikebuck had one of the large forts which one sees in pictures; there may have been another about two miles above Parkdale. Neither of them has enough left to make it recognizable. When I asked various people along the river, a lad named Jimmy Teezac at Texas Creek told me he and a friend had found a number of them. I went back a few days later - this was about August 1 of 1965 - and we looked for and located on the Cotopaxi and Royal Gorge quadrangles all the places we thought might be forts.

Some of them were sure, notably one three miles down the river from Texas Creek about 60 feet above the road on a rock. Among the others some are very likely, some not so. Jimmy pointed out several that we only saw from across the river well enough to rate them as probables. I crossed to a couple of them later on in a kayak and came back convinced about one. In subsequent trips - usually too fast to find out much, it has seemed to me that there are fewer than there were - that some of the wall-rocks have been pulled off. I would like it if we could preserve two or three good forts and perhaps restore one of the long ones in its original place (using photographs) as mementos of this extraordinary bit of railroad history. I have mapped about 30 locations of fortlets and possible fortlets with the idea that some one with some time and interest might like to bring in a more exact report.

The CANON CITY AND SAN JUAN RAILWAY COMPANY was the organization raised up by the Santa Fe to battle for the Royal Gorge right of way. The Santa Fe's allies on the ground were Canon City business men — Rockafellow, Clelland, Alling, Holbrook — who capitalized the venture at a modest $100,00 on February 19, 1877. The aim was to run through the Grand Canon and to South Arkansas Post Office. The Pueblo and Arkansas Valley Railroad absorbed this line and took over construction in September, 1878, the time when the P&AV was reincorporated with a proposed network that paralleled all existing branches of the D&RG.

The PUEBLO AND ARKANSAS VALLEY RAILROAD COMPANY was incorporated on March 24, 1875, to absorb and consolidate into a new plan two previous Santa Fe companies formed in Colorado. These previous companies were the Colorado and New Mexico Rail Road set up in July of 1873 by Santa Fe men to run from the Kansas-Colorado line across to Santa Fe and Albuquerque with branches to Trinidad and Pueblo, and the December, 1873, Pueblo and Salt Lake Railway Company formed by friendly Pueblans to run up the Arkansas from Granada to Pueblo and continue by way of Tennessee Pass to Salt Lake.

The walk through the Gorge along the track is a pleasant one. It is wiser to walk up than down because the down-trains can slip up behind you almost inaudibly, with the river making a good deal of noise. The lowest of the forts is on a shoulder of high ground, not visible but behind a visible old shack. The one not far beyond the high bridge is also on the right, and unmistakable. Near the Parkdale end there are signs of a camp which may have had a fort with it.

This fortlet in the Gorge covered a steep side canyon.

The Westcliffe Branch slices through ridgelets two miles south of West Creek

The WESTCLIFFE BRANCH of the D&RG via Texas Creek makes its best scene at the start, where you can see it cliff-hanging its way around a hill above you on the left as you approach Texas Creek on US 50. You can drive a mile south on Colorado 69, climb up left on foot near where it crosses Texas Creek, and follow a mile or so of it around the bend on that section. Most of the rest of the line is visible as you drive 69 to Westcliffe except the part between mile 6 and mile 12, where the highway leaves the creek.

The Wet Mountain Valley saw some fabulous silver mining. The reason there are two towns in the same mile there is that citizens of Silver Cliff, resenting the high water taxes there, put their houses and a store or two on beams and rolled them down the road to Westcliffe. The latter owes its terminal to English sportsmen who liked the valley. Its early settlers included a colony of Germans who were imported to make use of the land; nearby was another colony of Russian Jews who were given useless scrub-oak land near Cotopaxi in a bilking arrangement from which they had to be rescued.

A high fill cuts across the Howard Creek Road midway up the Calcite Branch

The CALCITE BRANCH of the D&RG climbed from about 18 miles southeast of Salida to a limestone quarrying area on both sides of Howard Creek. The D&RG exit, starting point of the line, is 1.2 miles up-river from where the Howard Creek Road starts off US 50. The road to Calcite and its foundations is open - forest access - but the land on both sides, where the railroad winds up and where the quarries are, is closed. You can see an impressive fill crossed by the road, 1.7 miles from US 50, another at mile 2.3, and some switch-backing and foundations at Calcite, but to prowl the upper part of the trackage and the quarries you can pay a fee at the upper Canterbury Ranch that entitles you to carry off a quantity of the calcite crystals which abound in the vast quarry area. For another dollar you can try for trout, if you tire of railroading.

The MONARCH BRANCH of the D&RG is not a ghost railroad but ghost buffs find it interesting because it alone preserves the mountain-climbing feature of switchbacking to make altitude in the steep canyon of the South Arkansas. The track follows the old Gunnison line, now standard gauged, as far west from Salida as Poncha Junction, and continues up the South Arkansas near US 50 to the large quarry there which supplies limestone for the Colorado Fuel and Iron Company's steel mill in Pueblo. As it climbs the railroad U-turns out of the South Arkansas, crosses the highway going east, and after the other half of the S curve, crosses to the creek to start the two laps of

switchback which bring it up close to the floor of the quarry. The D&RG freight agent at Pueblo could probably give you an idea about timing if you want to see the operation.

One day in 1958 I watched a load of 24 cars being taken down the switchback in two sections in a period of about 25 minutes. The brakeman, who had been with the narrow gauge for 26 years, said he had a better job then this with standard gauge and diesel power.

Switchbacking on the Monarch Branch - a Diesel unit comes back up the grade for another turn of the long trainload of limestone

Looking east along the single track

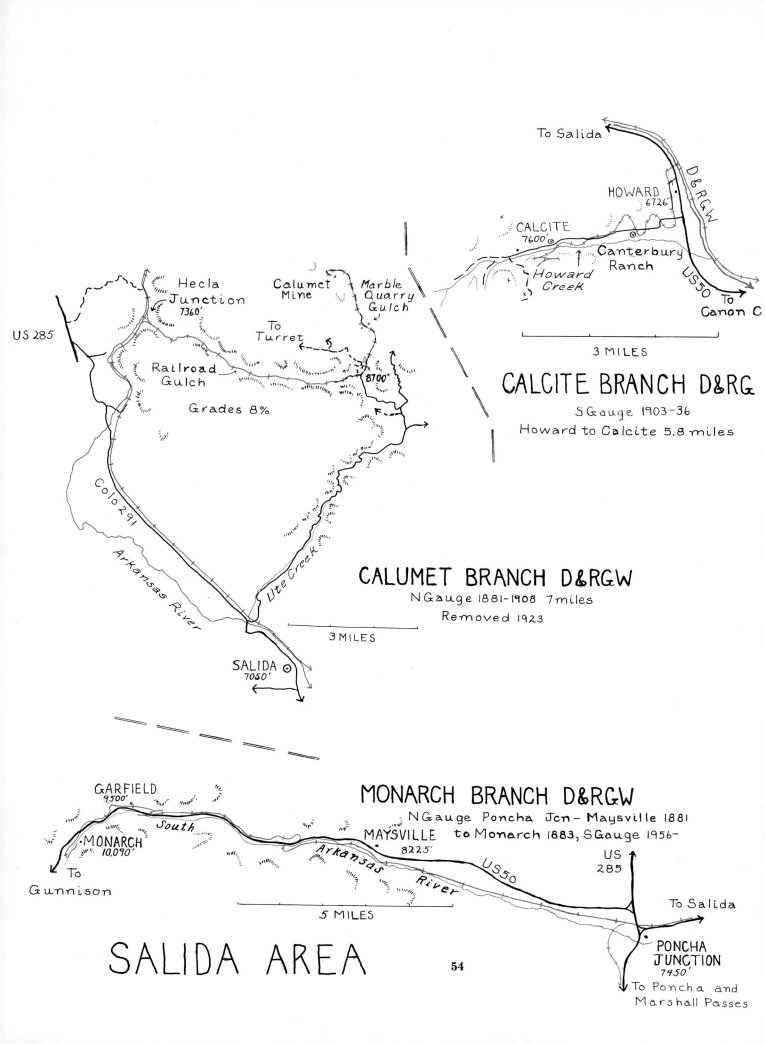

Hecla
Junction
7360'

Calumet
Mine

Marble
Quarry
Gulch

US 285

To
Turret

Railroad
Gulch

8700'

Grades 8%

Colo 291

Arkansas River

Ute Creek

SALIDA
7050'

CALUMET BRANCH D&RGW

N Gauge 1881-1908 7 miles

Removed 1923

3 MILES

To Salida

HOWARD
6726'

CALCITE
7600'

Canterbury
Ranch

Howard
Creek

D&RGW

US 50

To
Canon C

3 MILES

CALCITE BRANCH D&RG

S Gauge 1903-36

Howard to Calcite 5.8 miles

MONARCH BRANCH D&RGW

N Gauge Poncha Jcn - Maysville 1881
to Monarch 1883, S Gauge 1956-

GARFIELD
9500'

MONARCH
10,090'

South

MAYSVILLE
8225'

Arkansas
River

US 50

US
285

To
Gunnison

To Salida

5 MILES

PONCHA
JUNCTION
7450'

SALIDA AREA

54

To Poncha and
Marshall Passes

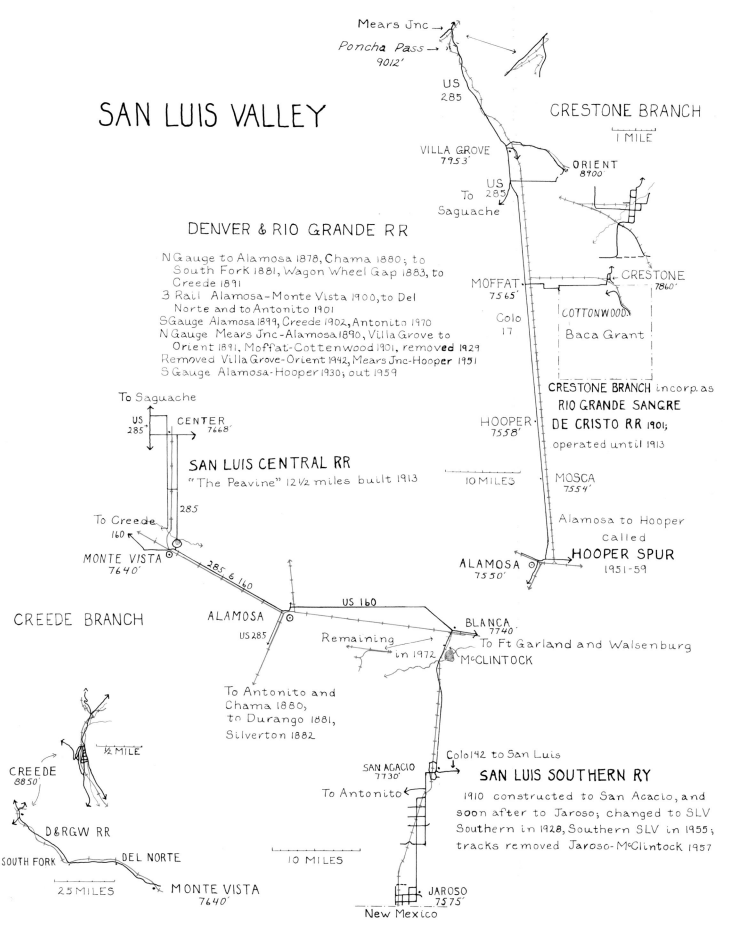

SAN LUIS VALLEY

Mears Jnc →

Poncha Pass →
9012'

US 285

CRESTONE BRANCH

|— 1 MILE —|

VILLA GROVE
7953'

ORIENT
8900'

US 285
To
Saguache

CRESTONE
7860'

DENVER & RIO GRANDE RR

N Gauge to Alamosa 1878, Chama 1880; to
  South Fork 1881, Wagon Wheel Gap 1883, to
  Creede 1891
3 Rail Alamosa-Monte Vista 1900, to Del
  Norte and to Antonito 1901
S Gauge Alamosa 1899, Creede 1902, Antonito 1970
N Gauge Mears Jnc-Alamosa 1890, Villa Grove to
  Orient 1891, Moffat-Cottenwood 1901, removed 1929
Removed Villa Grove-Orient 1942, Mears Jnc-Hooper 1951
S Gauge Alamosa-Hooper 1930; out 1959

MOFFAT
7565'

Colo
17

COTTONWOOD.

Baca Grant

CRESTONE BRANCH incorp. as
RIO GRANDE SANGRE
DE CRISTO RR 1901;
operated until 1913

To Saguache

US 285

CENTER
7668'

HOOPER
7558'

SAN LUIS CENTRAL RR

"The Peavine" 12½ miles built 1913

10 MILES

MOSCA
7554'

285

To Creede
160

MONTE VISTA
7640'

285 & 160

Alamosa to Hooper
called
HOOPER SPUR
1951-59

ALAMOSA
7550'

CREEDE BRANCH

ALAMOSA

US 285

US 160

Remaining
in 1972

BLANCA
7740'

To Ft Garland and Walsenburg

McCLINTOCK

To Antonito and
Chama 1880,
to Durango 1881,
Silverton 1882

½ MILE

Colo 142 to San Luis

SAN ACACIO
7730'

SAN LUIS SOUTHERN RY

To Antonito

1910 constructed to San Acacio, and
soon after to Jaroso; changed to SLV
Southern in 1928, Southern SLV in 1955;
tracks removed Jaroso-McClintock 1957

CREEDE
8850'

D & RGW RR

SOUTH FORK

DEL NORTE

25 MILES

MONTE VISTA
7640'

10 MILES

JAROSO
7575'

New Mexico

The CALUMENT BRANCH OF THE D&RG, sometimes referred to as the Calumet and Hecla Railroad, provided iron from Whitehorn and from Calumet, the mine at the end of the line, and presumably also limestone from Marble Quarry Gulch. Both commodities were used by the Colorado Fuel and Iron Company and its predecessors.

Walking the Calumet Branch near the upper end

The end of the Orient Branch is a steep pull over a deep red roadbed

It is a tempting railroad to explore because of its age, the rough winding valley in which it lies, and its inaccessibility. To see the upper end you take the Turret road. Drive north out of Salida on Colorado 291, exit at the first right turn-off to cross the Arkansas, cross the railroad track, and keep immediately left. After 6 miles up Ute Creek Road exit left for Turret, and keep left after another half mile. Another mile takes you NW over the hill into Railroad Gulch.

To see the upper end of the railroad, take the road marked Ute Trail running east across the Arkansas and D&RG tracks from Colo 291 a mile or so NW of Salida. About 6 miles up the road divides Take the left fork for a mile or so to Railroad Gulch, where you see quarrying. With some vehicles you can drive down the gulch a mile or so in dry weather. Dr. Lester Williams tells me the walk down to Hecla Junction is a long one if you have to return for a car. The road can be followed beyond Railroad Gulch on grade most of the way up Marble Quarry Gulch to the Calumet Mine.

The SAN LUIS VALLEY line of the D&RG, which followed the abandonment of the Grape Creek Branch in 1890, provided, along with a growing agricultural source for revenues, new sources for iron ore. It U-turned on Poncha Creek above Mears Junction to gain altitude, returned to near US 285 for a mile, then veered off right to return to the highway a little south of Poncha Pass. The old water tank at Alder Creek has disappeared but you can see some loading pens and most of the grade down to Villa Grove and can trace it most of the full length of the 52-mile Gunbarrel stretch to Alamosa.

The ORIENT BRANCH went southeast to the mountain base from just south of Villa Grove and about a mile north of the start of the above grand tangent. You can drive most of the grade to the mine by turning east at Villa Grove and after 2 miles angling a little south to find it. The mine, with its piles of brick-red ore up on the hillside is well worth a prowl.

The CRESTONE BRANCH wyes off the mainline .4 mile north of Moffat. It is on fenced land, a mile north of the 12-mile long road west from just south of Moffat to Crestone, and is far from conspicuous. Crestone itself is one of those near ghost towns where there are some live inhabitants to enjoy the atmosphere and keep the buildings in repair. To see what is left of the railroad at Crestone - vanishing grade running out west from a burnt - down station - you keep right on the dirt street instead of left on the pavement, and do your exploring on foot in the vicinity of a locked gate. Cottonwood, at the end of the line, is within the Baca Grant and requires permission and a four-wheel drive approach from the ranch headquarters. I was told in 1965 the road was rough and too sandy for ordinary cars.

The SAN LUIS SOUTHERN RAILWAY COMPANY opened a 31½ mile railroad from Blanca to Jarosa on September 1, 1910. It was started by a group of Colorado Springs men including Franklyn E. Brooks and Horace Lunt. Their purpose, expressed in a charter description of July, 1909, was to run a railroad from either Blanca or Fort Garland south to the Culebra River (at a spot where the Culebra doesn't run) and thence south to Taos and Santa Fe, with a branch east to San Luis from the Culebra. The first section, from Blanca to San Acacio, was opened April 14, 1910. The plan for the year was to take the road on to Jarosa, just short of the state line, and 8 miles into New Mexico, but it only went to Jarosa. The company went into receivership in 1924 and was reorganized four years later as the San Luis Valley Southern Railway by the Boettcher interests, who proposed to extend it to Taos and Santa Fe, and began by authorizing construction of the first 18 miles, Jarosa to Questa. The extension plan was not carried out by this group nor by a group under the name of the San Luis Valley Railroad who proposed lengthening the line again in 1953.

Since the major removal there have been a delapidated steam locomotive and a caboose standing on the track near the north end, and a little north of that there is a stretch of live trackage which serves as a spur from the D&RG siding. This remnant and a small diesel unit take care of loading from the packing sheds of the Mizokami Brothers. A good deal of the grade can be traced south to Jaroso, including the Trinchera Creek trestle which is now part of the automobile road. The SLS is the only railroad which ended exactly on the state line.

The old caboose is on the present end of the track southwest of Blanca

The SAN LUIS CENTRAL RAILROAD COMPANY began operating in 1913 with 15 miles - 2¹/₂ miles to the east from Monte Vista, perhaps with a D&RG spur only, and the 12¹/₂ miles north to a sugar factory at Center. The *Del Norte Prospector* of February 11, 1955, reported that the Central has "purchased a diesel electric engine to replace the old steam puffer, serving since 1913." The rails at Center were still shining on my last visit around 1968.

The CREEDE BRANCH, built in the David Moffat presidency of the Rio Grande and still intermittently active, is a pleasant drive along the rocky stretch of the Rio Grande. The slumbering station at Wagon Wheel Gap may still be there, and it has some curiosities at the upper end of Creede where an upper level of grade from one of the mines still remained (1967) as a walkable trestled roadbed from which ore must have been troughed to the cars below. The branch takes out ore and concentrates from the Imperius Mine as they collect.

Pleasing railroad architecture - the station at Wagon Wheel Gap

An upper-level of mine-gauge track delivered ore to the end of the Creede Branch

San Luis Southern's locomotive 105 - a museum piece

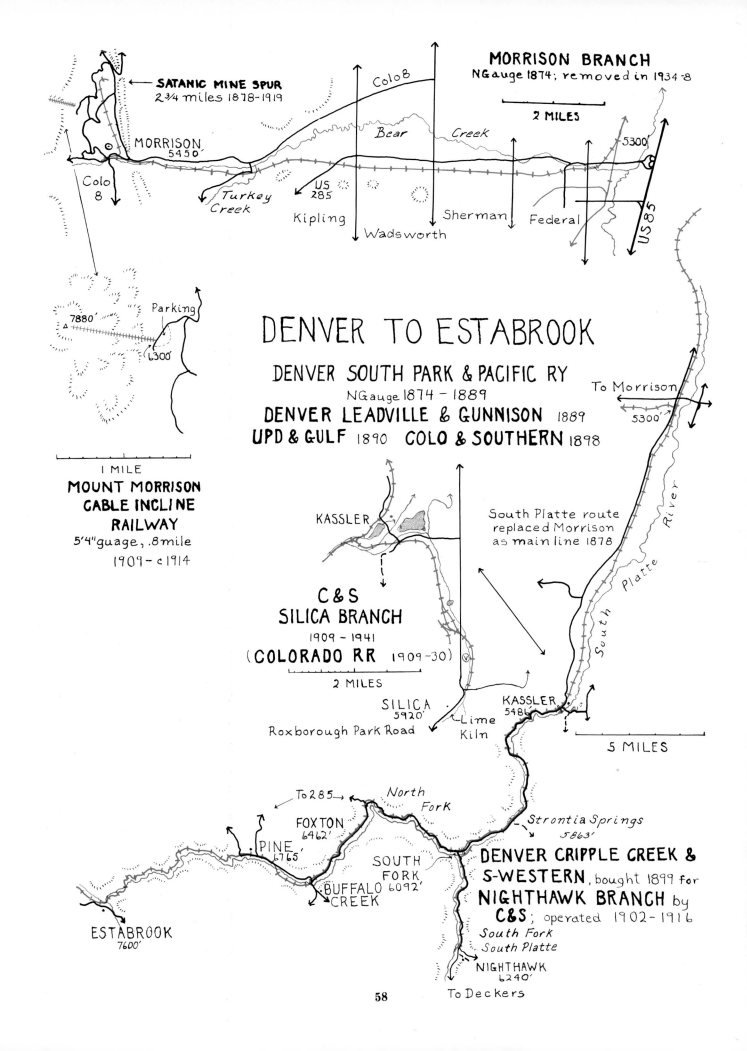

SATANIC MINE SPUR
2¾ miles 1878-1919

MORRISON BRANCH
N Gauge 1874; removed in 1934-8

Colo 8

2 MILES

Bear Creek

5300'

MORRISON
5450'

Colo 8

Turkey Creek

US 285

Kipling

Wadsworth

Sherman

Federal

US 85

7880'

Parking

6300'

1 MILE

MOUNT MORRISON CABLE INCLINE RAILWAY
5'4" guage, .8 mile
1909 - c 1914

DENVER TO ESTABROOK

DENVER SOUTH PARK & PACIFIC RY
N Gauge 1874 - 1889
DENVER LEADVILLE & GUNNISON 1889
UPD & GULF 1890   COLO & SOUTHERN 1898

To Morrison

5300'

KASSLER

South Platte route
replaced Morrison
as main line 1878

**C & S
SILICA BRANCH**
1909 - 1941
(COLORADO RR 1909-30)

2 MILES

South Platte River

SILICA
5920'

Roxborough Park Road

Lime Kiln

KASSLER
5486'

5 MILES

To 285

North Fork

FOXTON
6462'

Strontia Springs
5863'

PINE
6765'

SOUTH FORK

BUFFALO CREEK
6092'

DENVER CRIPPLE CREEK & S-WESTERN, bought 1899 for
NIGHTHAWK BRANCH by
C&S; operated 1902-1916

ESTABROOK
7600'

South Fork
South Platte

NIGHTHAWK
6240'

To Deckers

58

PART III
DENVER WEST

MAPS

This composite shows two main ways of making altitude: The Georgetown Loop and the Argentine's switch-backs.

The DENVER SOUTH PARK AND PACIFIC RAILWAY COMPANY was formed June 14, 1873, by a group including Hallack, Kountze, Cheesman, Clayton, J.W. Smith, and John Evans, the last its president and main drive. It was one of two spokes actually constructed by Evans in a vast wheel of which Denver was to be the hub, and aimed at a junction with the Southern Pacific at Fort Yuma in Arizona. The book, *Denver South Park and Pacific,* in which M.C. Poor relates the road's history, was published by the Colorado Railroad Club in 1949. It was soon out of print and now commands high prices as a railroaders' classic and collectors' item.

This railroad made its drive toward Leadville and the San Juan while the D&RG was still battling with the Santa Fe over the Royal Gorge and the upper Arkansas Valley, and it arrived in the Buena Vista area ahead of the D&RG. The South Park line, which was also headed for the Gunnison country and Leadville, came under the control of Jay Gould, who had helped to bail General Palmer out of some of his difficulties with the Rio Grande. Through his efforts the Rio Grande rented trackage rights to the South Park line between Buena Vista and Leadville and agreed not to build a parallel to the South Park's intended line to Gunnison, but instead accept a rental of DSP&P trackage for any business they developed there. In 1880 Jay Gould sold his interest in the DSP&P to the Union Pacific. Palmer stated that this liberated him to move into the Gunnison territory since he had made no arrangements with the UP. The DSP&P took a short cut route up Chalk Creek, through the Divide in an 1800-foot tunnel and down an expensive rock palisade to Quartz Creek, the Tomichi and Gunnison. The tunnel, instead of being solid rock as expected, had to be shored up with redwood 12x12's, and the railroad was a year later than the D&RG in reaching Gunnison.

The South Park line had one of the worst slide disasters in Colorado history when an avalanche crushed the station at Woodstock, on the west side of Alpine Pass, and killed 13 of 18 people who were swept down. In a suit by Mrs. Marcelle Doyle, who lost her family of three sons and three daughters, it was plausibly stated that the railroad company had created the hazard by cutting out the heavy timber above the station. There were tales of hardship caused by the deep snow on the east side, too, including a slide which knocked out a long section of the snowshed approach to the tunnel. The tunnel story is enlarged from Poor's treatment in a book by Dow Helmers entitled *Historic Alpine Tunnel.*

Instead of continuing through the San Juan country to Arizona, the road settled for the extension up Ohio Creek for about 20 miles to Baldwin and Kubler. Three or four more miles of track were laid north from Baldwin, and from there the grading that was to go to Floresta continued.

The grade in South Park is nearly all in evidence though not always in sight. Proceeding south from Trout Creek Pass, where it underpasses the Midland, it is the closer of the two grades you see. Where the road (US 24) turns from south to southwest you can look down on a long section that was converted to highway and still has remains of highway bridges. Parts near the bottom are less accessible but when you get to the Chalk Creek road you are soon on grade and follow the cuts and curves all the way to Hancock. Some people jeep it from there on to Alpine Tunnel but it makes a good walk of about 2½ miles with flowers between the ties. The tunnel mouth is closed. An old road makes it easy to climb to the pass crest and look down on the wye on the roomier valley head of the west side.

Coming up the west side from US 50 you don't see much of it

before you reach Pitkin, but from there you are on grade and after the snows melt you can take the fine drive up Quartz Creek to Sherrod and along the palisades to the tunnel mouth, where there is plenty to look at. Not much shows up between Parlin and Gunnison.

The grand palisade on the west side of Alpine Tunnel.

The SILICA BRANCH, which was attached to the South Park by the Colorado Railroad, another Colorado and Southern property, can be visited from US 85. A graveled road runs west from 4 miles south of the Blakeland underpass or 5½ miles northwest of Sedalia. After 3 miles it turns south for 4 miles. On this stretch the grade crosses from east of the road to west and remains visible on your left the rest of the way to Roxbury Park entrance. Right there you can find some half buried track and the kiln for brick-making which together with feldspar mining provided the basis for the town of Silica and the spur. One can walk the grade north from near the kiln but it is weedy.

The kiln at the end of the Silica Branch.

The DENVER CRIPPLE CREEK AND SOUTH-WESTERN RAILROAD COMPANY was formed in the beginning of 1896 to run southwest from Denver through Cripple Creek and Victor, through Silver Cliff and through the Territories of New Mexico, Arizona to tidewater. William G. Evans was one of the incorporators of this long cast to the southwest. Colorado and Southern records show that that railroad purchased the DCC&Sw franchise in 1899 as a basis for the 4-mile line built in 1902 from South Platte to Nighthawk. Morris Cafky tells us that it was to be the basis for a standard-gauge line to run from the projected Denver Leadville and Gunnison, where that left the Platte Canon to the Colorado Midland track at Florissant. By double-gauging the end of the DL&G and using the Midland system, they would get standard-gauge track from Cripple Creek to Denver for the price of 41 miles of new construction. There seems to have been a free-for-all over the part of this roadbed which is now covered by Cheesman Lake. The *Rocky Mountain News* of February 2, 1900, tells that C&S officials had been instructed to lay tracks as far as Horse Creek (Deckers) and claims that they were doing it; another clipping of the time states that the D&RG were surveying and grading above this point, and the *Denver Times* refers to the Denver Cripple Creek and Southwestern as a co-defendant with the D&RG, the Colorado Irrigation and Canal Company, and the Denver Lakewood and Golden and Colorado and Southern Railroads in a condemnation suit for the South Platte lands later inundated. At any rate the Denver Union Water Company ended up in control and built Cheesman Dam. The Denver to Cripple Creek project was eventually given up.

The NIGHTHAWK BRANCH served a small mining area during the 14 years of its existence. You are clearly on the grade between Nighthawk and South Platte.

The road-on-grade from Kassler to South Fork is closed, so that without permission and key all one can do is walk it, which is interesting enough for at least a stretch at the upper end. One rides or sees it off and on from South Fork to Pine, at Estabrook, and from Bailey over the pass to Como, with special interest points at Estabrook (a bridge), at Webster (a loop up Hall Valley), and at Como, where you can go south to King Mines.

Como is said to have had as many as twenty trains a day at one period but Cecil Graves remembers riding to Denver for Christmas vacation in 1917 when he was one of two passengers. It was a daytime trip, from 6 to 6.

The Boreas Pass road is one of the fine railroad drives on grade through the mountains. Except for the ends and a one-sided cut which you must walk to enjoy properly, you are on the track all the way. The great high snow fence at the top has been shot down by the winds, but you can trace out the wye and foundations at the summit. The tank on the north side reasserts the old atmosphere and the presence of an army of enthusiasts who want to keep what they can of the railroad days. Some of the roadbed can be found in the north parts of Frisco. From there to Climax there are occasional evidences of both railroads, particularly in a stretch about 2 miles long starting just south of the Vail Pass departure near Wheeler, and at Kokomo.

The KEYSTONE BRANCH represented indirectly the realization of plans of long standing to get through the Divide over or under Argentine Pass from Clear Creek and provide rail service for considerable mining areas there. Its 55-year life span indicates something of its usefulness.

The last time I visited the Keystone Branch there were ties

still there. To reach it from the Denver approach you drive off Highway 6 on the Peru Creek - Montezuma Road and take the first right turn to go 2 miles west. You may find a fellow named Peterson on his porch and across from his house a roadbed complete with ties and spikes. A few yards east there is a house which served as the station. You can trace the grade on west with some interruptions to where it crosses into Highway 6 with your road, about 2 1/2 miles west of the Montezuma exit.

Although the independent line to Leadville had been projected during the late 1870's when the railroad was crossing Kenosha Pass, it appears from Poor's book that the grading of Boreas Pass, which was started in 1881, was mainly with the purpose of reaching Keystone and perhaps Montezuma on the Snake River and perhaps making connection with the Georgetown Breckenridge and Leadville through Argentine Pass. The road went to Dillon, 30.7 miles from Como, in December of 1882 and made the turn from Dickey east 7 miles to Keystone in January, 1883. The D&RG had no sooner reached Leadville than it came over Fremont Pass and down the Ten Mile to Dillon. They graded stretches down the Blue River on a line described in an early incorporation called the Western Colorado, and were very much on the ground when the South Park officials decided to lay a parallel track into Leadville. The latter incurred litigation over the right of way, which was in part too close to that of the D&RG, and at Kokomo they were forced to over pass the prior line. The Leadville line, which twice crossed the Divide, gave its operators some more snow problems.

The most famous of the DSP&P legends is that of the circus elephants which were taken from their cars and set to work at the back end as helpers. M.C. Poor runs three versions of the story which agree as to what happened but assign different locations.

The 15 1/2 mile Garos to Alma line, which in the original thinking might well have served as the springboard for the Blue River and Leadville extension via Hoosier Pass, was instead terminated with two tracks that climbed high into the Mosquito Range. One was the 11 1/3 mile Horseshoe or Leavick Branch, surveyed in 1888 but not built until 1896 under the charter Denver South Park and Hilltop Railway and merged into the Denver Leadville and Gunnison under Frank Trumbull's management of the same. The other was known as the London South Park and Leadville Railroad, reorganized in April, 1885, after financial difficulties as the South Park and Leadville Short Line Railroad. Though *Poor's Manual* states that the Union Pacific advanced materials for the road in 1882-83, it was constructed as a separate organization and remained so. It was not constantly in use even through 1890, and before 1900 a new South Portal to the London Mine rendered it useless. Secondary motor roads now run on or next to both of these high valley railroad beds.

Two short coal feeders of the DSP&P went in near Como. The first according to M.C. Poor was named the Leckner Branch for its discoverer. It left the main line in a mile-long spur running northwest, and later became the start of the Boreas Pass route. The second started 3/4 mile short of Como and went south 3 miles to the King Mines. Both mines became the property of the South Park Coal Company which the railroad officials organized.

Among the South Park stories is one about Governor Evans, who was riding up front on the locomotive when it rounded a curve to reveal a little girl playing between the rails. The Governor possessed himself of a stick from somewhere and slid down the cowcatcher far enough to push her out of the way. I found it

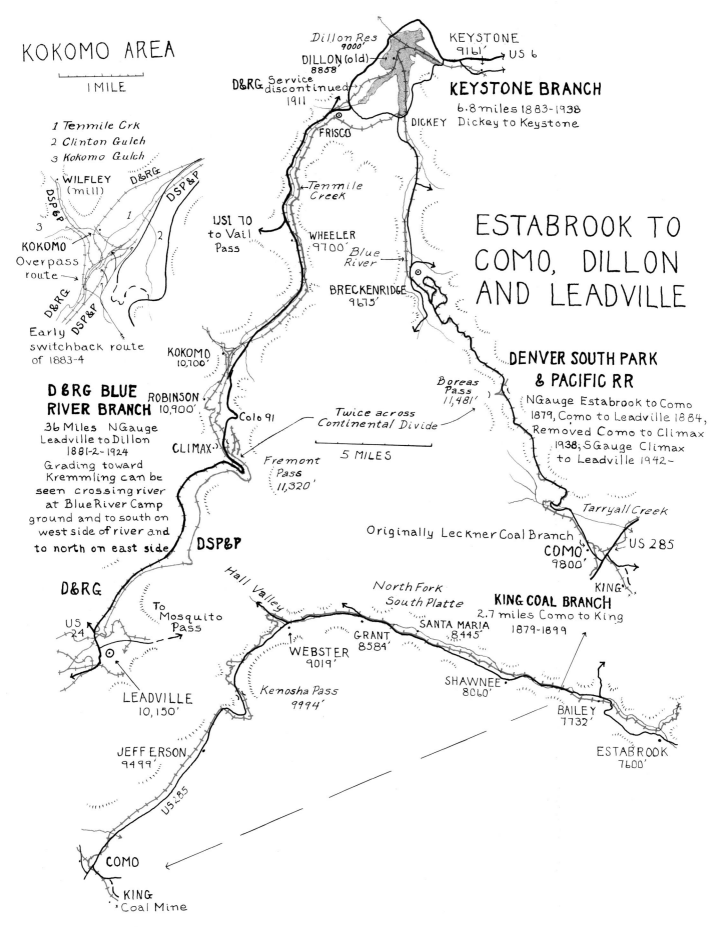

KOKOMO AREA

|——— 1 MILE ———|

1 Tenmile Crk
2 Clinton Gulch
3 Kokomo Gulch

WILFLEY (mill)

DSP&P

D&RG

KOKOMO
Overpass
route

D&RG   DSP&P

Early
switchback route
of 1883-4

KOKOMO
10,700'

ROBINSON
10,900'

Colo 91

CLIMAX

Fremont
Pass
11,320'

D&RG BLUE RIVER BRANCH

36 Miles N Gauge
Leadville to Dillon
1881-2-1924
Grading toward
Kremmling can be
seen crossing river
at Blue River Camp
ground and to south on
west side of river and
to north on east side

D&RG

US 24

To Mosquito
Pass

DSP&P

LEADVILLE
10,150'

JEFFERSON
9499'

US 285

COMO

KING
Coal Mine

Dillon Res
9000'
DILLON (old)
8858'

KEYSTONE
9161'   US 6

D&RG Service
discontinued
1911

KEYSTONE BRANCH

6.8 miles 1883-1938
Dickey to Keystone

DICKEY

FRISCO

*Tenmile
Creek*

US 70
to Vail
Pass

WHEELER
9700'   *Blue
River*

BRECKENRIDGE
9675'

*Boreas
Pass
11,481'*

Twice across
Continental Divide

|——— 5 MILES ———|

ESTABROOK TO COMO, DILLON AND LEADVILLE

DENVER SOUTH PARK & PACIFIC RR

N Gauge Estabrook to Como
1879, Como to Leadville 1884,
Removed Como to Climax
1938; S Gauge Climax
to Leadville 1942-

Tarryall Creek

Originally Leckner Coal Branch

COMO
9800'

US 285

KING

KING COAL BRANCH

2.7 miles Como to King
1879-1899

*North Fork
South Platte*

Hall Valley

SANTA MARIA
8445'

GRANT
8584'

WEBSTER
9019'

*Kenosha Pass
9994'*

SHAWNEE
8060'

BAILEY
7732'

ESTABROOK
7600'

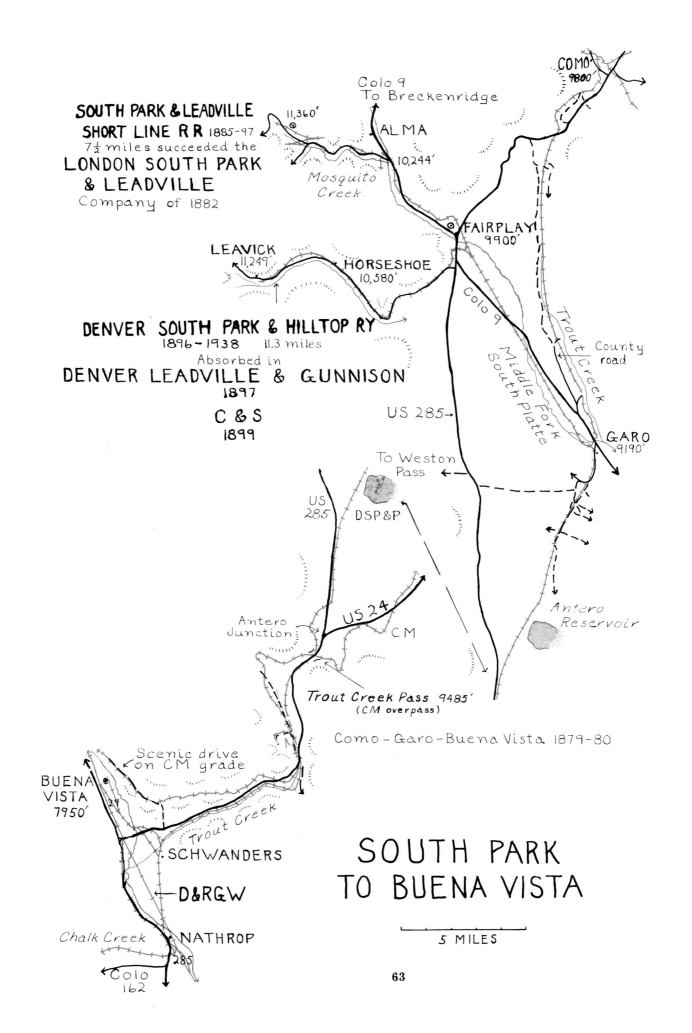

SOUTH PARK & LEADVILLE
SHORT LINE R R 1885-97
7½ miles succeeded the
LONDON SOUTH PARK
& LEADVILLE
Company of 1882

11,360'

Colo 9
To Breckenridge

ALMA
10,244'

Mosquito Creek.

COMO
9800'

FAIRPLAY
9900'

LEAVICK
11,249'

HORSESHOE
10,580'

Colo 9

Trout Creek

County road

DENVER SOUTH PARK & HILLTOP RY
1896-1938 11.3 miles
Absorbed in
DENVER LEADVILLE & GUNNISON
1897
C & S
1899

US 285→

Middle Fork South Platte

GARO
9190'

To Weston Pass ←

US 285

DSP&P

Antero Reservoir

Antero Junction

US 24

CM

Trout Creek Pass 9485'
(CM overpass)

Como - Garo - Buena Vista 1879-80

Scenic drive
on CM grade

BUENA VISTA
7950'

24

Trout Creek

SCHWANDERS

←D&RGW

Chalk Creek

NATHROP

285

Colo 162

SOUTH PARK
TO BUENA VISTA

5 MILES

63

easier to believe another tale told me by an old Breckenridge miner. It seems he and his sister were playing on a detached freight car when it started to move and carried them down at a fast rumbling rate to Dickey where the locomotives coaled before it slowed down and they could get off.

The MOUNT MORRISON CABLE INCLINE carried passengers from Morrison to the top of 7000-foot Mount Morrison on a cable road described in a 1911 issue of *Engineering News*. Like the Mount Manitou, it had two cars hung on the ends of a cable. The cable was wrapped around an electric-powered drum or driving sheave at the top, operated by electricity. A Burlington Route pamphlet whose cover shows one of the old rustic arched footbridges in Monument Valley Park with Pikes Peak in the background lists this trip, reached from the end of the Morrison line of the C&S, "Mt. Morrison and the Park of the Rocks," as one of those "reaching views not surpassed." Tracks were a wide gauge — 5-foot 4-inches — to accommodate wide cars that held 100 passengers. Unlike the Manitou, this had 3 rails to avoid the use of frogs in the 4-railed middle section where the cars passed. It was about .8 mile long, running west from a point 1.2 miles northwest of Morrison, or just north of the Red Rocks.

The MORRISON BRANCH began life with a locomotive dubbed the Fairplay as the DSP&P main line. It was still partly visible near the Morrison end in the middle '60's. Running from the town north you could also see scars of the Satanic Mine spur and the Mount Morrison Cable Incline.

D&RG grading on the east side of Blue River.

The BLUE RIVER BRANCH of the D&RG was part of Palmer's ramifications to forestall competition. The Union Pacific could get into Colorado's back country from Wyoming without crossing the mountain range west of Denver. The first goal on the line was in the active Kokomo area, which gave the general's road a farther-north entry to the western slope. The road was ironed down to Dillon, and had sections of grading beyond there along the Blue. I have not shown this on a map and there isn't much of it in evidence, but you can find some of it if you turn off Colorado 9 at the Rock Creek Campground, about 7 miles north of the US 6 exit for Kremmling. There are remnants of a bridge abutment at the river, and you can find some sketchy grade through the flats to the south of it for a little way. Driving on north and looking across the river you see what is probably more of this work through the next two miles.

The SOUTH PARK AND LEADVILLE SHORT LINE RAILROAD COMPANY was a successor to the London South Park and Leadville Railroad of February, 1882 and *Poor's Manual* carries an item for several years in the late eighties and early nineties which states that the railroad acquired at this company's incorporation in 1885 had been built by the London one with track which had been advanced by the Union Pacific. The UP owned the SP&Leadville, having paid prior obligations of $4490.01. The UP never listed it as operated railroad, but M.C. Poor indicates it carried ore in the '90's from the London Mine.

Like the London road, the SP&L was to go through to Leadville — this one specifically through the north ridge of Mosquito Gulch on a line governed by grades not to exceed 240 feet to the mile to the high-line track of the DSP&P in Birds Eye Gulch in Lake County, and thence down the Arkansas (East Arkansas) to Leadville. At 12,000 feet this would have meant a 2-mile tunnel; 400-feet higher, it would have meant a 1/2 mile tunnel through the sharp part of the ridge.

There is no problem for a small car in driving up the grade or finding its separation from the road at the upper end. If you have followed the railroad west from Fairplay (above or right of Colorado 9), you turn off about where it swings across Colorado 9 to the left side and take the Mosquito Pass road.

The DENVER SOUTH PARK AND HILLTOP RAILWAY ran from Hilltop Junction, between Fairplay and Alma on the Denver South Park and Pacific, west to Leavick, a distance of 11 miles. The charter, dated September 1, 1896, called for a road from Fairplay to Leavick, and the road was built in that year. It was merged with the Denver Leadville and Gunnison a year later and became part of the C&S in the beginning of 1899. The branch is included in the line to be revived by the 1932 attempt — the Denver Leadville and Alma Railroad. M.S. Wolle states that the road profited by the 1901 boom as a carrier of tie lumber and also brought down high-grade zinc carbonate ore from the mine at Leavick.

The end of track at Leavick is still conspicuous where it turns off the road to head for a few yards toward the big horseshoe for which the gulch is named. The Horseshoe Branch, as it was sometimes called, had 6% grades.

The DENVER AND RIO GRANDE, after 1920 the D&RG Western, has been almost from the beginning the chief mountain railroad of the nation and the only surviving railroad through the Colorado mountains. The story of its difficulties and of its emergence as a strong modern road has been drawn together in a 1962 Yale University Press book by Robert G. Athearn: *Rebel of the Rockies*. For the account below we are indebted to this work and to the several more specialized and less complete ones which preceded it, among them the Logan and Wilson theses, George Anderson's small book on Palmer and the early D&RG, William S. Jackson's discussion of rivalries in the eighties, the McMechen book on the Moffat Tunnel, the Brayer book on early financing, and such books as Overton's Marshall's, etc., primarily about other roads.

Summary of Management and Corporate History

William J. Palmer makes something of a hero, complete with tragic frailty, for the narrative of the early Rio Grande. As a Union officer in the Civil War, he was caught behind enemy lines in civilian clothes. At the Richmond prison he had to fight off recognition by anyone among the successive waves of new inmates lest he be shot at sunrise. He was exchanged, became a general, and after the war set out as an officer of the Kansas Pacific, for which he surveyed through the Southwest. He took over construction of that railroad for its last jump — Limon to Denver — and then formed his own company. Instead of living in Denver and aligning himself with the business men there, he set up his home in a mountain glen so hidden that no one can even see into it except from the mountain behind. It is five miles from the town he founded, and he is remembered for living there in his later days in the remote grandeur of a large castle, from which he doled out parks to Colorado Springs, and buildings and ground to Colorado College, and indulged in such little personal benevolences as bringing his cavalry regiment out from Pennsylvania for a party in his hotel and passing out a million - dollar largess to his former railroad employees.

Palmer incorporated his railroad in 1870 and remained its president for 13 years. Financial difficulties caused him to lease it to the Santa Fe in December, 1878, during the war for the Royal Gorge. He forced the road into the receivership of L.C. Ellsworth beginning in August, 1879, in order to escape self-interested Santa Fe management, and achieved surrender of the lease in the Boston Treaty, early in 1880. The U.S. Supreme Court had awarded him victory in the Gorge and the treaty deflected his road westward. With vastly improved credit rating, he expanded over Colorado and built up a continuing system in Utah, the D&RGW (later RGW) which he leased to the D&RG. An aggressive policy of route explorations and pre-emptive grading in strategic mountain valleys brought on disfavor with the eastern owners who in 1883 replaced him in the presidency with Frederick Lovejoy. Lovejoy condemned the terms of the RGW lease, by which the D&RG had to guarantee interest on the RGW bonds. Lovejoy tried to gain management of the RGW, and when he failed, cut the rail connection between the two. He also refused to carry freight for the Colorado Coal and Iron Company, a Palmer organization in Pueblo, and thus contributed to strengthening the (later) Colorado and Southern, an east-slope rival of the D&RG. Bond defaults took both D&RG and RGW into receivership in 1884, at which time W.S. Jackson took over for the D&RG and promptly re-established connections. Receivership ended with an 1886 sale which returned the property to its owners under the name change from Railway to Railroad. Jackson remained in office as president for another year, long enough to persuade the conservative eastern owners to return to some of the Palmer aggressiveness and counter the various threats of competition in western Colorado: the Union Pacific entry, through a northern back door from Fort Steele, the UP and also Burlington exploring and grading activities in the Colorado Canon, and the actual building of the Colorado Midland Railroad from Colorado Springs through Leadville and over the divide to Aspen.

When Jackson retired in 1887, David Moffat followed him as president. His policy reflected his interest in the metal mines and his long association with business leaders in Denver. He built the Creede Branch for the D&RG and the Florence and Cripple Creek, and carried out the surveys from which he later selected the route for his own railroad over Rollins Pass. One of Moffat's schemes, said to have been acceptable to the directorate though it was never pushed, was the Denver Short Line — a railroad that would follw the same route as the Denver South Park and Pacific from Denver to Buena Vista except for using the south fork of the South Platte instead of the north fork. This would save 100 miles over the Pueblo route and compensate for some of the greater altitude by cutting out the 3000-foot climb over the Palmer Lake divide — at an estimated cost of $8 million.

Other Moffat surveys were carried over Argentine, Georgia, Grizzley, and Montezuma Passes, farther south in general than the possibilities earlier explored by the Union Pacific, at a com-

bined cost reported by Arthur Ridgway as $106,000. He also set up the main line shift from the Gunnison to the Colorado River and the change, with Palmer's cooperation, to standard gauge in 1890. His policies were a little too much like Palmer's for the management, who replaced his regime with the long economy rule of E.T. Jeffery, 1891-1912.

The latter of these two decades began with a shift of ownership to the Gould family, represented by George Gould. His father, Jay Gould, had in 1879 come to Palmer's financial rescue with the double purpose of fighting the Santa Fe out of Union Pacific and Denver South Park and Pacific territory — he had an interest in both roads — and of working his way into a raiding position in the Rio Grande. As Athearn shows, he threatened the Santa Fe with a rival road to be built down the Arkansas parallel to their own by the Rio Grande — this just before the Boston Treaty — and then when he could not bluff his way into control of the D&RG over Palmer's head he sold out and tried to depress the price of the stock, presumably so he could buy up the road at a bargain. Before 1900 the Gould interest had shifted from the Union Pacific to the Missouri Pacific, and George Gould set about organizing a trans-continental system. He brought about D&RG purchase of the Rio Grande Western from Palmer, and then when the Harriman-Hill combination flanked him out at Ogden he built his way to San Francisco with the Western Pacific between 1905 and 1910. The D&RG, which had been meeting its obligations, was made the chief guarantor of Western Pacific indebtedness.

B.F. Bush, president of the Missouri Pacific and the Western Pacific, succeeded Jeffery in the Rio Grande. Gould had lost control of the system as a whole to Kuhn Loeb and Company, but in 1915 he installed George Coppell as Rio Grande president, and a few days after him Henry Mudge, whose presidency saw some rehabilitation in the badly run-down road but no improvement in its hopeless financial burden. Default brought about the 1918 receivership of Edward Brown and Alexander Baldwin, which lasted until shortly after the wartime period of government control ending in 1920. In the reorganization sale the owners of the Western Pacific obtained control for a court upset price of $5 million. The new name is that which has held since — the Denver and Rio Grande Western. Joseph Young served as president for the first year, and when default forced another receivership in 1922 he continued as receiver. Thomas Beacom replaced him in this position in 1923, and after another year the railroad was purchased in effect for the Western Pacific and Missouri Pacific together by a group called the Reorganization Managers for the upset price of $18 million. James S. Pyeatt served as president until the Depression brought about another default and the 1935-1947 trusteeship of Henry Swan and Wilson McCarthy. During this long period the court, which had become attentive to Colorado protests against predatory outside management, encouraged all expenditures necessary for a complete physical modernization, and at its end recognized no Missouri Pacific and Western Pacific control through stock ownership. The management was thus transferred into the orbit of Colorado and Utah business interests. McCarthy continued with the road as president from 1947 until his death in 1956, when G.B. Aydelott succeeded.

Modernizations of the Swan-McCarthy-Aydelott period have included a large pruning of the narrow-gauge system, notably the entire Gunnison line, the Santa Fe line: and the line from Antonito line to Durango, and reductions of double track in favor of CTC, installations of protective warning fences, the change to Diesel power on all standard lines, and a number of innovations resulting from the most progressive laboratory in the

NATHROP TO GUNNISON

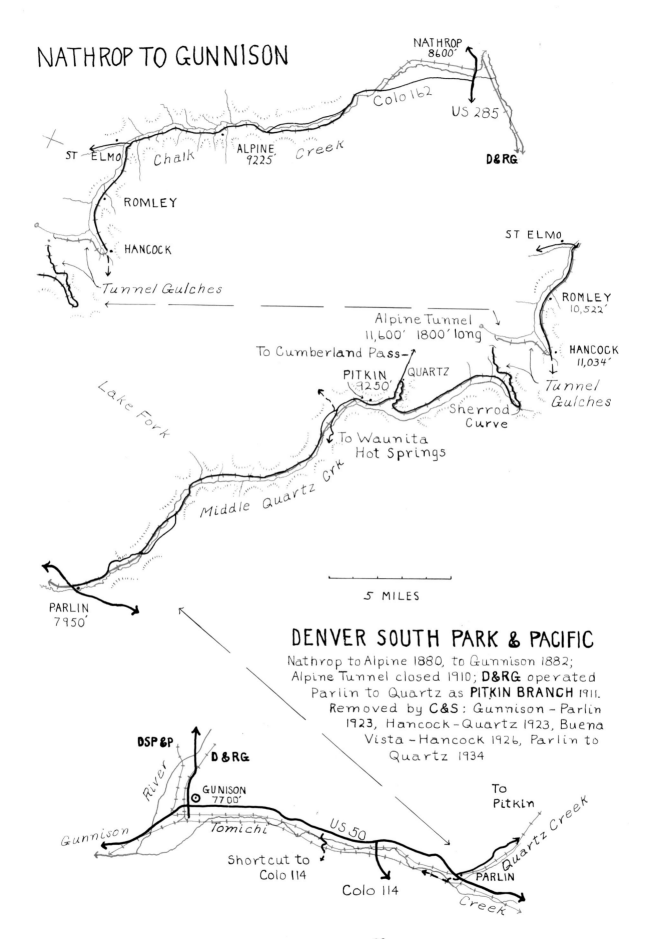

NATHROP 8600'

Colo 162

US 285

D&RG

ST ELMO

Chalk   ALPINE   Creek
        9225'

ROMLEY

HANCOCK

Tunnel Gulches

ST ELMO

ROMLEY
10,522'

HANCOCK
11,034'

Tunnel Gulches

Alpine Tunnel
11,600' 1800' long

To Cumberland Pass

PITKIN   QUARTZ
9250'

Sherrod
Curve

Lake Fork

To Waunita
Hot Springs

Middle Quartz Crk

5 MILES

PARLIN
7950'

DENVER SOUTH PARK & PACIFIC
Nathrop to Alpine 1880, to Gunnison 1882;
Alpine Tunnel closed 1910; **D&RG** operated
Parlin to Quartz as **PITKIN BRANCH** 1911.
Removed by **C&S**: Gunnison – Parlin
1923, Hancock – Quartz 1923, Buena
Vista – Hancock 1926, Parlin to
Quartz 1934

DSP&P   **D&RG**

River

GUNISON
7700'

Gunnison

Tomichi   US 50

Shortcut to
Colo 114

Colo 114

To
Pitkin

Quartz Creek

PARLIN

Creek

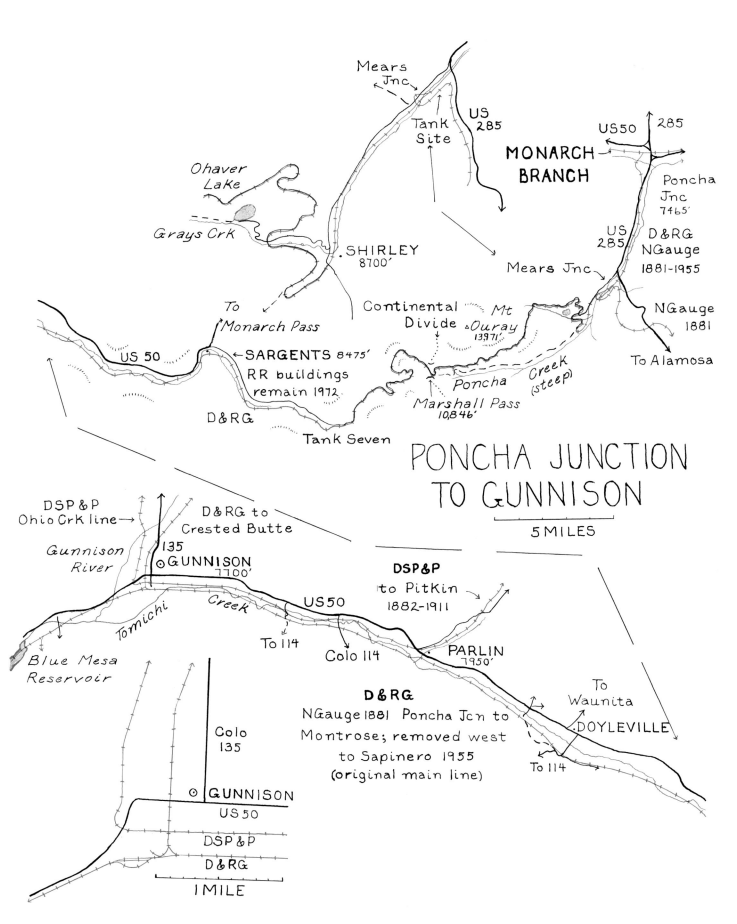

Mears Jnc

Tank Site

US 285

MONARCH BRANCH

US50   285

Poncha Jnc 7465'

Ohaver Lake

Grays Crk

SHIRLEY 8700'

US 285

Mears Jnc

D&RG N Gauge 1881-1955

N Gauge 1881

To Monarch Pass

Continental Divide

Mt Ouray 13,971'

Poncha Creek (steep)

To Alamosa

US 50

←SARGENTS 8475'
RR buildings
remain 1972.

D&RG

Tank Seven

Marshall Pass 10,846'

PONCHA JUNCTION TO GUNNISON

5 MILES

DSP&P Ohio Crk line →

D&RG to Crested Butte

Gunnison River

135

GUNNISON 7700'

US50

To 114

Colo 114

DSP&P
to PitKin
1882-1911

PARLIN 7950'

To Waunita

DOYLEVILLE

Blue Mesa Reservoir

Tomichi Creek

D&RG
N Gauge 1881 Poncha Jcn to
Montrose; removed west
to Sapinero 1955
(original main line)

To 114

Colo 135

GUNNISON

US 50

DSP&P

D&RG

1 MILE

67

industry. The laboratory has made useful studies of combustion, of wear in moving parts, of lubricants, of gas filled signal lights, and of fuels, including an exploration of atomic power for locomotives.

D&RG officers tend to associate the narrow-gauge line with the days when the whole railroad was obsolete. We hope they will come to treasure it more as a man would who has a 1912 car in the garage beside his modern one.

The Geographic Recapitulation

Palmer hoped to build his railroad from Denver to Mexico City, making use first of a piedmont line in Colorado and second of the Rio Grande Valley, which he intended to follow to El Paso and perhaps farther. The piedmont line would connect the towns that gave access to the mountains; the river route recognized the importance of water in the arid West. Palmer was too late for a land grant railroad; his line would have to depend on the development of the country it went through. He envisioned a complex that would connect the growing Colorado cities with piedmont coal, mountain forests, river agriculture, metal mining in such places as western Colorado, southern New Mexico, and Durango, Mexico, and finally the large labor supply promised by populous Mexico.

The general wished to be independent of other roads, and expressed this bent both in the north-south idea, which ran counter to the main trend of ambitious roads to reach the Pacific, and in his firm insistence upon narrow gauge at a time when gauging was pretty well standardized. He had of course the argument that narrow gauging could go farther for less cost anywhere and more particularly in the mountains, which require heavy cutting and filling and drastic curvatures.

By a series of moves the road gradually swung through 90 degrees to westward orientation. First (1878), the Santa Fe seized the best pass into New Mexico from Trinidad, and the D&RG moved slightly to the west to cross the same barrier on Chicken Creek; second, the boom at Leadville brought a much more violent and lasting rivalry for the Arkansas Canyon, particularly the Royal Gorge; third, the D&RG built track across the frontal mountains of the Sangre de Cristo to the Rio Grande from a spur at La Veta during this battle for the Royal Gorge route to the San Juan and Leadville, and after the battle sent out prongs toward both Santa Fe and the southern San Juan; fourth, and most decisive of the steps (1880), the D&RG won the Gorge route from the Santa Fe, and in a treaty which ended the war with the Santa Fe gave up its New Mexico ambitions in return for the Santa Fe's promise to keep out of the Colorado mountains; fifth (1880-81), Palmer built his line to Leadville and also into the north side of the San Juan at Gunnison and took other steps toward cutting off rivalries and gaining dominance in the mountains; sixth (1881-83), he built and organized from other roads a system in Utah which would serve as a ready-made continuation and brought about linkage by extending the D&RG to a junction point and then leasing to it his new RGW; seventh (1887-90), after Palmer's regime the D&RG shifted its main line to the more northerly Colorado River valley and brought about standard-gauging for the main system; eighth (1901 and 1908), the D&RG bought the Utah road and eventually brought about full consolidation; ninth (1905-10), the building of the Western Pacific extended the system, now including the Missouri Pacific, to San Francisco; and tenth (1934), with the acquisition of the Moffatt railroad, the use of the Moffat Tunnel and the construction of the Dotsero Cut-off, the Rio Grande ended its full swing from Denver-south to Denver-west. Minor steps in this change include the abortive movement southwest from Durango, the various contractions in

southern Colorado trackage, and the assimilation of the Moffat's line to Craig.

Many ironies marked the several stories of the progress. Palmer carried out a first intention in building the narrow-gauge Mexican National Railway in the eighties, but it came to the U.S. border at Laredo and there turned east to connect with Corpus Christi; meanwhile his one-time enemy A.A. Robinson of the Santa Fe built the Mexican Central from the capitol. He also made passes at a system through New Mexico with the New Mexico Central south to El Paso. The success with a north-south road was achieved by another early rival, the Denver and New Orleans and the companies which succeeded to its line. As D&RG president, Palmer fought the new line almost to extinction by refusing it Colorado Coal and Iron Company freight between Denver and Pueblo. Afterward, however, his RGW became an ally of the new road in a joint purchase of the Midland, which posed a threat to the D&RG as a by-passing system. Moffat, too, cooperated with the southbound road during his D&RG presidency since he had long-standing business associations with the Denver business men interested in it. Trackage agreements between the two roads date from his time.

Curiuosly, too, the D&RG's incorporation into a large system with the Missouri Pacific was the cause of decades of financial distress and wretched physical condition, and almost caused frustration of those who wished to profit by the Moffat Tunnel.

Although Leadville was a primary objective of the D&RG during the Gorge War, and was the first extension to be built after the settlement, the main line for westward expansion was that to Gunnison, completed the following year. It was continued in 1883 to Grand Junction and Crevasse to connect with roads already built and purchased in Utah, and it remained the main line until a new rival - the Colorado Midland - caused William S. Jackson to prod the lethargic owners into extending the Leadville line west down the Colorado River and standard gauging. The Gunnison line gave access to coal branching on the north side and to the metal mine branching on the south.

The Rio Grande on the west side of Marshall Pass (Jackson Collection - State Historical Society Library)

One sees the grade of the Gunnison line on the hillside on the right soon after leaving Poncha Springs and heading south on US 285, and can follow its progress to Mears Junction. From a little past there he can follow it over Marshall Pass on a very pleasant drive (summer only) over the Continental Divide. It can be a little bumpy but it gets some attention from county road crews. You stay on the grade for about 10 miles on the west side to about where Tank Seven was; then the road leaves the grade to stay on the hillside. This part can be slippery in wet weather. The old tank at Mears Junction was good for a picture against the background of Antora Peak, but it is no more. At Sargents however, where you rejoin US 50, you will see the most complete and real of all the ghost railroad towns. It should become a state historic center.

Sargents, now cluttered, was a beautifully preserved station in 1965.

West from Sargents there are some places where grade can be seen by the road (at least until it is widened) and also by making excursions from 50 on roads that cross the meadows to the south. Parts have become roads or 4-wheel routes for farmers, parts are used for a pipeline and some segments serve as mounds for fencing.

The CRESTED BUTTE BRANCH of the D&RG is not much in evidence at the Gunnison end, but from four or five miles north of Almont to the mines north of Crested Butte you can see most of it. Louisa Ward Arps has an article in the June 1956 *Trail and Timberline* which tells something of the grade to Anthracite Mesa and the mine and tram there, and also speculates about a possible preliminary grade north of Pittsburg for a railroad which was to cross the range into Yule Creek. The Yule Creek Pass road, running west from Paradise Divide has the uniform grade of a railroad.

A TINCUP PASS TUNNEL was apparently started in the early 1880's from a point below the pass on the west side. Francis Rizzari, who had heard about the tunnel, found the mouth in 1958 or 1959 and identified it as a railroad effort by the ties and a pair of wheels on an axle from a muck car which showed a gauge of three feet instead of te 18 to 24 inch gauge of mine trackage. He was unable to find any corporate history of the effort, but D&RG records show that a Cottonwood Pass line was planned to link Buena Vista with Crested Butte.

The RUBY ANTHRACITE BRANCH was a westward extension of the Crested Butte one. It makes one of the best pedestrian excursions in the state. You drive the first part on Colorado 135 from Crested Butte to just short of Kebler Pass, where a road turns off left for nearby Ohio Pass. A little way down this road you can see on your right in a meadow across from a sawdust pile a wye where there was a ghost town. You can start your walk here with a drop and climb across the creek to the south, or you can drive a little farther south on the way to Ohio Pass, take a turn in to the right on a side road as far as a locked gate, and start there by dropping north to the grade. You will specially enjoy seeing where the line cut through a rock ridge and turned south, and the quiet, wild-flowered valley where the Floresta Mine was. From the above gate one can walk the closed private road over the hill and drop to the mine by a shorter

From Crested Butte D&RG trains went up the Slate to the Coal Breaker Mine under Anthracite Mesa. (Jackson Collection - State Historical Society)

route, then walk out on the grade to make a round trip of it.

A FLORESTA BRANCH was planned for the Denver South Park and Pacific Railroad as well. It was an extension of what became of the Baldwin and Kubler Branch, and would presumably have been completed had not the D&RG reached Floresta first. The story of the discovery of this grade by W.R. Richardson is told in *The Denver South Park and Pacific Supplement,* published in 1959 by the Colorado Railroad Club. As it climbs toward Ohio Pass some of this intermittently graded route crosses ribs of cliff and a precipitous mountainside. To follow the line out on foot would be a delicate and rugged operation.

The ABERDEEN QUARRY RAILROAD, which brought out granite for the Colorado State Capitol and other buildings, runs through the Lewis Ranch. To see this D&RG branch you drive US 50 to a point 3 miles west of the Gunnison River crossing just west of Gunnison, turn down the Gold Basin

Elk Range

PITTSBURG
Smith-Hill Mine 9850'
ANTHRACITE 1880-1903
9000'

Cr Butte -Anthracite
4 mile spur
1882-1947

CRESTED BUTTE

Ruby Range

Slate R.

Lake Irwin

135
To Paonia

Coal Creek

Colo 135

FLORESTA

Grade
on
cliffs

Anthracite Range

Graded c 1893

KUBLER SPUR DSP&P

1 MILE

KUBLER
8800'

BALDWIN
8600'

Ohio Creek

8400'

BALDWIN

KUBLER
1896 Rocky
Mtn Fuel
Company

CASTLETON

**CRESTED BUTTE
BRANCH D&RG**
N Gauge
1881-1954

5 MILES

East River

Ohio Creek

ALMONT

**OHIO CREEK BRANCH
DENVER SOUTH PARK
& PACIFIC RY**

N Gauge 1883, operated 1911 by
D&RG when Alpine Tunnel
closed; acquired 1937 as

**CASTLETON
BRANCH D&RG**
Abandoned 1954

**RUBY ANTHRACITE BRANCH
D&RG** Cr Butte -Floresta
11 miles
1893-1929

Ruby Anthracite Crk

Colo 135

Kebler Pass
9980'

Ohio Pass
9990'

FLORESTA
9800'

2 MILES

Colo 135

*Gunnison
River*

GUNNISON
US 50 7700'

GUNNISON
NORTH

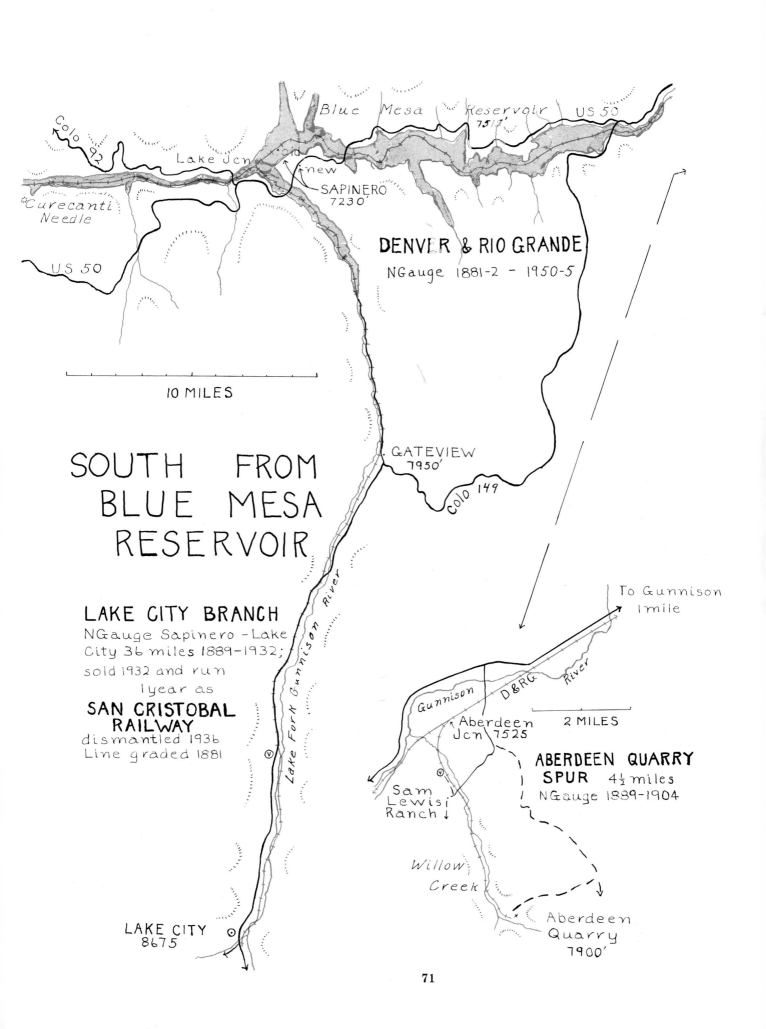

Colo 92

Blue Mesa Reservoir US 50

Lake Jcn. Old
new
SAPINERO
7230'

Curecanti Needle

US 50

DENVER & RIO GRANDE
NGauge 1881-2 - 1950-5

10 MILES

**SOUTH FROM
BLUE MESA
RESERVOIR**

GATEVIEW
7950'

Colo 149

LAKE CITY BRANCH
NGauge Sapinero - Lake
City 36 miles 1889-1932;
sold 1932 and run
1 year as
**SAN CRISTOBAL
RAILWAY**
dismantled 1936
Line graded 1881

Lake Fork Gunnison River

To Gunnison
1 mile

Gunnison D&RG River

Aberdeen
Jcn 7525

2 MILES

**ABERDEEN QUARRY
SPUR** 4½ miles
NGauge 1889-1904

Sam
Lewis
Ranch

Willow
Creek

Aberdeen
Quarry
7900'

LAKE CITY
8675

Near end of track at the Aberdeen Quarry.

Resource road, and at mile 1.6 south of 50 take a jeep road south for 3½ miles. Turn right (west) on a sketchy powerline road for 2 miles to leave car at top of hill and work your way south down hill to quarry. To see the other end or some of the middle ground of the railroad, go in to the ranch (main traveled road instead of jeep road) and ask. I was permitted to drive north in the field as far as feasible and walk on down to the junction near the river, and at some seasons you can go north from the ranch. This is one of those obscure lines that will give you a kick. I would not chance the jeep road in wet weather.

The D&RG main line crosses the road down to Aberdeen; a little west of there it goes under the serene surface of Blue Mesa Reservoir, visible only to fish and divers others. You can look down from the reservoir dam on a small bit of the stretch that fishermen used between Sapinero and Cimarron. The grade between Cimarron and Cerro Summit is generally along the highway and sometimes absorbed by it; from Cerro Summit down to the flats it is on the opposite (south) side of the draw.

The LAKE CITY BRANCH has more to see in its terminus than in the grade itself, for Lake City still has a good deal of the old left. The grade has become a secondary road from Gateview down to where it is submerged in the reservoir, and south of Gateview it is partly absorbed by the wider road until you reach the place where it made a high crossing of the river. I remember looking down on the Sapinero end of the line from the high US 50 bridge and picturing Captain Gunnison and his wagons struggling with the deep trough the Lake Fork created there. Gunnison's route must have been pretty close to that of US 50 from where the Cochetopa road (Colo. 114) runs into the Tomichi to the Uncompahgre River.

Lake City mines were an early stimulus of the D&RG-AT&SF rivalry. C.K. Holiday sent Santa Fe surveyors over Cochetopa Pass and also got reports on a Poncha-Marshall Pass Route, and he urged the road's officers to build into Lake City and the San Juan so as to have a permanent source of traffic when the Leadville bubble shoud burst. The branch had its most prosperous years before the silver panic of 1893 and seems to have been the least profitable of the D&RG's 3 penetrations into the heart of the San Juan.

The SAN CRISTOBAL RAILWAY succeeded the D&RG as owners in 1931 when M.B. Burke bought the line for $16,000. It was operated for a year or so but not removed until 1936. As late as 1951 there was an RGS type galloping goose in the shop at Ridgway with the San Cristobal name painted on it. The Jeffrey two-headed spike was used on this line.

The OURAY BRANCH and the Lake City Branch which followed it entered the San Juan mining country several years after Palmer had taken his road into the San Juan city of Silverton from the line farther south; these belonged to the regime of David Moffat. Moffat's ambitions were aggressive like those of Palmer, but somewhat different: he sought with numerous surveys to find a route that would relate the westward expansion and the mountain empire of the railroad with Denver, and he took more interest in the metal mining where he had made a fortune than in the more stable product of coal.

US 550 used to cross and re-cross the Ouray branch continually on the flats south of Montrose. Now the railroad is always on the west. South of Ridgway it is visible across the valley from the highway at points 3 and 7.3 miles south of the Ridgway exit.

Crossing the high bridge below Lake City. (Abby Kernochan Collection.

A breakdown on the Eldora line. (Martha Carlson photo)

The COLORADO AND NORTHWESTERN RAILWAY COMPANY, chartered in 1897, built a going line on the route of the Union Pacific's Greeley Salt Lake and Pacific from Boulder to Sunset, which had been washed out four years earlier. They used for this stretch and for the continuation to Ward a survey made for the Inter-Mountain Railway for a 22-inch gauge line, adapting it to 3-foot width. This alignment reduced the number of bridges from 66 to 17. The Eldora route, like the one to Ward, doubled back eastward from Sunset on the Mountain Flank to make altitude. Maximum grades were generally 4¹/₂% , with a 7% stretch near Salina; curves reached highs of 40⁰, to earn the name of the Whiplash Route.

The DENVER BOULDER AND WESTERN RAILROAD COMPANY was formed in April, 1909, to take over the foreclosed Colorado and Northwestern. The new corporation shows no ambitious intentions beyond operating the line from Boulder to Sunset and the branches from there to Ward and Eldora, with wyes at Boulder and at Sulphide Flats, the latter for an eastward spur to the Barker Dam at Nederland, being constructed by the Eastern Colorado Power Company. The line down to the dam was short-lived, but it provided the only period of steady earnings the railroad ever enjoyed. Elder citizens remember riding the trains to Mount Alto Park, where there was picnicking and a dance hall, or beyond to the mine camps. The story of the road is told in Forrest Crossen's book *The Switzerland Trail,* and in a brief treatment by M.C. Poor in Bulletin 65 of the *Railway and Locomotive Historical Society.*

Crossen notes that there are Greeley Salt Lake and Pacific bridge abutments still visible, some used by the Boulder water system. You can find the first of these by following Arapahoe Road west from town to the first bridge that crosses Boulder Creek. Others are harder to distinguish from the later DB&W ones. Grade of the latter is off and on visible or under your wheels between Boulder and Sunset. From there to the ridges both the climb-out roads use the grade, which is on gravel and generally smooth, and they make a pleasant tour. On the Ward line one leaves the good grade at Gold Hill Station, but can go on for some distance farther NW with a small car. Up at the Ward end one can drive around the hill from a little way from the town of Ward. Students of mine followed in 1972 the grade from a little beyond Glacier Lake down to the Bluebird Mine on foot. They also covered the stretch between Sulfide and Cardinal, reporting both as fine walks with plenty of cuts and fills.

The BOULDER LEFT HAND AND MIDDLE PARK RAILROAD AND TELEGRAPH COMPANY. This company planned a "broad or narrow gauge" line to run from Boulder to the mouth of Left Hand Canon, up it to the foot of Bald Mountain presumably on its east side, south of Ward, and then through Middle Boulder Pass to the headwaters of the Grand.

Some grading done by this organization but not shown on my map is mentioned in Crossen's *Switzerland Trail* as visible to the north of Boulder. You see it on the hillside to the west where Colorado 7 and 36 meet. From 36 you can drive in west .7 mile on the Lee Hill Road, where it is visible running south. It dies out on the north of there about 1.5 miles up the road.

The Gilpin Tramway hairpins out of North Clear Creek to climb around above Central City.

The GILPIN TRAMWAY COMPANY was formed in 1886 by A.N. Rogers and associates, to run by air, electric, compressed air, horse, or other means of power from near the western boudary of Gilpin County to Blackhawk, with branches to Russel Gulch and the mines and railroad stations in Central City and Blackhawk.

Two books have come out on the tram: Frank R. Hollenback's *The Gilpin Tram,* and the more recent *Gilpin Gold Tram* by Mallory Hope Ferrell. This relic grade of the mining days is largely traceable in a happy combination of driving and walking. A little way up North Clear Creek from Blackhawk you see the lazy V where the road switchbacked at a rock abutment on the west or left side of the canyon and climbed around the hill toward Chase Gulch. The USGS 15' Blackhawk Quadrangle shows the spur which continued up Clear Creek above the lazy V for most of a mile, and you can find traces of this grade on the west side of the creek.

From the lazy V you can walk the main line around into Chase Gulch and up the north side of that to the stream crossing, then east around the hill to the slope above Central City. Some of the latter grade north of Central City is accessible for driving if you go up the side street at the Opera House corner, or up the Main Street to where the grade crosses it in Gregory Gulch. Some of the next part going south may be posted but you can drive up toward Nevadaville and walk the grade and switchbacks to the north. Likewise with Russel Gulch. There is a lot more railroading as you work south to Pleasant Valley and Pewabic Mountain, much of the way on drivable grade, or work your way down the mixup in Willis and South Willis Gulches. I

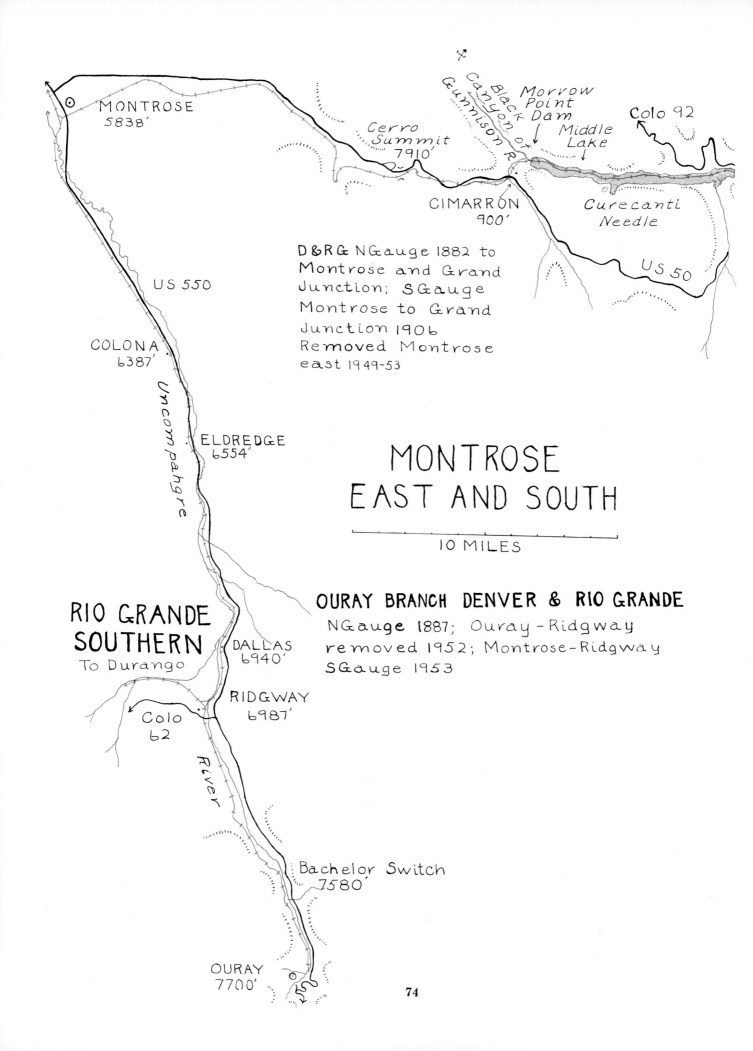

MONTROSE
5838'

Cerro
Summit
7910'

Black Canyon of
Gunnison R.

Morrow
Point
Dam

Middle
Lake

Colo 92

CIMARRON
900'

Curecanti
Needle

US 50

D&RG N Gauge 1882 to
Montrose and Grand
Junction; S Gauge
Montrose to Grand
Junction 1906
Removed Montrose
east 1949-53

US 550

COLONA
6387'

Uncompahgre

ELDREDGE
6554'

MONTROSE
EAST AND SOUTH

10 MILES

RIO GRANDE
SOUTHERN
To Durango

DALLAS
6940'

OURAY BRANCH DENVER & RIO GRANDE
N Gauge 1887; Ouray-Ridgway
removed 1952; Montrose-Ridgway
S Gauge 1953

RIDGWAY
6987'

Colo
62

River

Bachelor Switch
7580'

OURAY
7700'

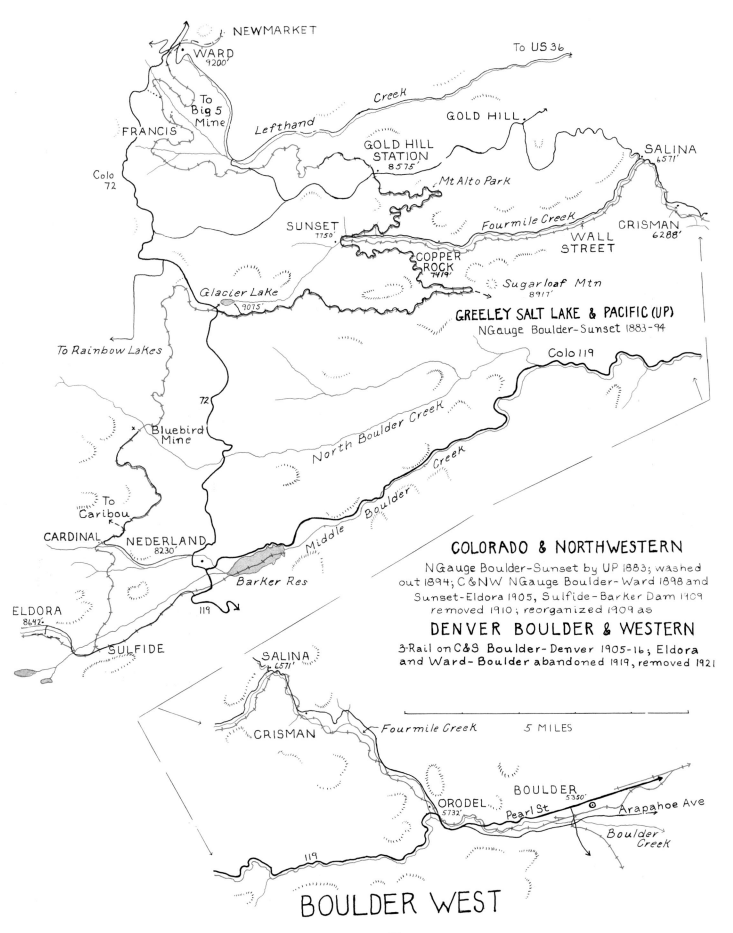

NEWMARKET

WARD
9200'

To
Big 5
Mine

FRANCIS

Colo
72

Creek

Lefthand

GOLD HILL

GOLD HILL
STATION
8575'

Mt Alto Park

SALINA
6571'

SUNSET
7750'

Fourmile Creek

CRISMAN
6288'

WALL
STREET

COPPER
ROCK
7479'

Sugarloaf Mtn
8917'

Glacier Lake
9075'

GREELEY SALT LAKE & PACIFIC (UP)
N Gauge Boulder-Sunset 1883-94

To Rainbow Lakes

Colo 119

72

Bluebird
Mine

North Boulder Creek

Creek

To
Caribou

Boulder

Middle

CARDINAL

NEDERLAND
8230'

Barker Res

COLORADO & NORTHWESTERN
N Gauge Boulder-Sunset by UP 1883; washed
out 1894; C&NW N Gauge Boulder-Ward 1898 and
Sunset-Eldora 1905, Sulfide-Barker Dam 1909
removed 1910; reorganized 1909 as

ELDORA
8642'

119

SULFIDE

DENVER BOULDER & WESTERN
3-Rail on C&S Boulder-Denver 1905-16; Eldora
and Ward-Boulder abandoned 1919, removed 1921

SALINA
6571'

CRISMAN

Fourmile Creek

5 MILES

BOULDER
5350'

ORODEL
5732'

Pearl St

Arapahoe Ave

*Boulder
Creek*

119

BOULDER WEST

have come far short of covering or understanding all the grade on these hills in four or five scattered full days of driving and walking, but with never a dull moment to complain of. My map is copied from the USGS Central City District quadrangle of 1906 reprinted in 1949, with additions based on some further explorations and reference to the Hotchkiss map of 1913.

The GILPIN COUNTY TRAM RAILWAY, incorporated in 1872 to carry wood from the hills east of James Peak to Blackhawk and Nevada, is perhaps the only remnant to be found in Colorado of an all wooden railroad. Louisa Ward Arps wrote up in the 1968 *Brand Book* what she had found out about the line and its promoters, and with this the results of sleuthing it out with her husband Elwyn Arps, one of their visits being accomplished on skis. The rails were logs 6 to 8 inches in diameter, some chosen for their natural curvature.

The Arpses discovered certain evidence along North Clear Creek, all or mainly between Miners Gulch and Pecks Gulch, of the line to Black Hawk, but she does not believe the Nevada line was built.

The GILPIN AND CLEAR CREEK DISTRICT RAILWAY COMPANY was formed in 1904 to connect Pactolus east of Rollinsville on the Denver Northwestern and Pacific with Central City and Blackhawk. It would be 17 miles long and serve the communities of Gilpin, Gold Dirt, Perigo, and Wide Awake. *The Clear Creek Weekly Register Call* of July 14, 1905, reports the line as being cnstructed standard-gauge so that transfer to narrow-gauge cars would be unnecessary for the 60,000 tons of coal consumed in the District each year.

Using the 1931 Hotchkiss map and the Tungsten, Blackhawk and Central City Quadrangles and a map of the projected railroad before it was graded, a seminar group of mine from Colorado College attempted to find what was left of this challenger to the narrow-gauge supply road for the mining community.

Following the road up South Beaver Creek from Pactolus, they saw a good deal of the grade below and across from them, and identified in the S-curve area of the Peak to Peak Highway some parallel railroad line of less tight curvature. They found more on the south side of Dory Hill (on a route different from that planned on their map) and they thought perhaps they found some more on the side of Clear Creek and Chase Gulch but were uncertain. The railroad line on the map represents a combination of actual findings and guessing. They could not see anything in the Missouri Gulch drainage.

The COLORADO CENTRAL RAILROAD was a broad and narrow centered in Denver's rival town of Golden, reaching on the one hand into the mining country to the west of Denver and

34 INSPIRATION POINT, CLEAR CREEK CANON.

A Colorado Central train - copied from a giant colored postcard in the Abby Kernochan collection.

on the other to the Union Pacific. Its affairs are recorded in a University of Colorado thesis by Ralph N. Traxler, Jr., *Some Phases of the History of the Colorado Central Railroad, 1865-1885,* and in Richard C. Overton's 1953 *Gulf to the Rockies.* In this account we have borrowed from Overton and even more heavily from Traxler, whose paper is not in a form for general circulation.

While the Union Pacific's Grenville Dodge explored northern Colorado and southern Wyoming for the best through route, another company, the Colorado and Clear Creek Railroad, was formed with the idea of building a segment which would take the Pacific road up to and over the mountains and put it into coasting position on the other side. The Colorado and Clear Creek was incorporated in February of 1866 to run from Golden west to Blackhawk and Central City and east to Kiowa and Bijou Basin, but its plan was amended shortly afterward to run over Berthoud Pass and exclude the east line. Late in the year Dodge decided against the mountain route for the UP. A new plan, the Colorado Central and Pacific, was formulated by Loveland in January of 1868 to build a connecting road from the UP somewhere near Julesburg to the mountain communities. This company included five UP directors. Loveland got bond issues voted in Weld County, Denver, and the mountain communities. When Denver discovered she was to be on a mere branch of the main line from Julesburg to Golden, the plan fell through. However, the UP people in it supported still another version set up by Loveland — the Colorado Central Railroad, formed with an 1869 amendment of the Colorado Central and Pacific name — and the UP furnished rails and equipment for the railroad that was built.

Loveland had got tracks and a handcar on his road and held a 200-foot run so as to prove up on a franchise in 1867. The first serious building was the 15-mile segment from Golden to Cutoff Junction, meeting point of the DP and the KP tracks just north of Denver, finished in the summer of 1870. The three miles from this point to Denver were run on KP track. The line went 20 miles up Clear Creek to Black Hawk early in 1872, and Loveland put in grading for a road to meet the D&RG at Littleton, the aim being to cut Denver out of the line of communication between Golden and the territory to the south.

Traxler says the narrow-gauge lines — to Blackhawk and to Georgetown from Golden — cost $2,430,000 or $60,000 a mile, partly because of floods requiring reconstruction, partly because of other delays, and of course largely because of the tunnels and heavy blasting of the rock walls of Clear Creek. The extension from Blackhawk to Central City — 4 1/2 miles of track for one mile of distance — was laid out by the Central's Swiss engineer, Edward L. Berthoud, in May of 1877. When opened a year later it included a 175-foot bridge built in Chicago for local assembly to cross Selack and Gregory Streets. Cost of the segment was $25,000 a mile.

Isabella L. Bird tells of riding the Central to Idaho Springs and taking a Concord stage from there to Georgetown. This was in the fall, after the tourist season was supposed to be over, and she reports that the railroad employees were uncivil to the passengers, and for lack of coach space put them in the baggage car, where she sat in the door to watch the scenery go by. She would have liked to ride her horse up Toughcuss Creek (Clear Creek), but had to leave the animal in Golden because the railroad had monopolized the canon. She talks of the road as gouged from the mountain wall and sometimes built up on stones piled into the Creek itself. "There was mining everywhere along that grand road ... and up all along the seemingly inaccessible heights were holes with their roofs log-supported, in which solitary and patient men were selling their lives for treasure. Down by the stream, all among the icicles, men were sluicing and washing, and everywhere along the heights were scars of hardly passable trails, too steep even for pack-jacks, leading to the holes, and down which the miner packs the ore on his back. These mines with their stamping and crushing mills, and the smelting works ... fill the district with noise, hubbub and smoke by night and day..." Maybe some of Bird's enthusiasm got to the conductor: on the way back he gave her his chair.

Crofutt's 1881 Gripsack Guide to Colorado lists the Colorado Central as offering two among eight scenic trips. First he describes the trip from Denver to the Union Pacific, $5 extra in a Horton Chair. The second, the mountain trip, is described more fully. Running out to Golden on the three-rail, you pass through Arapahoe, already a ghost town of the placer era. At Golden, the narrow-gauge trains are separated into two parts, which will go two directions from the Forks - to Georgetown and to Blackhawk and Central City. On this tour you can see Chinese who are living in the abandoned Whipple and Excelsior Mills, jumping the placer claims left by white men. Blackhawk you see from the bridge over its main street and from the zigzags above. Blackhawk passengers were requested not to shoot sheep from the speeding trains. The CC grade is visible in Clear Creek, mainly where it is across the creek from US 6, or where it is bypassed by tunnels. There are two or three places in North Clear Creek where the grade separates itself from the highway.

The Colorado Central grade can be traced by foot from Blackhawk to near the end in Central City, though the station area is said to lie beneath the Chain O'Mines tailings structure. There are other places where grade has been destroyed by later operations. Some of the lower parts of the line along Clear Creek were not obliterated by US 6 and so can be seen from that road.

Further extensions of the narrow gauge was planned in the Georgetown Leadville and San Juan late in 1878 by the Golden-UP combine, and in January of 1879 Loveland went east and interested Jay Gould. This road was to go through Leadville and on to Lake City. The UP leased the Central that year and then consolidated it by purchase in 1880, and in 1881 set up the successor company for the extension, the Georgetown Breckenridge and Leadville, which pushed the road up and around the Georgetown Loop to Graymont.

The GEORGETOWN BRECKENRIDGE AND LEADVILLE was formed in February of 1881 and used the survey made by the Georgetown Leadville and San Juan to run its 8 1/2-mile line west up Clear Creek from Georgetown, end of the Colorado Central, to Graymount. The reported cost of the line was $428,000. It included the Georgetown Loop, and in it the Devil's Gate Viaduct, which is perhaps the most famous piece of track of the nostalgic narrow-gauge days.

The Loop is under reconstruction and has already seen partial operation.

The ARGENTINE CENTRAL RAILWAY COMPANY. This narrow-gauge line from Silver Plume to the top of Mt. McClellan was the only traction railroad in the world of comparable height outside the Andes. Its 4500-foot climb from about 9100 to 13,644 feet was accomplished on a track about 16 miles long with an average grade of $5 1/3\%$. The road was started in 1905 and finished by August of the next year. It connected with the terminus of the Georgetown Breckenridge and Leadville which had been completed over the Georgetwon Loop to Silver

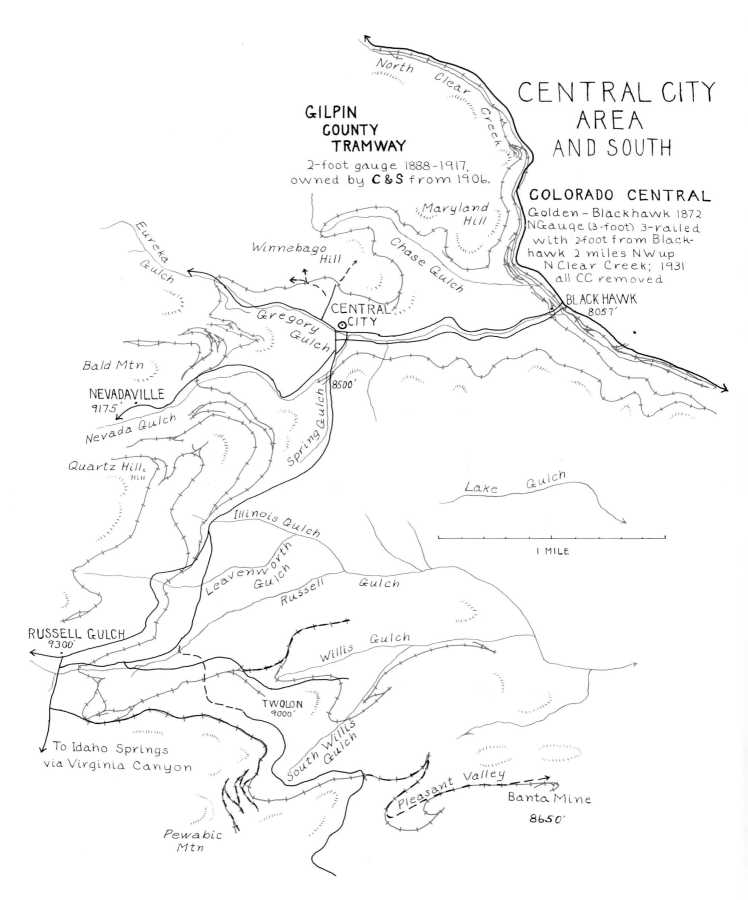

CENTRAL CITY
AREA
AND SOUTH

North Clear Creek

GILPIN
COUNTY
TRAMWAY
2-foot gauge 1888-1917,
owned by C&S from 1906.

Maryland
Hill

Chase Gulch

COLORADO CENTRAL
Golden – Blackhawk 1872
N gauge (3-foot) 3-railed
with 2 foot from Black-
hawk 2 miles NW up
N Clear Creek; 1931
all CC removed

BLACK HAWK
8057'

Eureka Gulch

Winnebago
Hill

Gregory Gulch

CENTRAL
CITY

Bald Mtn

Spring Gulch

8500'

NEVADAVILLE
9175'

Nevada Gulch

Quartz Hill
Hill

Lake Gulch

1 MILE

Illinois Gulch

Leavenworth
Gulch

Russell Gulch

RUSSELL GULCH
9300'

Willis Gulch

TWOLON
9000'

To Idaho Springs
via Virginia Canyon

South Willis Gulch

Pleasant Valley

Banta Mine
8650'

Pewabic
Mtn

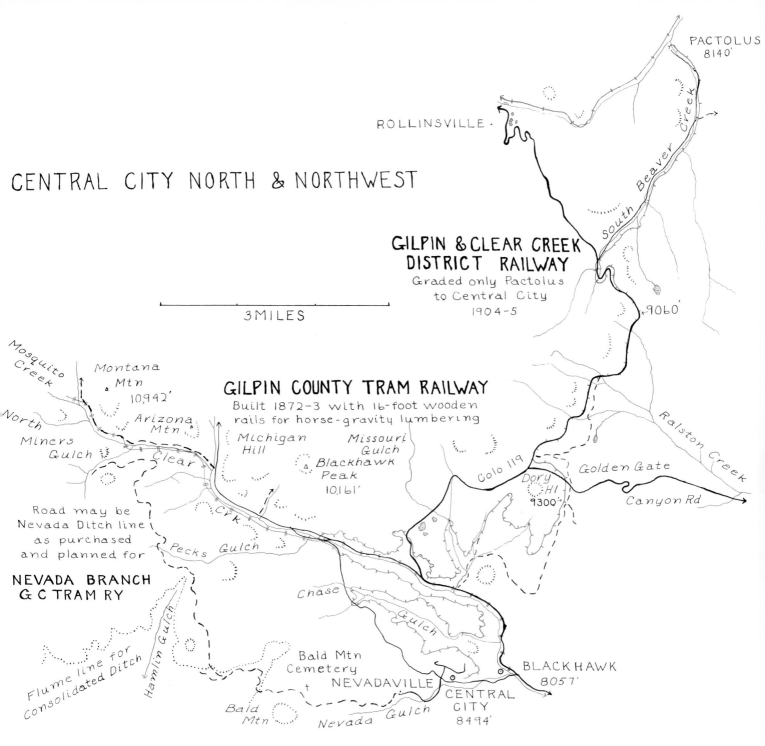

CENTRAL CITY NORTH & NORTHWEST

PACTOLUS
8140'

ROLLINSVILLE ·

**GILPIN & CLEAR CREEK
DISTRICT RAILWAY**
Graded only Pactolus
to Central City
1904-5

9060'

3 MILES

Mosquito
Creek

Montana
Mtn
10,942'

GILPIN COUNTY TRAM RAILWAY
Built 1872-3 with 16-foot wooden
rails for horse-gravity lumbering

North

Arizona
Mtn

Michigan
Hill

Missouri
Gulch

Ralston Creek

Miners
Gulch

Clear

Blackhawk
Peak
10,161'

Colo 119

Golden Gate

Dory
HI
9300'

Road may be
Nevada Ditch line
as purchased
and planned for

Ck

Pecks Gulch

Canyon Rd

**NEVADA BRANCH
G C TRAM RY**

Flume line for
Consolidated Ditch

Hamlin Gulch

Chase

Gulch

Bald Mtn
Cemetery
+
NEVADAVILLE

BLACKHAWK
8057'

CENTRAL
CITY
8494'

Bald
Mtn

Nevada Gulch

*Colorado's earliest gondola ride - from Silver Plume to
timberline.*

79

The Dumont end of the Georgetown Breckenridge and Leadville Railroad.

Waldorf, business end of the line.

Plume two decades earlier. At its inception the Argentine was not designed to carry out the aim of multitudes of other roads and cross the continental divide. Its function was to serve the East Argentine Mining District centering at Waldorf, and to climb Mount McClellan, then published as a 14,000-foot peak. The Grays Peak Scenic Development Company, organized in June of 1909 to do a business with loop-the-loops, merry - go - rounds and gravity and pleasure railroads, possessed 3/5 of the

Argentine's $500,000 worth of stock, and planned to extend the road to the 14,274-foot summit of Grays Peak, some 2 1/2-miles farther west. The ridge between Mount McClellan and Grays Peak would take a railroad, but one could hardly imagine a bleaker line. Poor's Manual of 1910 lists 5 locomotives and 16 freight cars, but the wildest dreamer could hardly imagine anything more than passenger service beyond Waldorf.

The Grays Peak Railroad was incorporated the year before the Argentine Central with the idea of following the same route as the AC did out of Silver Plume but continuing to Keystone, Minturn, and Wolcott on the western slope. There were at least two plans to connect the Argentine Central with the western slope: the Argentine Tunnel and the Waldorf-Vidler Tunnel Railway Companies. The latter had a half-mile of 3-foot gauge track. Poor's Manual for 1915 states that the line and its rolling stock of 3 locomotives and 16 freight cars were leased to and operated by the Georgetown and Grays Peak Railway. We wonder whether these 16 freight cars were the same as those reported by the Argentine Central in 1910.

The tunnel companies would have bored through into Peru Creek. The Denver South Park and Pacific did some grading upstream from its Keystone Branch in anticipation of connection with the Argentine, and there was also a Montezuma and Western Railroad Company effort to drive a shortcut through the big ridge.

The prime mover of the Argentine Central was Edward John Wilcox, a Canadian who came to Colorado in 1878 and to the Argentine district in 1900. A summit one and a half miles south of the Waldorf Mine was named for him in 1948. His associates in the venture included Magee, Filius, and others. But the successor companies were organized by a five-man group including the William Rogers of the 1904 Grays Peak scheme and one William Iliff. Vidler of the tunnel company was a Colorado Springs mining man. The Argentine Tunnel Railway Company was formed by a different group including two Norwegians.

Wilcox, being an ordained minister, would not permit operation of trains over his highly scenic road on Sunday, the only day when many people could have traveled it.

The Georgetown and Grays Peak Railway Company bought

Top of the Argentine, but never on Sunday.

the AC in 1913 and a few months later reincorporated it as the Argentine and Grays Peak Railway Company. The latter was simply the 16-mile AC; the Georgetown and Grays Peak was the owner company, and it scheduled trains over the 60 miles from Denver to the top fo Mount McClellan, using other narrow gauge trackage to Silver Plume. The freight business did not amount to much, and the line was only operated in summer. The Argentine company was dissolved in 1917, the owner organization in 1920.

The Argentine's route is described as climbing from Silver Plume up to and over the ridge of Leavenworth Mountain to get into the upper part of Leavenworth Creek where Waldorf and the East Argentine Mining District were. Switchbacks, on which the engines alternately pulled forward and pushed backward their loads up a zigzag course, were used to make altitude on the steep slopes of both Leavenworth Mountain above Silver Plume and Mount McClellan above Waldorf. At present writing the D&RG still operates this sort of a climbing device on its Monarch branch. A look at the USGS maps of Montezuma and Georgetown Quadrangles will show why switchbacking was used to get up the mountains. They are long slim ridges with little opportunity to loop into lateral valleys. The altitude has to be made on a tilted plane instead of the grooves of drainage.

Looking southeast from Silver Plume you see the roadbed high on the hill, and by going south from Georgetown toward Grant you can turn right and follow it as far as Waldorf or beyond.

The first treatment of this railroad that we know about is that of M.C. Poor in *Bulletin No. 64* of the Railway and Locomotive Historical Society, a source from which we have borrowed in this short account. See F.R. Hollenbeck's more recent book, published by Sage Books, *The Gilpin Tramway*.

There is a book titled *Over the Loop* containing a store of pictures of both this railroad and the Georgetown Loop. If your lungs and legs are in shape for it there is no finer railroad walk than that up to Mount McClellan. At the top you are rewarded with a stretch of grade where ties are still in place, and a look across the abyss at Grays and Torreys Peaks. I have seen trail bikes go all the way up the grade too. When you drive back down you can keep on the grade for a mile or so beyond where the proper road leaves it, and you can walk much farther than that.

The SUNRISE PEAK AERIAL TRAMWAY was Colorado's pre - ski - age cable ride designed for tourists. A 1911 *Engineering News* called it "perhaps the only one in this country" though there were many like it in Europe. It carried 26 300-pound cars on a continuous 1½-inch cable supported on 18- to 60-foot towers spanned from 80 feet to 485 feet from Silver Plume, about 9200 feet above sea level, to Sunrise Peak at 12,500 feet. Sunrise is a lower north point of the same Mt. McClellan reached farther south and higher by the Argentine Central Railroad. I met a lady in her eighties who had lived in Silver Plume since her girlhood. She spoke with enthusiasm of the tramway and denied that the Argentine Central had ever existed. I would like to credit *Engineering News* for the picture copied from its pages. This 1911 source tells us that the round trip took 46 minutes, that there were three watch towers along the line connected to the engine house at the top by a bell system. Power came from a hydroelectric plant, where it was reduced from the 10,500 carrying voltage to 440 for the motor. Oil electric switches were used to cut off power in electric storms. In July of 1911 the line was carrying in its 4-passenger cars an average of a little over 500 fares a day. The hauling cable was slightly smaller than the stationary one and hemp cored. Its

safety factor was 10, that of the hanging cable 16, considerably larger than the allowances for ore tramways.

I can give no information on any remnants of the line, but it should be possible to find the string of tower foundations from the top down.

Another way to make a loop. (State Historical Society Library.)

The DENVER NORTHWESTERN AND PACIFIC realized a long - standing hope of Denver businessmen to take a railroad directly west from Denver over the mountain barrier which had deflected the Union Pacific. David Moffat, as president of the D&RG in the latter eighties had authorized numerous surveys over the range and doubtless selected this one for the relative smoothness of the crest in the James Peak sector. Moffat was the prime mover in the effort to build it and keep control of it. The story of the road and Moffat's difficulties is told 'in *The Moffat Road* by Ed Bollinger and Fred Bauer, which replaces an earlier book *Rails that Climb* by Bollinger.

The surveys called for a 2.6-mile tunnel under Corona, but that had to wait for money that was never available. Even without that, the eastern approach was the tunnelingest piece of road in the Rockies, requiring Orman and Crook to bore 28 tunnels through Boulder Canon, 26 of them in a 10-mile stretch. Their contract price between Leyden Junction and Tolland was $78,000 a mile.

In Boulder Canon men suspended on ropes from the cliff tops while they drilled pins into the rock to hang a tie footbridge on. Bollinger says that Chief Engineer Sumner's survey payroll in 1902 showed 9 parties in the field drawing $10,000 a month. Four roads surveyed the Gore Canon for roads before the DNw&P got there: The Denver Utah and Pacific, the Colorado Railway, the D&RG, and the Union Pacific through its UP and Western Colorado. Some of the DNw&P surveys were designed to avoid dropping all the way down the Gore Canon and instead crossing Mesa country or circling mountainsides farther north. Bollinger understands that the choice of the water route was made in part because it would afford a means of connecting the road with the D&RG. Whether or not this is the case, it was a piece of good fortune.

Between Yankee Doodle Lake on the east side of Rollins Pass and the trestle-over-tunnel loop on the west, operators had heavy work to battle the snow and ice. Farther down there were combustible tunnel timbers on one side and intense cold on the other.

Moffat died in 1911 and the reorganization company pushed

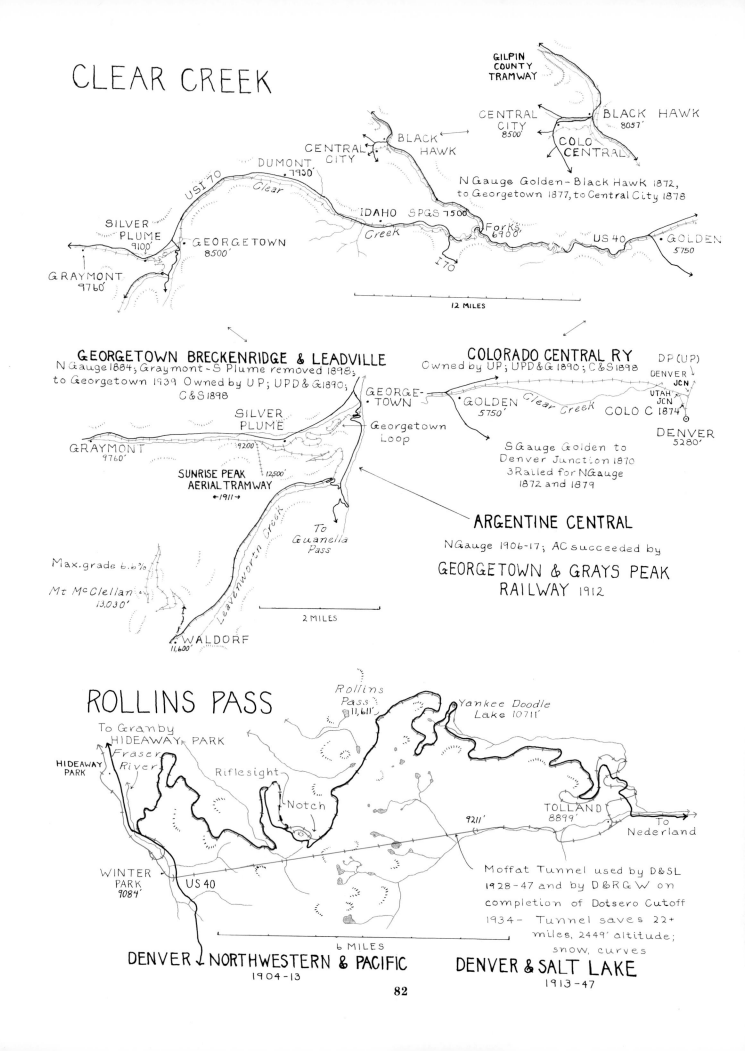

CLEAR CREEK

GILPIN
COUNTY
TRAMWAY

CENTRAL
CITY
8500'

BLACK
HAWK
8057'

COLO
CENTRAL

N Gauge Golden-Black Hawk 1872,
to Georgetown 1877, to Central City 1878

DUMONT
7950'

CENTRAL
CITY

BLACK
HAWK

US I 70

Clear

SILVER
PLUME
9100'

GEORGETOWN
8500'

IDAHO SPGS 7500

Creek

Forks
6900'

US 40

GOLDEN
5750'

GRAYMONT
9760'

I 70

12 MILES

GEORGETOWN BRECKENRIDGE & LEADVILLE

N Gauge 1884; Graymont-S Plume removed 1898;
to Georgetown 1939 Owned by UP; UPD & G 1890;
C & S 1898

GEORGE-
TOWN

SILVER
PLUME

Georgetown
Loop

GRAYMONT
9760'

9200'

SUNRISE PEAK
AERIAL TRAMWAY
←1911→

12500'

To
Guanella
Pass

Max. grade 6.6%

Mt McClellan
13,030'

Leavenworth Creek

2 MILES

WALDORF
11,600'

COLORADO CENTRAL RY

Owned by UP; UPD & G 1890; C & S 1898

GEORGE-
TOWN

GOLDEN
5750'

Clear Creek

COLO C 1874

DP (UP)

DENVER
JCN

UTAH
JCN

DENVER
5280'

S Gauge Golden to
Denver Junction 1870
3 Railed for N Gauge
1872 and 1879

ARGENTINE CENTRAL

N Gauge 1906-17; AC succeeded by

GEORGETOWN & GRAYS PEAK RAILWAY 1912

ROLLINS PASS

Rollins
Pass
11,611'

Yankee Doodle
Lake 10711'

To Granby
HIDEAWAY PARK

Fraser
River

HIDEAWAY
PARK

Riflesight

Notch

TOLLAND
8899'

9211'

To
Nederland

WINTER
PARK
9084'

US 40

Moffat Tunnel used by D&SL
1928-47 and by D&RGW on
completion of Dotsero Cutoff
1934- Tunnel saves 22+
miles, 2449' altitude;
snow, curves

6 MILES

DENVER NORTHWESTERN & PACIFIC
1904-13

DENVER & SALT LAKE
1913-47

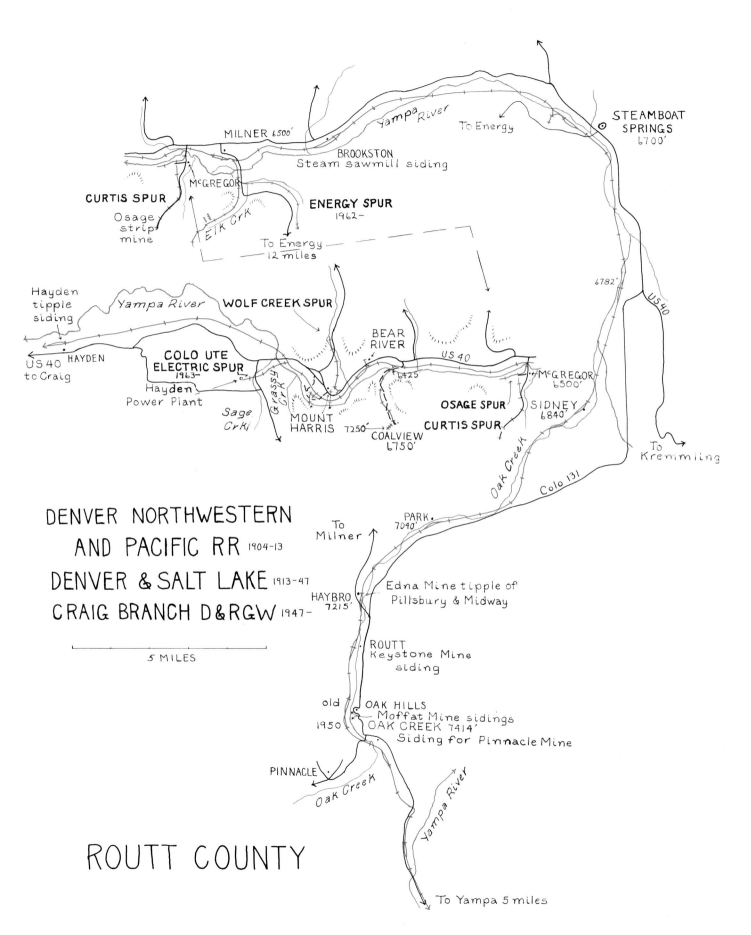

STEAMBOAT SPRINGS 6700'

MILNER 6500'

Yampa River

To Energy

BROOKSTON
Steam sawmill siding

McGREGOR

CURTIS SPUR

Osage strip mine

Elk Crk

ENERGY SPUR
1962-

To Energy
12 miles

6782'

US 40

Hayden tipple siding

Yampa River

WOLF CREEK SPUR

BEAR RIVER

US 40

US 40
to Craig

HAYDEN

COLO UTE
ELECTRIC SPUR
1963-

Hayden
Power Plant

Sage
Crk

Grassy Crk

MOUNT HARRIS

7250'

L425

COALVIEW
6750'

OSAGE SPUR

CURTIS SPUR

McGREGOR
6500'

SIDNEY
6840'

Oak Creek

Colo 131

To Kremmling

DENVER NORTHWESTERN
AND PACIFIC RR 1904-13
DENVER & SALT LAKE 1913-47
CRAIG BRANCH D&RGW 1947-

5 MILES

To Milner

PARK
7040'

HAYBRO
7215'

Edna Mine tipple of
Pillsbury & Midway

ROUTT
Keystone Mine
siding

old

1950

OAK HILLS
Moffat Mine sidings
OAK CREEK 7414'
Siding for Pinnacle Mine

PINNACLE

Oak Creek

Yampa River

ROUTT COUNTY

To Yampa 5 miles

Moffat's railroad climbed high on the canyon wall; Tunnel 7 (Jackson photo - State Historical Society)

easily. The Hayden one was built for plant construction purposes and its rails are still in though apparently little or not at all used. The Osage gives a view of extensive mining and is easy to find and drive. The Wolf Creek one appears to have stopped a mile or so short of the mine though this may not be the case. At Mount Harris one gets off the highway on a side road and finds the understructure of the old bridge. The interesting thing here is to realize that there were some 5½ miles of track belonging to the spur, but all except the bridge and a little piece to the north was underground. To reach Coalview you would have to find the owner of the access land and get his permission to go in; if the water is low and your courage high you can ford the river and drive up there.

The line to Energy, a recent addition to the D&RGW system, would show you that coal is not dead.

Across the Yampa and straight into Mount Harris on standard guage.

his railroad on to Craig. There had been, according to Arthur Ridgway, three levels considered for a tunnel to replace the highest railroad pass in the country. The Moffat Tunnel would not have been justified for the Denver and Salt Lake Railroad, but with the prospect of linking it into the D&RGW system, Denver business could have its western outlet as a through line. The tunnel was arranged for as an enterprise of the state. This was made politically possible by including in the bond issue a benefit for Pueblo: an Arkansas River floodway through Pueblo to replace the mess and menace of the 1921 flood. The story of this large undertaking is told in *The Moffat Tunnel* by E.C. McMechen. The Denver and Salt Lake Western Railroad was incorporated to connect the two roads between Orestod and Dotsero.

The drive over Rollins Pass is on a sound roadbed but can be very choppy and rough, especially on the east side. It is a splendid trip, however, with a great deal to see. Highlights are Yankee Doodle (the lake in the loop), the Needles Eye Tunnel, the tundra area at the top, and most especially the full loop, trestle over tunnel, high on the west descent. Some shortcutting is possible on the lower west end.

The COAL SPURS ALONG THE DENVER AND SALT LAKE, later the Craig Branch of the D&RG, west and south of Steamboat Springs, have served a large number of mines whose history has not been put together in any one place. The Osage Spur from McGregor, the Wolf Creek Spur, and the Hayden Power Plant Spur are the only ones of any length one can travel

The MIDDLE PARK LUMBER COMPANY RAILROAD and its operations are described in the 1954 Brand Book in an article by Frank A. Eastom. Fraser, formerly Eastom for George A. Eastom, father of the author, was headquarters for a 5½ mile railroad. A Climax geared locomotive number 684 pulled the flat cars, of which there were 14, up a maximum 6% grade to and along the mesa north of St. Louis Creek. Fuel for the first two years was wood slabs. The incorporation of the railroad as the Colorado Utah and Southwestern expressed an intention to build west if the Moffat did not do so. The Omaha Lumber Company bought the business in 1908 but were foreclosed in 1912.

The locomotive survived the railroad for 20 years on a siding at Fraser before it was junked. Now the railroad is an old but unmistakable path through the trees. I had no luck finding the upper end, and a midsection was blocked off by a ditch, but I found my spike (always it is the last one left) and did some tracking soon after the road climbs to the mesa and closely parallels the grade. You should allow time and take to the woods.

The ROCKY MOUNTAIN RAILWAY COMPANY was a 1907-08 lumber road from Granby to Monarch with 14 miles of main line, a 1-mile spur at the Switzer Ranch, and a generous notion of its destiny. The first plan, written in April of 1905, described the road as it materialized - from the Denver Northwestern and Pacific at Granby, east to Monarch Lake - and a branch north to Grand Lake from about the middle. A 1906 amendment planned additional lines (1) from Granby north through Walden to the state line, (2) a branch east to Fort Collins, or Loveland, and (3) a branch from somewhere near Walden southwest to the town of Hahns Peak and thence west to the state line. Organizers included two Waltemeyer brothers and Charles Wolcott. Frank Wolcott, a brother, set down a valuable record of his memories of the road and lumbering operations for the *1954 Westerners Brand Book,* under title "Monarch of Grand County." To summarize briefly, Monarch was being settled in the winter of 1904-05, and the box factory and lumber mill were built the following year. Freight came over the Moffat road as far as Arrowhead and was hauled from there on wagons. The Monarch Lake dam and a canal leading from it were built in order to float logs to the mill from chutes on the mountain sides. A home-made steampowered end wheeler pushed logs around in the day and served fishermen after hours. J.J. Argo of the Moffat surveyed a line with few cuts and fills for the standard-gauge railroad in from Granby. It was partly built when Frank Wolcott and his bride arrived, and they went from the end of the rails to Monarch on a sled.

The brevity of this railroad's life is explained by a fire which destroyed the box factory in 1908. Members of a Railroad Seminar tried in vain to find any sure vestiges of this line, but it appears that 7 miles are under water, somewhere between 4 and 6 are under roadway and at least part of the rest is dammed hard to find. I believe I drove a little stretch of it on an approach to Monarch Lake before Granby Lake came into being.

The LARAMIE HAHNS PEAK AND PACIFIC, chartered February 27, 1901, was built from Laramie into Colorado to bring out North Park coal. It has been written up by Frank R. Hollenback in a small Sage Books volume of 1960 called *The*

Laramie Plains Line, which has interesting information about the shift of terminus from Encampment to the North Park in Colorado, about Van Horn, the promoter, Fred Miller, and others connected with the road, notably a Mrs. Gladys Ceuphf Wilson, long the Laramie station master. The first segment, in operation in 1903, was a 7-mile link between Laramie and some grading which continued west to Centennial. Other installments followed: 3 miles in 1905, 7 in 1906, 13 in 1907, 10 in November of 1908, 10 in 1909, and 5 in 1910. These 55 miles took the line west through Centennial and south through Fox Park to the state line. At this time it boasted 3 locomotives, 18 cars, and a rotary.

Meanwhile a sister corporation was formed in 1907, the Larimer and Routt County Railway to go from the end of LHP&P through North Park to "near Grizzley Creek." The road was built first to Hebron, and afterwards south to Coalmont, just northwest of Grizzey Creek. The LHP&P went into receivership in 1912, and two years later the newly formed Colorado Wyoming and Eastern took over both properties. The 111-mile standard gauge line ran for a decade under this name, for two months of 1924 as the Northern Colorado and Eastern, and then from 1924 as the Laramie North Park and Western. Since January of 1936 the Union Pacific has controlled and operated the road through stock ownership. Petition for abandonment was denied in 1941.

The mine at Coalmont was flooded out and the railroad service benefits only a large but thinly populated ranch area. Its scenic quality and the desultory nature of its business has caused me to include it in this collection. The UP management made possible a buff trip in a recent year, and a friend of mine rode it as one of two passengers on a mixed train. A parley seemed to be going on about the bridge, but the true cause turned out to be that the crew needed to catch some trout for dinner.

Early piggyback on the Laramie Hahns Peak and Pacific. (Denver Public Library)

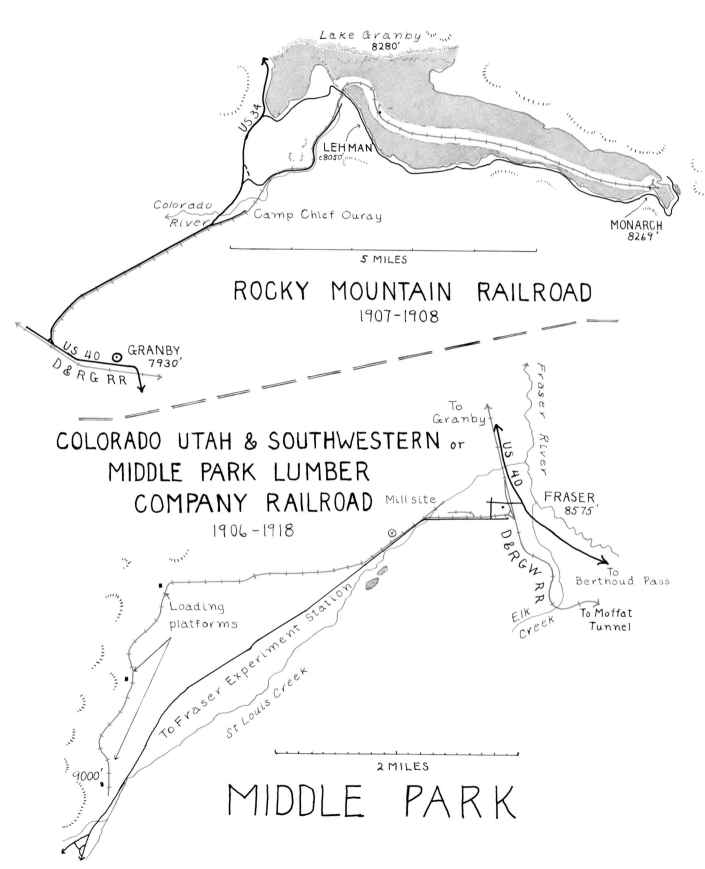

Lake Granby
8280'

US 34

LEHMAN
c 8050

Colorado
River

Camp Chief Ouray

MONARCH
8269'

5 MILES

ROCKY MOUNTAIN RAILROAD
1907-1908

US 40   GRANBY
7930'

D & R G RR

To
Granby

Fraser River

US 40

Mill site

FRASER
8575'

COLORADO UTAH & SOUTHWESTERN or
MIDDLE PARK LUMBER
COMPANY RAILROAD
1906-1918

D & R G W RR

To Berthoud Pass

Elk
Creek

To Moffat
Tunnel

Loading
platforms

To Fraser Experiment Station

St Louis Creek

2 MILES

9000'

MIDDLE PARK

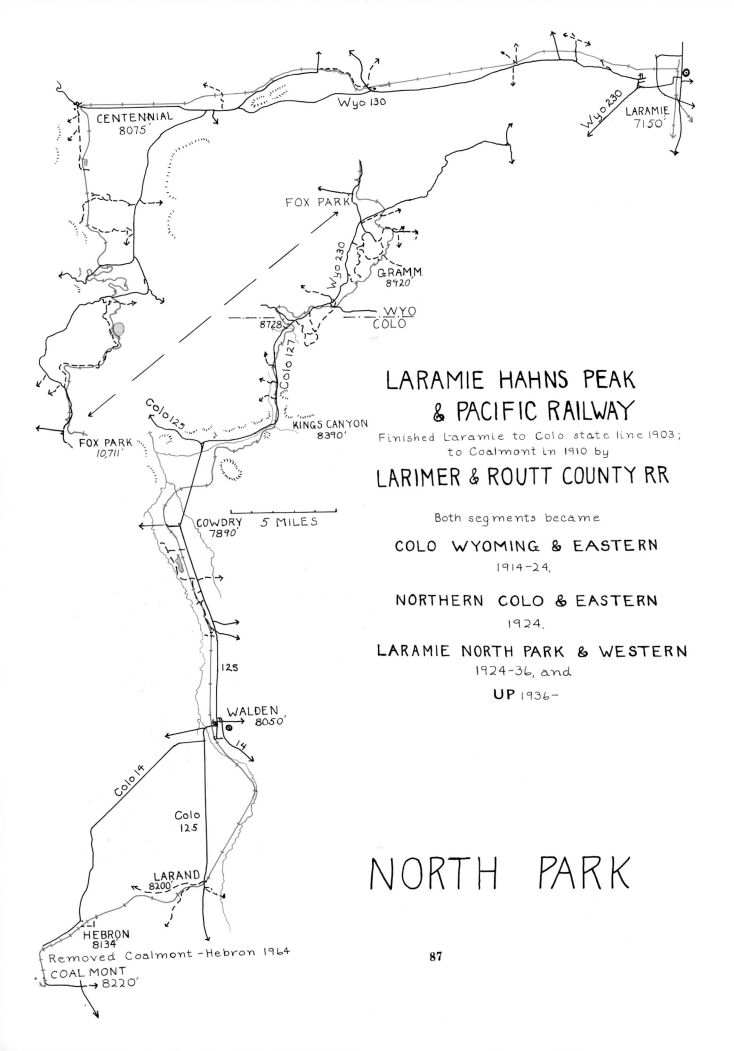

CENTENNIAL
8075'

Wyo 130

Wyo 230

LARAMIE
7150'

FOX PARK

Wyo 230

GRAMM
8920'

WYO
COLO

8728'

Colo 127

LARAMIE HAHNS PEAK
& PACIFIC RAILWAY

Finished Laramie to Colo state line 1903;
to Coalmont in 1910 by

LARIMER & ROUTT COUNTY RR

Both segments became

COLO WYOMING & EASTERN
1914-24,

NORTHERN COLO & EASTERN
1924,

LARAMIE NORTH PARK & WESTERN
1924-36, and

UP 1936-

Colo 125

KINGS CANYON
8390'

FOX PARK
10,711'

5 MILES

COWDRY
7890'

125

WALDEN
8050'

14

Colo 14

Colo
125

LARAND
8200'

NORTH PARK

HEBRON
8134'

Removed Coalmont - Hebron 1964

COAL MONT
→ 8220'

Deep cuts and high fills were almost continuous on the Cripple Creek Short Line.

PART IV
COLORADO SPRINGS AND WEST

MAPS

Early train on the Pikes Peak Cog Railway. (Courtesy Mr. and Mrs. Harold Seely)

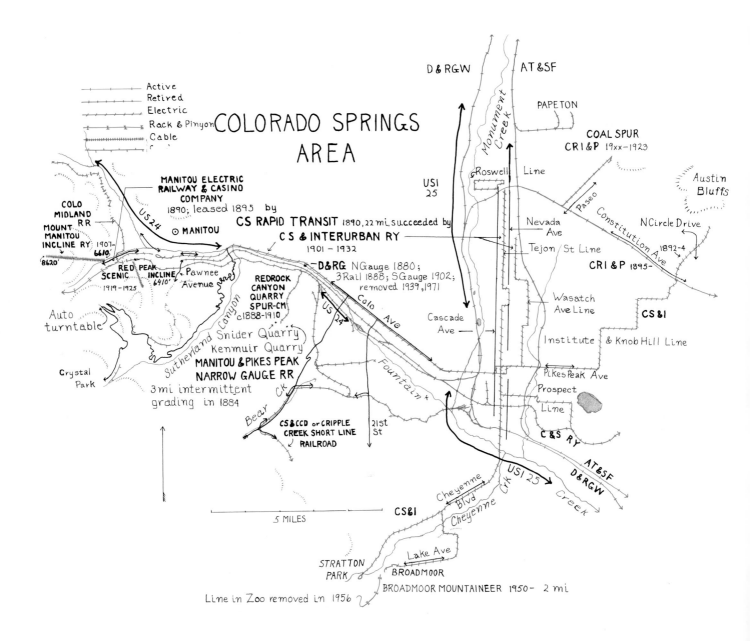

COLORADO SPRINGS
AREA

Active
Retired
Electric
Rack & Pinyon
Cable

MANITOU ELECTRIC
RAILWAY & CASINO
COMPANY
1890; leased 1895 by

CS RAPID TRANSIT 1890, 22 mi, succeeded by
CS & INTERURBAN RY
1901 - 1932

COLO
MIDLAND
RR

MOUNT
MANITOU
INCLINE RY 1907-
6610'

8620'

US 24

⊙ MANITOU

RED PEAK
SCENIC
1919-1925

INCLINE
6410'

Pawnee
Avenue

Sutherland Canyon

REDROCK
CANYON
QUARRY
SPUR-CM
c1888-1910

Snider Quarry
Kenmuir Quarry

MANITOU & PIKES PEAK
NARROW GAUGE RR
3 mi intermittent
grading in 1884

Auto
turntable

Crystal
Park

Bear Ck

CS & CCD or CRIPPLE
CREEK SHORT LINE
RAILROAD

US 24

D&RG N Gauge 1880;
3 Rail 1888; S Gauge 1902;
removed 1939, 1971

Colo Ave

21st
St

Fountain

CS&I

STRATTON
PARK

Cheyenne Blvd
Cheyenne Crk
Lake Ave
BROADMOOR

USI 25 Creek

Line in Zoo removed in 1956

BROADMOOR MOUNTAINEER 1950- 2 mi

5 MILES

D & RGW   AT & SF

PAPETON

COAL SPUR
CRI&P 19xx-1923

Roswell   Line

USI
25

Nevada
Ave

Tejon St Line

Cascade
Ave

Paseo   Constitution Ave

Austin
Bluffs

N Circle Drive

1892-4

CRI & P 1895-

Wasatch
Ave Line

CS & I

Institute
& Knob Hill Line

Pikes Peak Ave

Prospect

Line

C & S RY

AT & SF
D & RGW

Monument Creek

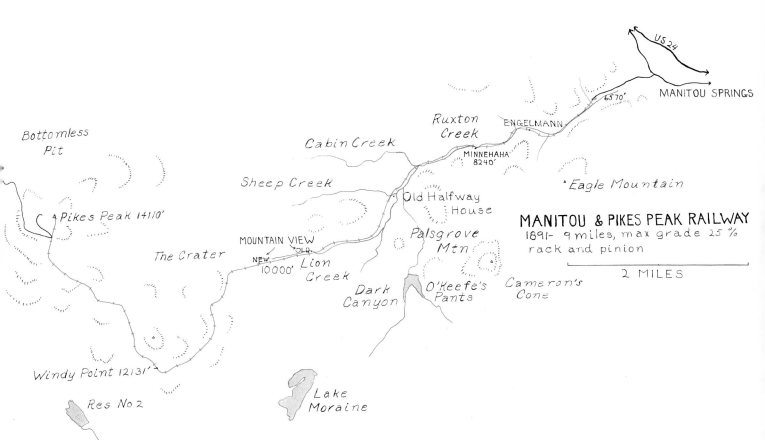

Bottomless
Pit

Cabin Creek

Ruxton
Creek

ENGELMANN

US 24

6570'

MANITOU SPRINGS

Sheep Creek

MINNEHAHA
8240'

Pikes Peak 14110'

Old Halfway
House

Eagle Mountain

MANITOU & PIKES PEAK RAILWAY
1891- 9 miles, max grade 25%
rack and pinion

MOUNTAIN VIEW
OLD

The Crater

NEW
10000' Lion
Creek

Palsgrove
Mtn

2 MILES

Dark
Canyon

O'Keefe's
Pants

Cameron's
Cone

Windy Point 12131'

Res No 2

Lake
Moraine

A watering car runs east to get around the Colorado College campus (Clarence Coyle photo)

The COLORADO SPRINGS AND INTERURBAN RAILWAY COMPANY came into being in August of 1902. The first idea was to run lines to Pueblo and to Cripple Creek and Victor as well as to the places where it actually did run — Colorado City, Manitou, Cheyenne Canon, and Prospect Lake — and also to the Garden of the Gods. This line was associated with Stratton and the Stratton estate down to its discontinuation in 1932. The company as formed was a consolidation of the earlier Colorado Springs Rapid Transit Company formed in 1890 and the 1901 CS&Suburban.

As kids we loved the open street cars used in summer. Instead of an aisle they had two levels of running board on each side, so we could walk them, swinging ourselves from pew to pew by hanging on to the upright posts. Also on hot days we rushed out from the curb to get into the spray of the watering cars. The only remainder of the Interurban that I know of is a hill-climbing stretch from the present Three Eagles Development Company to the east part of the Broadmoor Mesa, using a double-back on a bit of shelf roadbed on a 5% gradient. This railroad must have inherited some of its right of way from an older Colorado Springs and Manitou Street Railway Company incorporated in 1886 by J.J. Hagerman, W.S. Jackson and Jefferson A. Hayes. The earlier Company laid down 6 miles of 18-pound rails and by 1890 were operating between the points named with a fleet of cars and 42 horses.

Locations for the CS&I and several other grades in the area were taken from a recently published map titled *Railroads of the Pikes Peak Region,* drawn by Tom Daniels with compilations by Bill McKenzie, Harold Seeley and Dr. W.B. Crouch of the Colorado Midland Chapter of the National Railway Historical Society.

The Santa Fe and Rock Island coal spurs to the northeast of Colorado Springs served rather shallow lignite mines. Real estate developments have eliminated the opportunities for exploration but we have heard of a case or two where people discovered the quaint old mines when their houses began to tilt, and then quietly slipped into the sink-holes.

The MANITOU ELECTRIC RAILWAY AND CASINO COMPANY started operating in June of 1895, two years after incorporation, and for many years ran a little trolley car from the Loop in central Manitou, up the steep and winding Ruxton Avenue to the Iron Springs Pavilion and the stations of the cog road up Pikes Peak and the Manitou Incline.

It was consolidated into the CS&Interurban. Some grade and

a short piece of track remain visible where it cut from the road into the hillside to the south, .4 mile up Ruxton Avenue from Manitou's "Loop." As children we considered this line a gyp because the fare was 10¢ for the half mile when the main line all the way to Manitou was only two 5¢ fares.

The MANITOU INCLINE RAILWAY COMPANY was organized in 1907 to take over and operate for tourist and recreation purposes the already constructed cable railway which had been built to carry pipe and other materials for the Colorado Springs water and hydroelectric power generating systems on the south and east slopes of Pikes Peak. It has been a Penrose (El Pomar) interest since 1923. Lloyd Shaw, steer-bulldozing and square dancing principal of Cheyenne Mountain School, who paid for his education by conductoring on the line, flavored his spiel to the tourists with statements like the one about the gravel on the road-bed: it was an annual crop, sent to Battle Creek where it was ground up and sold as grape nuts.

The RED PEAK SCENIC RAILWAY COMPANY was formed on June 11, 1919, and built a cable railroad from the sidewalk of Ruxton Avenue in Manitou to a ridge spur 750 feet higher and a half a mile south. The Manitou Incline, starting farther up the street, had been operating at a profit since 1907, but this venture had only one thing in its favor, competitively speaking: people walking up the street reached it first. There may have been other difficulties, as we find in the April 3, 1925, edition of the *Colorado Springs Evening Telegraph* a story about an official of the company, involving embezzlement and a penitentiary sentence.

The staircase from the sidewalk is still there with some of the lettering on the smooth wall, .25 mile up Ruxton Avenue from Manitou Springs's "Loop," the latter named for the old street car loop, end of the main CS&I Ry line. Some of the Red Peak grade is too steep and rough to follow, but one can drive up Pawnee Avenue from the main street (Library corner of the main street) as far as the road goes and then climb the steep hillside to the west to reach the concrete foundations at the summit, or if he is exploring the grade of the Pikes Peak Narrow Gauge Railway he can descend to the top of the incline from the point where that grade comes into the Crystal Park Road.

The PIKES PEAK RAILWAY AND IMPROVEMENT COMPANY was formed in 1883 to build a narrow gauge adhesion railroad from Manitou to the summit of Pikes Peak by way of Crystal Park, Lake Moraine, Seven Lakes and Satchet Mountain. Money was raised and some grading was done - part of it on the route later used by the Crystal Park Road. Ulysses Grant was one of those interested, and company funds were deposited in a New York Bank which promptly closed, at least partly because of a failure in the Grant and Ward Company. Morris Abott's *The Pikes Peak Cog Road,* source for these statements, has a fuller account of the venture.

I have used this handy grade as a training place for Colorado College railroad seminar students to map the grading and to project intended grading on a USGS quadrangle. We start in a canyon at the upper limit of Pawnee Avenue, where we find the grade running east about the level of the uppermost house. Where it peters out we return to the canyon, follow the trail up it until we meet the Crystal Park road, then go east again on a downhill stretch of the grade and continue on intermittent bits of grade till we meet the trail again.

The REDROCK CANYON QUARRY SPUR was built by

the Colorado Midland to bring out the red sandstone from strata that are a continuation of those in the Garden of the Gods. As children we played on the giant steps of the deserted quarry before the rails were taken out but after operations had ceased. (The stone was too soft for satisfactory building material).

We know little about this spur except that the Snider Lime and Stone Company acquired a new hoist and boiler in 1891 and in 1893 a misguided locomotive knocked the derrick over - these items from the *Colorado City Iris.*

Train and tank high on the slope of Pikes Peak.

The MANITOU AND PIKES PEAK RAILWAY COMPANY had its story told in a 1962 book, *Pikes Peak by Rail,* authored by Frank R. Hollenbeck and William Russell, and more completely in the 1972 volume of Morris Abbott, *The Pikes Peak Cog Road.* The standard gauge track is right where it was in 1891 and it is at least as live an operation now as an El Pomar (Penrose) property as it was then. Some people are nostalgic about the old steam locomotives, but the diesel - powered cars give a far smoother and cleaner ride. Old locomotives are on display on Manitou's main street (US 24 business route) and at the lower terminal of the cog railway on Ruxton Avenue.

High altitudes make for fine views all along the eastern end of the line.

The COLORADO SPRINGS AND CRIPPLE CREEK DISTRICT RAILWAY COMPANY, owned the Cripple Creek

Extensive rock work was needed to cross the broad slab called Devil's Slide. (State Historical Society)

District interurban trolleys and built the third railroad into the gold camp. Reasons for this standard gauge "short line" to Colorado Springs were two-fold: the mines were about to swing into their richest ($18,000,000) year of production, and the two railroads serving the camp — the Florence and Cripple Creek — and the Midland Terminal — could not handle all the traffic. The Colorado and Southern posed a threat by buying the partly graded Denver Cripple Creek and Southwestern which would be able to take ore down the South Platte to Denver.

The trestle at Cathedral Spires near Clyde - for later trains the woodwork was replaced by a fireproof gravel fill.

The Gold Camp Road follows the grade all the way to Victor with slight exceptions. Most of it is closed during the winter, but in summer it makes a fine drive, more scenic than the water line routes preferred by engineers in gentler topography. It is graveled and so never slippery in rain but it can be dusty on week ends. You reach the road by following 26th Street south from Colorado Avenue or from the Midland Expressway, or you can shortcut into it from Cheyenne Boulevard and North Cheyenne Canyon. It is narrow but wide enough for passing ex-

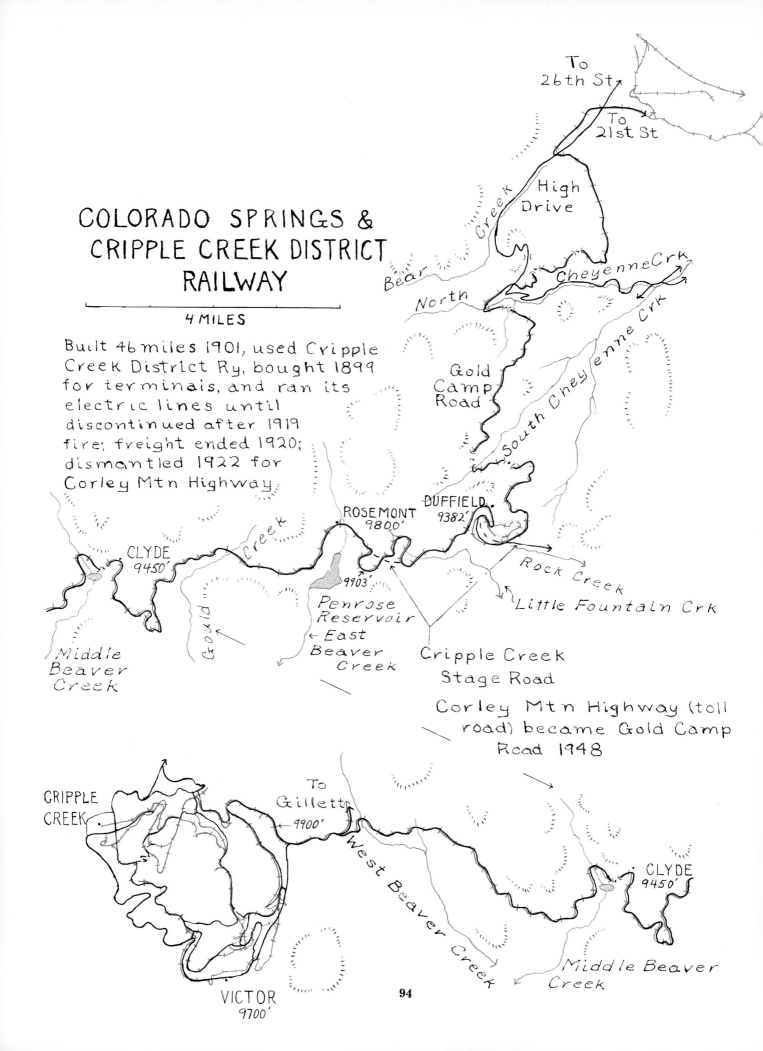

COLORADO SPRINGS & CRIPPLE CREEK DISTRICT RAILWAY

4 MILES

Built 46 miles 1901, used Cripple Creek District Ry, bought 1899 for terminals, and ran its electric lines until discontinued after 1919 fire; freight ended 1920; dismantled 1922 for Corley Mtn Highway

To 26th St

To 21st St

Bear Creek

High Drive

Cheyenne Crk

North

South Cheyenne Crk

Gold Camp Road

DUFFIELD 9382'

ROSEMONT 9800'

9903'

Penrose Reservoir

← East Beaver Creek

CLYDE 9450'

Gould Creek

Middle Beaver Creek

Rock Creek

Little Fountain Crk

Cripple Creek Stage Road

Corley Mtn Highway (toll road) became Gold Camp Road 1948

CRIPPLE CREEK

To Gillett
← 9900'

West Beaver Creek

CLYDE 9450'

Middle Beaver Creek

VICTOR 9700'

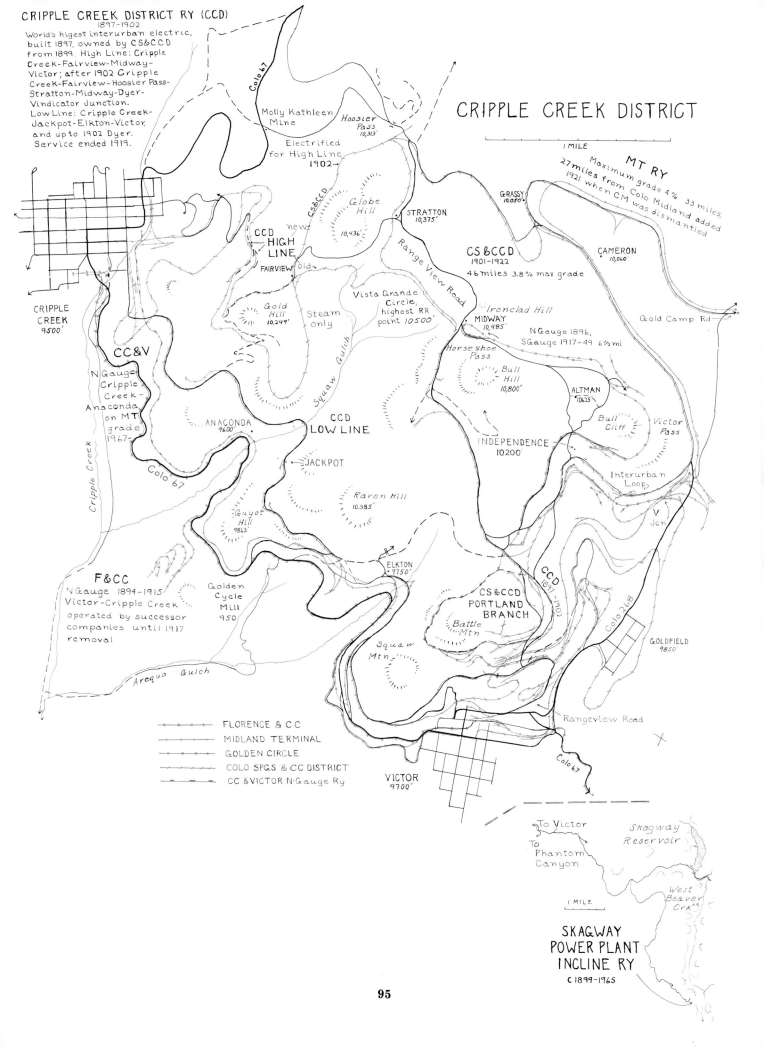

CRIPPLE CREEK DISTRICT RY (CCD)
1897-1902
World's higest interurban electric,
built 1897, owned by CS&CCD
from 1899. High Line: Cripple
Creek-Fairview-Midway-
Victor; after 1902 Cripple
Creek-Fairview-Hoosier Pass-
Stratton-Midway-Dyer-
Vindicator Junction.
Low Line: Cripple Creek-
Jackpot-Elkton-Victor,
and up to 1902 Dyer.
Service ended 1919.

CRIPPLE CREEK DISTRICT

1 MILE

Colo 67

Molly Kathleen
Mine

Hoosier
Pass
10,313'

Electrified
for High Line
1902→

MT RY
Maximum grade 4% 33 miles,
27 miles from Colo Midland added
1921 when CM was dismantled

GRASSY
10,050'

CS&CCD

Globe
Hill
10,436'

STRATTON
10,375'

CAMERON
10,060'

CCD
HIGH
LINE

new

FAIRVIEW old

CS & CCD
1901-1922
46 miles 3.8% max grade

Gold Camp Rd

CRIPPLE
CREEK
9500'

Range View Road

Gold
Hill
10,249'

Steam
only

Vista Grande
Circle,
highest RR
point 10500'

Ironclad Hill

MIDWAY
10,485'

N Gauge 1896,
S Gauge 1917-49 6½ mi

CC&V
N Gauge
Cripple
Creek-
Anaconda
on MT
grade
1967-

Squaw Gulch

CCD
LOW LINE

Horseshoe
Pass

Bull
Hill
10,800'

ALTMAN
10,625'

Bull
Cliff

Victor
Pass

ANACONDA
9600'

JACKPOT

INDEPENDENCE
10200'

Interurban
Loop

Colo 67

Raven Hill
10,385'

V
Jcn

F&CC
N Gauge 1894-1915
Victor-Cripple Creek
operated by successor
companies until 1917
removal

Guyot
Hill
9863'

Golden
Cycle
Mill
950

ELKTON
9750'

CS&CCD
PORTLAND
BRANCH

Battle
Mtn

CCD
1897-1902

Colo 268

GOLDFIELD
9850'

Squaw
Mtn

Rangeview Road

Arequa Gulch

Colo 67

VICTOR
9700'

FLORENCE & CC
MIDLAND TERMINAL
GOLDEN CIRCLE
COLO SPGS & CC DISTRICT
CC & VICTOR N-Gauge Ry

To Victor

To
Phantom
Canyon

Skagway
Reservoir

West
Beaver
Crk

1 MILE

SKAGWAY
POWER PLANT
INCLINE RY
C 1899-1965

95

A photo Craft Shop picture from the Harold Seely collection.

cept in a few of the cuts. Many of the long curving fills on this railroad replaced earlier trestles which had been less stable and also subject to burning.

The line was purchased in a surprise bid by W.D. Corley in what was probably intended as a reorganization auction by the owners. Corley junked it out and set up a toll road which was called the Corley Mountain Highway until his franchise ran out and it reverted to public land. It makes a good round trip coupled with either the Phantom Canyon Road south to US 50 on Florence and Cripple Creek grade, or north, partly on Midland grade to US 24. It ranks as one of the best of the drives on preserved railroad grade. Early drivers, especially from the flatland, were horrified at having to drive the high curving trestles on a roadbed consisting of two planks laid on the ties, but these have all been eliminated and dismantled. There are several stories of Cripple Creek and its people: Marshall Sprague's *Money Mountain,* Frank Waters' *Midas of the Rockies,* and more specifically for the railroads Morris Cafky's *Rails Around Gold Hill* being the most complete.

Cripple Creek provided a long period of good profits for railroading. The lines shown on the map are not complete, being largely taken from a special quadrangle of the USGS that probably omits several spurs taken up earlier or not yet built. To explore the district you might start with Colorado 69 between Cripple Creek and Victor, with a return over the Range View Road to the road junction north of Stratton and then a turn south on the east side over Victor Pass for further prowling. You can then come back north on the low line road. It is cool high country, with fringe benefits of mine structures and views of the Sangre de Cristo Range to the west.

The CRIPPLE CREEK AND VICTOR NARROW GAUGE RAILROAD is an operating tourist line built in 1967 on the roadbed of the Midland Terminal. It runs south from Cripple Creek to Anaconda on 60 cm or 22.2 inch gauge track, usually with power from a former Climax Molybdenum Company locomotive used in Mexico. The full story is told by Roger Appleton in his 1970 booklet on the line.

The SKAGWAY POWER PLANT INCLINE was a one-car cable railway dropping 1200 feet in 2300 feet of length. It ran over two trestles and through a tunnel and had a slight curve, managed by tilting the rollers over which the cable ran. It was the only means of reaching the Southern Colorado Power Com-

Mount Pisgah and Cripple Creek from broken grade of the High Line.

A sloping tunnel and a sloping trestle enlivened the Skagway Power Plant's cable railroad.

The perfectly level grade suggests that this was one of the many unmapped mine spurs between Cripple Creek and Victor.

pany's hydroelectric plant. The trestle section had a 40% grade; near the bottom it reached 60%. The penstock, dropping altogether 1600 feet from Skagway Reservoir, lay under the tracks like that on the Mount Manitou Incline. My only ride, taken in 1957 with Mayor John Vanderwalker of Victor, was full of surprises, one of which was a bighorn that rose from basking between the rails as we came down, and proudly walked off. To see where this curiosity of mountain railroading was, drive 1.25 miles south from Victor toward Phantom Canyon, take the Skagway road, and after 4 miles keep right. It is 5 miles more, this last part probably requiring 4-wheel drive. The abandonment was decided on after a flood which destroyed part of the reservoir and several hundred feet of the wooden pipe line.

The MIDLAND TERMINAL RAILWAY COMPANY, running from Colorado Springs to the Cripple Creek District, was organized in 1892 and opened in 1895. Until the Colorado Midland was pulled out, this was a feeder to that road, then 5 years old, running only from a high point of Divide to Victor and Cripple Creek. Like the mother road, it was standard-gauge. By many years the last survivor among the three roads into the gold camp, it is remembered for the 3-, 4-, and even 5-engined trains of empty cars which puffed up through south Manitou,

squealed around the big trestle above Ruxton Avenue, and climbed up through the Ute Pass tunnels across the brook from Highway 24. The story of this road and its Cripple Creek fellows as handsomely told in Morris Cafky's *Rails Around Gold Hill* can be briefly reviewed here. The Santa Fe, which controlled the Colorado Midland at the time the gold camp began to show real promise, grew interested enough to ask J.J. Hagerman, prime mover of the Midland, to investigate the wisdom of building a branch in. Hagerman was ill, and in his stead went Irving Howbert, president of Colorado Springs' First National Bank. This was in 1892, and Howbert found people mining gold in various parts of the district, but even discounting the fake boom caused by gold seeding at Cripple Creek's Mount Pisgah, he remembered that many of the camps had been too ephemeral to justify a railroad, and he recommended building only after a six-months' waiting period in which to see whether the camp had the prospect of some permanence. Without waiting, the Santa Fe took some first steps in surveying and grading, and then it began to lose interest, so that on August 2 a separate company, partly made up of Colorado Springs people, was incorporated. Meanwhile Collbran, the manager of the CM, kept after Santa Fe's president Manvel until September 1, when it was announced that the Santa Fe had let a building contract. The MT organization planned their road as a narrow-gauge to keep costs down; when the Santa Fe's CM started to build, it turned out they were only going to creep up with their branch to Midland,

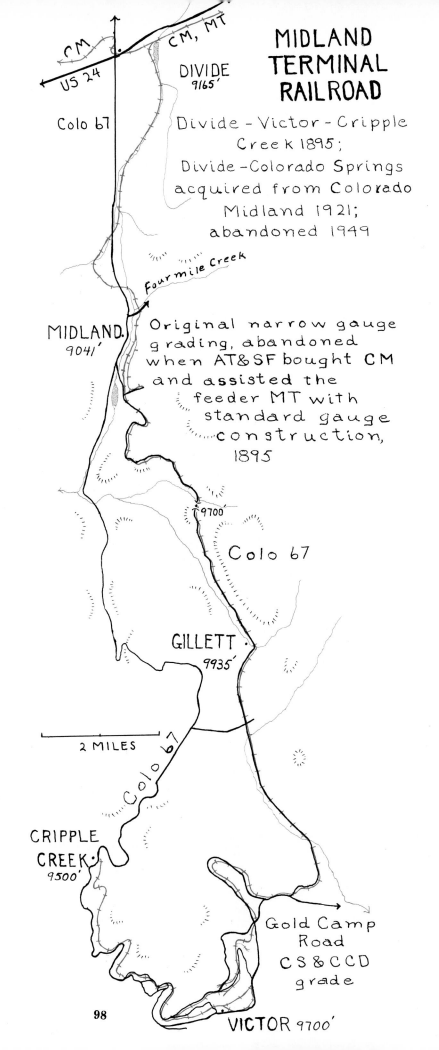

MIDLAND
TERMINAL
RAILROAD

Divide - Victor - Cripple
Creek 1895;
Divide - Colorado Springs
acquired from Colorado
Midland 1921;
abandoned 1949

CM

CM, MT

US 24

DIVIDE
9165'

Colo 67

Fourmile Creek

MIDLAND.
9041'

Original narrow gauge
grading, abandoned
when AT&SF bought CM
and assisted the
feeder MT with
standard gauge
construction,
1895

9700'

Colo 67

GILLETT .
9935'

2 MILES

Colo 67

CRIPPLE
CREEK .
9500'

Gold Camp
Road
CS&CCD
grade

VICTOR 9700'

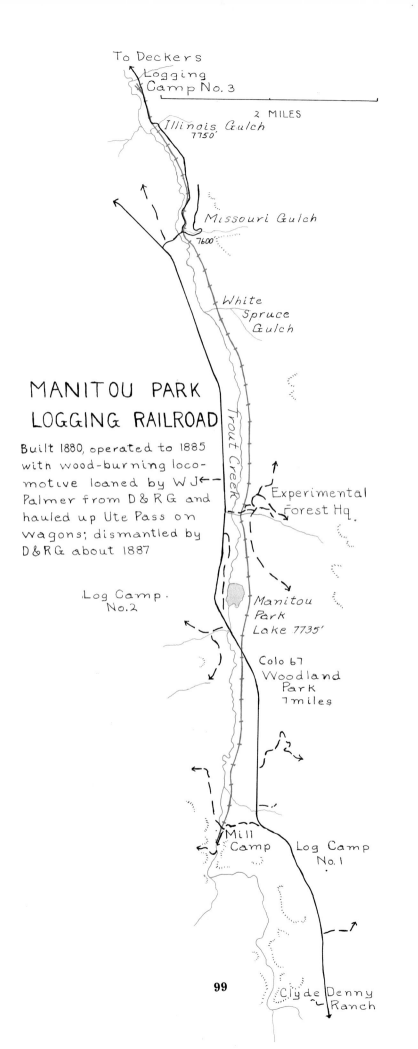

To Deckers
Logging
Camp No. 3

2 MILES

Illinois Gulch
7750'

Missouri Gulch

7600'

White
Spruce
Gulch

MANITOU PARK
LOGGING RAILROAD

Built 1880, operated to 1885
with wood-burning loco-
motive loaned by WJ
Palmer from D & R G and
hauled up Ute Pass on
wagons; dismantled by
D & R G about 1887

Trout Creek

Experimental
Forest Hq.

Log Camp.
No. 2

Manitou
Park
Lake 7735'

Colo 67
Woodland
Park
7 miles

Mill
Camp

Log Camp
No. 1

Clyde Denny
Ranch

99

End of the MT's narrow-guage grading, just off Colorado 67.

the point about halfway in to the edge of the district where the terrain begins to roughen up. From here on they would prefer to let the local company build its narrow-gauge. Shortly afterward the Santa Fe withdrew and conveyed what standard-gauge it had to the MT, which proceeded to grade for a narrow-gauge line all the way from Divide south. When the threat of competing roads became apparent, the Santa Fe persuaded and assisted the MT toward regrading for a standard-gauge line so as to obviate the expensive transshipping process the narrow-gauge line would require. Cafky finds that the iron for the MT was provided by the CM on a loan basis, for which the only repayment was probably in increased traffic.

In its 800-foot climb from Midland to 10,000-foot Gillett, mining town named for one of the Santa Fe's men who had become interested in the MT, the line side-hilled southward along the west slopes of Pikes Peak on 4-, 3-, and 2-percent grades. David Moffat's narrow-gauge Florence and Cripple Creek, though organized later, arrived in Cripple Creek in the beginning of July, 1894, just before the MT reached the camp's northern outpost of Gillett, and was draining most of the ore from the area off southward to the 3-railed D&RG line between Pueblo and the Royal Gorge. Gillett is only about 3 miles from Cripple Creek, but the last two of these miles have a 750-foot drop. The railroad went on building, but stayed high, running first down through Upper Beaver Park, then up Grassy Creek to Grassy, later Cameron, where passengers could stage west over Hoosier Pass to Cripple Creek, then south around Bull Cliff to the 10,200-foot Victor Pass before it began the descent past Victor, and back north on a winding route parallel to and above the F&CC line from Victor to Cripple Creek.

Rivalry between the two roads came to a head with a curious incident in Victor involving trespass, and induced wreckage. This was in 1897; two years later a holding company — the Denver and Southwestern Railway Company — was formed to take over the control of both properties along with the Golden Circle Railroad, the Canon City & Cripple Creek, and some non-railroading businesses.

The Midland Terminal enjoyed heavy traffic both before and after the camp's peak year of 1900 despite the appearance of a third railroad into Cripple Creek — the CS&CCD, which was also standard-gauged and saved 10 miles in the distance to Colorado Springs,. But the holding company went into receivership and was replaced by another one in 1904 — the Cripple Creek Central Railway Company. At the end of 1904 the CS&CCD was bought by the C&S company, and in 1905 all

three were operated under a single management to eliminate competition and duplication of passenger service.

In 1918 the Colorado Midland ceased operations west of Divide, where the MT junction was. Three years later all the CM's track except this 27-mile east end was torn up, and that was purchased and incorporated into the MT. Business was poor during the 1920's, but the depression lowered the cost of labor and materials and increased the price of gold, and the road operated profitably as part of the Golden Cycle Mining and Milling Company which purchased it from the Cripple Creek Central in 1934. All were among the Carlton interests.

The profit in gold mining declined with rising production costs, and the MT was abandoned early in 1949, and the Golden Cycle Mill moved to Cripple Creek.

From Midland to Gillette you are on the MT grade. You should take a run up to the section of narrow gauge grade half a mile beyond the road split, curio of an earlier purpose. If at Cripple Creek you take the Cripple Creek and Victor Narrow Gauge Railroad, whose freight now consists entirely of sightseers, you will be on Midland grade again. The sound of its whistle, coming over the hill from Anaconda, will remind you as nothing else could of the joys and griefs of the great gold camp.

The MANITOU PARK RAILROAD is an arbitrary name for an 8- or 10- mile lumber road running north from Fisher's Sawmill at Cantrells Gulch about 5 miles north of Woodland Park, northward down the stretch of the Trout Creek Valley known as Manitou Park to Drury Gulch. The sawmill was named for H.D. Fisher, employed by Palmer's friend William Bell to oversee the lumbering activity. Fisher later became a pusher for the Midland Railway. The lumbering railroad came from the D&RG, which furnished them with discard rails and a narrow-gauge wood-burner that was hauled west from Colorado Springs to Manitou and up the grades of Ute Pass by mules. Gordon Parker tells of the lumber business and the resort which Bell had in the park in his "Scrapbook pertaining to the history of the Colorado School of Forestry" in the Colorado College Library.

Mr. Claude Denny knows how to find some of the south end of the railroad. He has cut into spikes while haying in the meadows farther north. Grade is distinctly visible just north and south of Illinois Gulch. I pulled one spike out of the grass there and found another which a road grader had turned up, but I think to find any more you will have to scratch the ground.

Mr. Denny knew Henry Jones, both senior and junior, who had worked for the outfit, the elder mainly as a filer of saws. The mill, which he can locate, had two ponds, one for ice for food storage at the camp of Thornton, near the present lake, the other for washing the logs. The north end of the line had a switching place with two tracks but no wye.

The COLORADO MIDLAND RAILWAY, a late comer and early goer among Colorado railroads, is remembered as the first standard-gauge line over the main mountain crest and as the largest rail project anywhere in the world to be abandoned. The road was built by a dynamic bearded fellow named John J. Hagerman, who had made his fortune in iron mining in Michigan and then had come west to recover from tuberculosis.

Hagerman employed as general manager the H.D. Fisher who

The Midland ran these wildflower excursions on summer Sundays for several years. (Harold Seely Collection)

had supervised Dr. Bell's lumbering operation in Manitou Park, as chief engineer Thomas Wigglesworth, and as attorney H.T. Rogers.

Bell got into the picture and suggested the name Midland Railroad. It seems likely that as he was a Palmer friend and an associate his main interest here may have been to keep in touch with the aims of the new railroad. It was certainly to his interest to see a road go up Ute Pass as far as Woodland Park; there it could connect with his little lumbering railroad 7 miles to the north. Bell did not remain interested.

Green Mountain Falls - the pond is still there but the hotel is gone and the trees are crowded with housing. (State Historical Society)

Spike collecting, which I have done extensively, is doubtless one of the stupider patterns of acquisition, since with a very few minor exceptions the only thing that distinguishes one spike from another is the railroad or branch that it came from - a Book Cliff spike, for example, or an Aberdeen Quarry Spur spike being a great rarity, yet looking exactly like all the rest. The grand exception in shape is the Jeffry Spike which Otto Meas used on his RGS line. It is double-headed, like an exceptional

Building a steel bridge over Manitou's Ruxton Creek and Avenue - the CM expected to last. (State Historical Society).

calf.

101

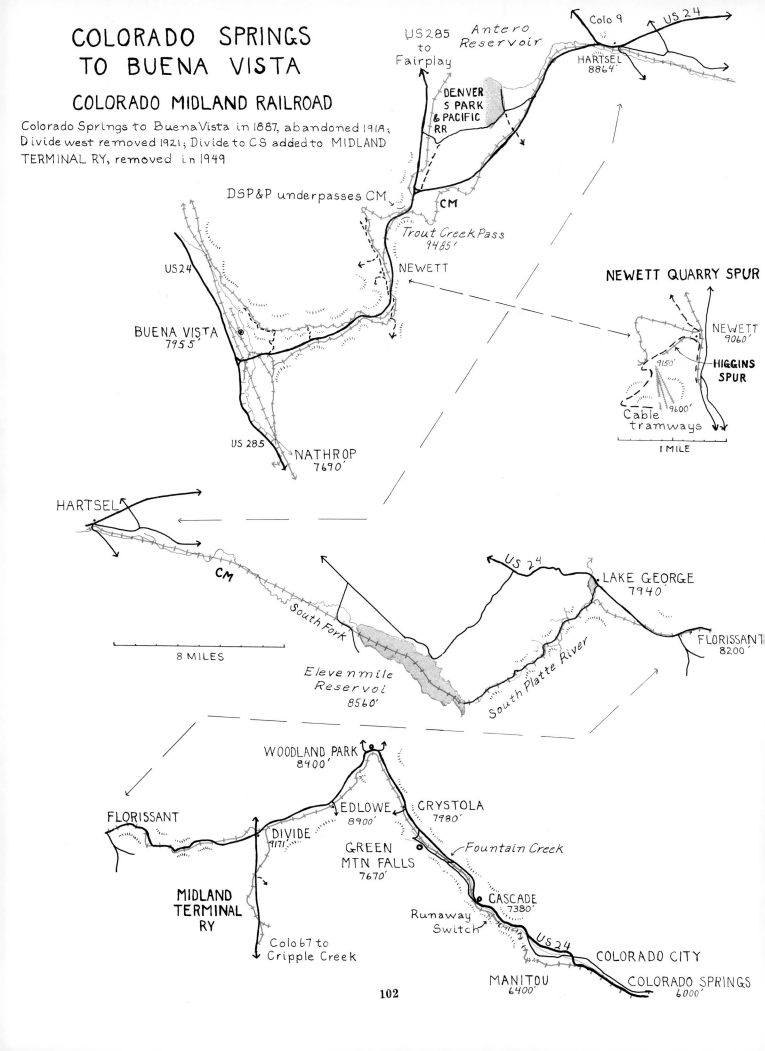

COLORADO SPRINGS
TO BUENA VISTA

COLORADO MIDLAND RAILROAD

Colorado Springs to Buena Vista in 1887, abandoned 1918;
Divide west removed 1921; Divide to CS added to MIDLAND
TERMINAL RY, removed in 1949

US285
to
Fairplay

Colo 9

US 24

Antero
Reservoir

DENVER
S PARK
& PACIFIC
RR

HARTSEL
8864'

DSP&P underpasses CM

CM

Trout Creek Pass
9485'

US 24

NEWETT

NEWETT QUARRY SPUR

NEWETT
9060'

9150'

HIGGINS
SPUR

9600'

Cable
tramways

1 MILE

BUENA VISTA
7955'

US 285

NATHROP
7690'

HARTSEL

CM

South Fork

8 MILES

Elevenmile
Reservoi
8560'

US 24

LAKE GEORGE
7940'

South Platte River

FLORISSANT
8200'

WOODLAND PARK
8400'

FLORISSANT

EDLOWE
8900'

CRYSTOLA
7980'

DIVIDE
9171'

GREEN
MTN FALLS
7670'

Fountain Creek

MIDLAND
TERMINAL
RY

CASCADE
7380'

Runaway
Switch

COLORADO CITY

US 24

Colo 67 to
Cripple Creek

MANITOU
6400'

COLORADO SPRINGS
6000'

102

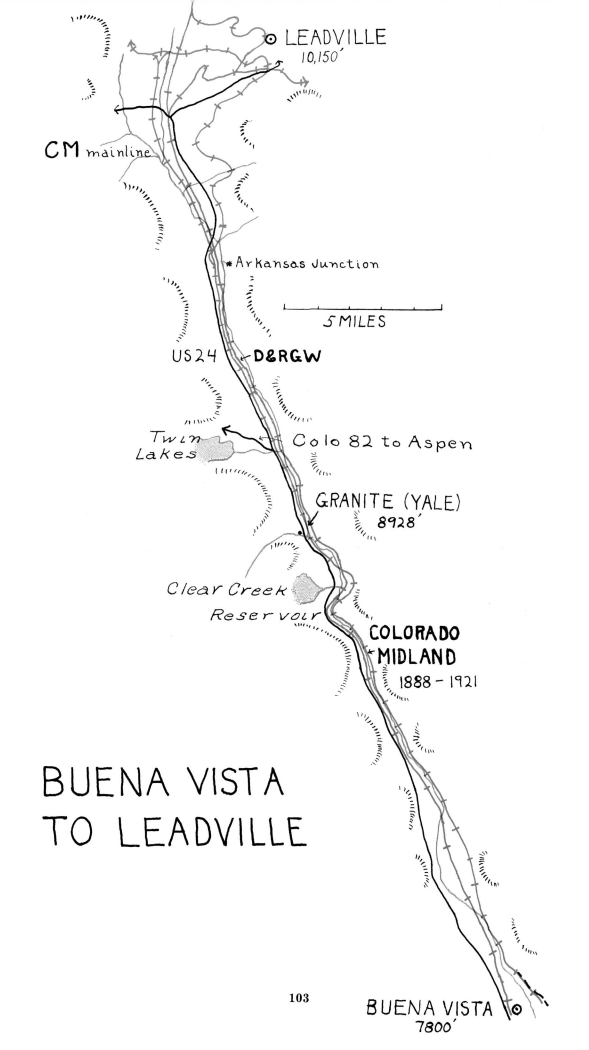

⊙ LEADVILLE
10,150′

CM mainline

✳ Arkansas Junction

5 MILES

US24   ← D&RGW

Twin
Lakes

Colo 82 to Aspen

GRANITE (YALE)
8928′

Clear Creek
Reservoir

COLORADO
← MIDLAND
1888 – 1921

BUENA VISTA
TO LEADVILLE

BUENA VISTA ⊙
7800′

You can still find the runaway end of this safety switch a mile below Cascade. (State Historical Society)

This stretch of the Midland's "Scenic Drive" near Buena Vista takes you around northwest to end at the embankments for a high trestle, long since gone. (State Historical Society)

Two railroads: on Trout Creek Pass the Midland overpasses the South Park line.

Concentric tunnels on the east side of the Arkansas Valley - now driveable. Inquire at Buena Vista. (Colorado State Historical Society.)

In 1885, while the Midland was being located by Wigglesworth down the Frying Pan, the Burlington became interested in it as the means of extending their railroad westward. The Burlington had trains running to Colorado Springs and engineers surveying the Colorado River below Glenwood Springs. The panic of 1887 dried up this and a lot of other ambitious railroad planning in western Colorado. Hagerman made the alliance with the D&RG and sat tight. In 1893, the Santa Fe bought his road for what John Lipsey says brought a profit to the associates who had begun the railroad's activity with a $3,000,000 subscription raised in J.J. Hagerman's North Cascade Avenue home (now the Russ-Amer Apartments) in a period of 15 minutes. The Santa Fe took it over as the reorganized Colorado Midland Railroad Company, a consolidation of the CMRy with the 6.6-mile Aspen Short Line. The

Santa Fe went into receivership, and the Midland with it, in 1894, but through a separation of the receiverships as the CMRailway Company. In 1900 the Rio Grande Western of Utah and the two-year-old Colorado and Southern bought each a 50-percent interest in the Midland. With merging the next year of the RGW into the D&RGW, the latter fell heir to this half interest in its rival. Despite some efforts during the first 20th century decade to get rid of it, these two roads were still the owners when the A.E. Carlton interests bought it in 1917 for $1,400,000. Carlton seems to have entertained a plan to link the Midland with two other railroad segments he controlled — the Grand Junction and Grand River Valley road from the Junction west to Fruita, and the narrow-gauge Uintah from Mack northwest to Dragon, Utah, with surveys and plans that went through to Salt Lake City. But the Carltons ceased to operate in July of 1918, and after some legal obstacles had been surmounted they pulled out all except the 27 miles between Divide and Colorado Springs. This was sold to the Midland Terminal, serving other Carlton interests in the gold camp of Cripple Creek.

Some of the Midland trackage was absorbed by the Midland Expressway in west Colorado Springs, and some by the westbound lanes of US 24 in Ute pass above Manitou Springs, but parts can be found in upper Manitou Springs, including the station, now home of the Nelson Hunts (Mrs. Inez Hunt is a historian), and some tunnels between Ruxton Creek and Fountain Creek. The runaway train trap is still visible on the southwest hillside a mile southeast of Cascade. One can see the grade generally from Cascade on to Lake George, drive it to Elevenmile Reservoir, and pick it up again between Hartsel and west of Trout Creek Pass. The Newett Quarry offers a detour to the curious cable tram there - still much in evidence - and below that there are stretches where you can get up to but not follow the grade in a car. The last access, at the foot of the pass on 24, is marked, and takes you around to a high broken bridge above Buena Vista. You continue to see grade occasionally on the far side of the Arkansas as you drive on to Leadville.

My love of railroads dates back to the annual round trip to our summer cabin at Crystola covering the period from Commencement to Labor Day. We children seldom failed to go down near the tracks to watch the noon train come through, and we flattened the heads of spikes by putting them in between the rail ends for trains to run over. This came to an end when a track walker followed us up the canyon trail. We were ready for him - we assembled a lot of rocks on a little cliff top above the trail and waited there, prepared to defend ourselves. Fortunately he disappointed us. Instead of coming up to our fort, he stopped and told our parents something about the dangers of derailment due to heat expansion.

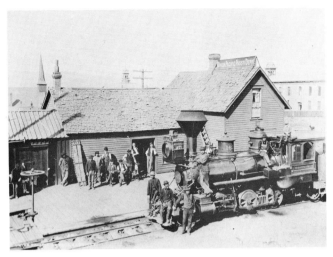

A South Park locomotive at the Union Pacific station in Leadville. (State Historical Society)

IN LEADVILLE most of the (old) grades can be identified. The map is based on three USGS maps of different periods and different scales, and some track has been dump-covered or in other ways obliterated. The long line west up Evans Gulch and around south to the timberline country of Ibex is the most enjoyable to explore. Some mining goes on up there now but there are plenty of old properties to prowl around, and a fine view of the mountain country across the Arkansas and beyond Tennessee Pass. Most of these roads do not require a 4-wheel drive and the ones I have tried were all drivable when wet. There is a lot of railroading to be done around Leadville, and staying at the old Vendome Hotel will help to flavor the experience.

The LEADVILLE MINERAL BELT RAILWAY was chartered by organizers of the Colorado and Southern and shortly after laying some track to the district mines was absorbed in that road. The rails came out with those of the main line east of Climax in 1938.

The DENVER SOUTH PARK AND PACIFIC had access to Leadville via the D&RG north from Buena Vista from 1881 to 1883 while Jay Gould was involved with both railroads, but with the lease cancelled they built their way over the mountains from South Park.

An Evans Gulch bridge east of Leadville.

The Ibex Branch had numerous mine spurs.

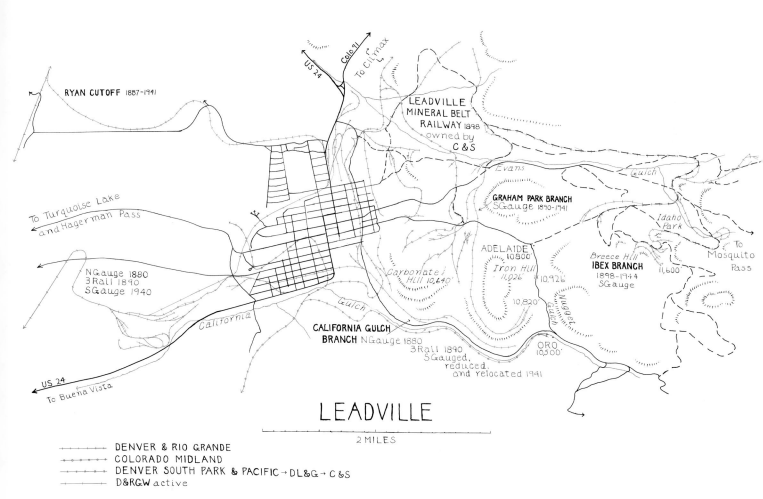

RYAN CUTOFF 1887-1941

US 24

To Cil'max
Colo 91

LEADVILLE
MINERAL BELT
RAILWAY 1898
owned by
C & S

Evans
Gulch

GRAHAM PARK BRANCH
SGauge 1890-1941

Idaho
Park

To Turquoise Lake
and Hagerman Pass

To Mosquito
Pass

NGauge 1880
3 Rail 1890
SGauge 1940

Carbonate
Hill 10,640'

ADELAIDE
10800'
Iron Hill
11,026'   10,926

10,820'

Breece Hill
11,600

IBEX BRANCH
1898-1944
SGauge

California

Gulch

CALIFORNIA GULCH
BRANCH NGauge 1880

3 Rail 1890
SGauged,
reduced,
and relocated 1941

Nugget
Gulch

ORO
10,500'

US 24
To Buena Vista

LEADVILLE

2 MILES

DENVER & RIO GRANDE
COLORADO MIDLAND
DENVER SOUTH PARK & PACIFIC → DL&G → C&S
D&RGW active

*The Cripple Creek's station
before it became a museum.*

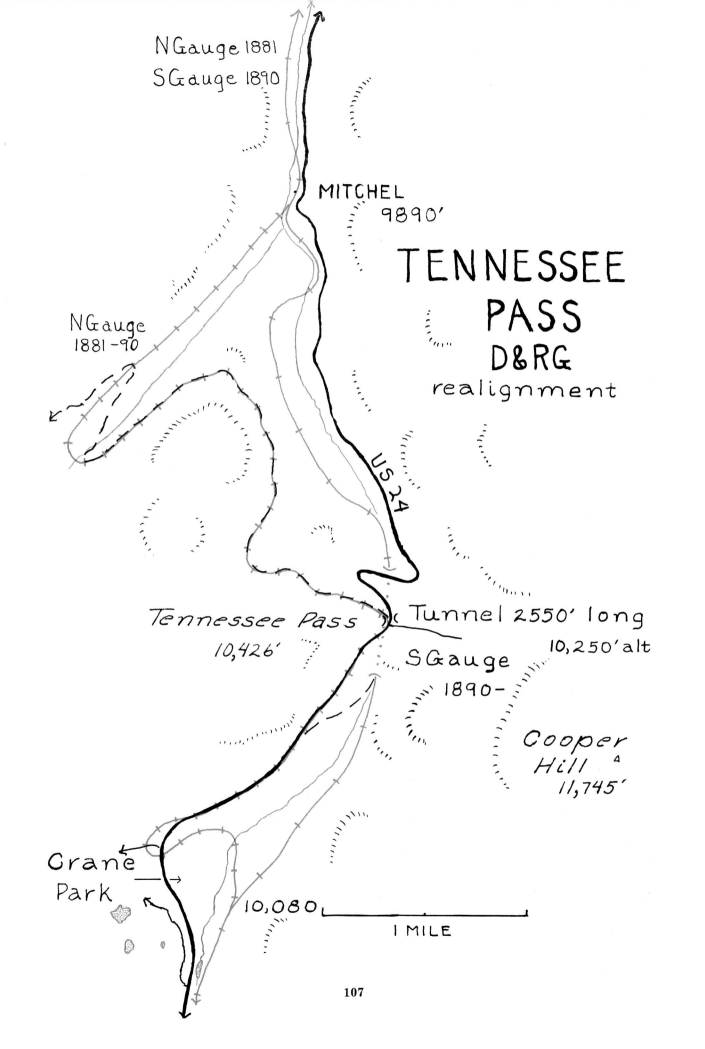

N Gauge 1881
S Gauge 1890

N Gauge
1881-90

MITCHEL
9890'

TENNESSEE
PASS
D&RG
realignment

US 24

Tennessee Pass
10,426'

Tunnel 2550' long
10,250' alt

S Gauge
1890-

Cooper
Hill
11,745'

Crane
Park

10,080

1 MILE

The DENVER AND RIO GRANDE'S first concern after winning the Gorge from the Santa Fe was to build the branch to Leadville, and the same year they extended it down the Blue and put in the spur to Oro City, scene of the district's earliest gold rush. I have seen references to this line as the Iron Silver Mine Branch.

The TENNESSEE PASS REALIGNMENT, as well as the original Tennessee Pass route, though it is in the heart of the snows in winter, is one of the reasons for the D&RG's success in the railroad competition. Snow problems were never like those of the Midland, the South Park line, the Moffat, or even those of the D&RG's own Divide crossings at Marshall and Cumbres Passes. All these had to give up the water line for miles of high, exposed hillsides. The tunnel effected a saving of 4 1/2 miles.

The COLORADO MIDLAND, whose eastern half appears in this series with the Pikes Peak Region material, can be studied historically in Morris Cafky's *The Colorado Midland,* in a later manuscript book on *The Colorado Midland in the Plans of Major Railroads* by William McKenzie (a Colorado College thesis), and in John Lipsey's "Hagerman Builds the Midland" and "How Hagerman Sold the Midland" in the *Denver Westerners' Roundup* for 1954 and their 1956 *Brand Book* respectively.

The Midland first went through the Continental Divide with the 2061-foot Hagerman Tunnel, at 11,258-feet altitude. In June of 1890 the Busk Tunnel Company was organized to build the lower tunnel. According to *Engineering News* of November 4, 1898, this tunnel was 1.78 miles long, and saved 580 feet of climbing, 13 snowsheds, 12 bridges and trestles — one of them 180 feet long and 84 feet high — and 2000 degrees in curvature. The tunnel was finished in 1893, the year the Santa Fe took over. The original agreement called for payment of $70,000 a year by the railroad, this being 7 percent of the expected cost of the tunnel, but when the cost turned out to be $1,250,000 instead of $1,000,000, the Midland paid instead $.25 per passenger and $.25 per ton as a bonus. The receiver, appointed the next year, dickered for lower payments; when he could not get them he relaid tracks on the old Hagerman tunnel route above and operated the trains over that line for a period. The tunnel company came to terms and the Midland acquired the tunnel in the 1897 reorganization. It was called the Carleton Tunnel in the period after abandonment when motor traffic went through in alternating east-west and west-east strings of cars.

With only the Hagerman tunnel the Midland construction averaged $80,000 a mile, more than any road had cost up to

The east portal of the Busk Ivanhoe Tunnel.

Rocky Country on the upper Frying Pan.

Colorado's grandest trestle - east of the old Hagerman Tunnel. (State Historical Society)

Big ovens still stand on the meadow at Seller.

108

that time. Oak ties shipped in from Missouri and standard-gauge rails brought from Chicago to Leadville by unfriendly roads added a large freight cost to the normal difficulties of mountain building. Snows kept the maintenance costs high over the Sawatch Range in the rough months of winter and spring, traffic being stopped from January 27 to the middle of April in 1899.

The D&RG, despite all its financial troubles, was far better equipped to compete for business than the Midland. Service was abandoned through government order in 1918 and never resumed after the war. In 1921 the rails came out all the way from Divide, where the Midland Terminal came in, west to New Castle. The Rio Grande Junction railroad passed into D&RG hands and the east end was sold to the Midland Terminal to keep that road complete to Colorado Springs from Cripple Creek.

The Midland abandonment, the largest in railroading up to that time, gave Colorado some auto roads — from Divide to Hartsel, and from Leadville through the one-lane Busk-Ivanhoe Tunnel (later called the Carleton Tunnel) to Basalt. Parts of these are still in service as by-roads, and on the Roaring Fork much of the Midland route is that of Colorado 82. The drive to the Busk-Ivanhoe Tunnel mouth from Leadville puts you in a position for exploring on foot the remarkable older line to the higher Hagerman Tunnel. You can also climb to the top of Hagerman Pass on a steepish road, but the descent to Ivanhoe Lake on the west side is on a powerline route, too rough for ordinary cars. From Basalt to Ivanhoe Lake is a fine long ride which uses the grade all the way except for obstacles like the Ruedi Dam.

The CM coked not only at Cardiff but here, high on the hillside near the Spring Gulch Mine.

The CARDIFF BRANCH of the Midland, also called the Jerome Branch, is interesting hunting. For the lower coal mines you take off right from Colorado 82 at the south end of Glenwood Springs on the Sunlight Ski Area road; for the upper ones you go southwest from Carbondale. I received considerable help in the track locations on the Cardiff from Mr. Jacinto Moda who lives on the Sunlight road.

The Midland line is still drivable for a stretch east from New Castle. West from Glenwood the D&RGW lies atop the Midland and USI-70 lies atop the former D&RGW.

The ASPEN AND WESTERN RAILWAY was a creation of the Colorado Coal and Iron Company. Western history libraries have various books or booklets on the Crystal River, Redstone,

Rock work on the Thompson Creek line. (Photo by R.J. Adair)

etc., telling the parts played by J.C. Osgood, J.A. Kebler, John L. Jerome, and others. The 13-mile line to the Thompson Creek coal mines from Carbondale had two incorporation papers, dated June 7 and June 17 of 1886. The second of these gives us the impression of a railroad that was designed to climb around and explore the country for coal outcrops rather than settle down and do business. For a million dollars it was to run from Aspen to Glenwood and down the then Grand to Utah. Up the Crystal River to Crystal. Up Thompson Creek to the forks and thence up North, Middle and South Thompson Creeks to their sources. To the source of Coal Creek from Redstone. From west of Glenwood up South Canyon Creek to the source. From New Castle up Elk Creek to the Carbonate Mining District with spurs. From Rifle to Meeker via Rifle Creek and Flag Creek. They had a Four mile Creek project which was realized in the Midland's Cardiff Branch.

It was possible some years ago to drive up to and along the grade well above Thompson Creek on the north side, but I don't think this route is open for a useful distance now. Students of mine have driven west and south from Carbondale to a higher part of the line and walked some of it. They photographed some segments of grade and a well-rocked bridge abutment. Len Shoemaker, a grand old forest service man of Carbondale, remembers seeing a tram tunnel coming down the hill from a mine in Willow Park.

The COAL CREEK BRANCH of the Crystal River Railroad, like the Aspen and Western, served the Colorado Fuel and Iron Company mining. Much of the coal was coked in the ovens which you can see along the road bank so that coal from narrow gauge cars didn't have to be trans-shipped into standard gauge. The road to this mine area was built on the old grade, and to drive it when I did you have to keep left so the coal trucks can the hug the bank. Complying with this requirement gave me a strong feelings of guilt, and I got out of there without a very thorough look.

The ELK MOUNTAIN RAILWAY COMPANY was formed in 1887 by Denver and Colorado Springs men who had connections with the Colorado Midland. Frank Hall's *History of Colorado* indicates that grading was done in 1892 from Sands, 12 miles above Glenwood Springs on the Midland, to Marble, but Bryant McFadden of the Colorado Railroad Club says that no track was laid and that the grade was sold to Orman and Crook under a mechanics lein. The line was a standard-gauge,

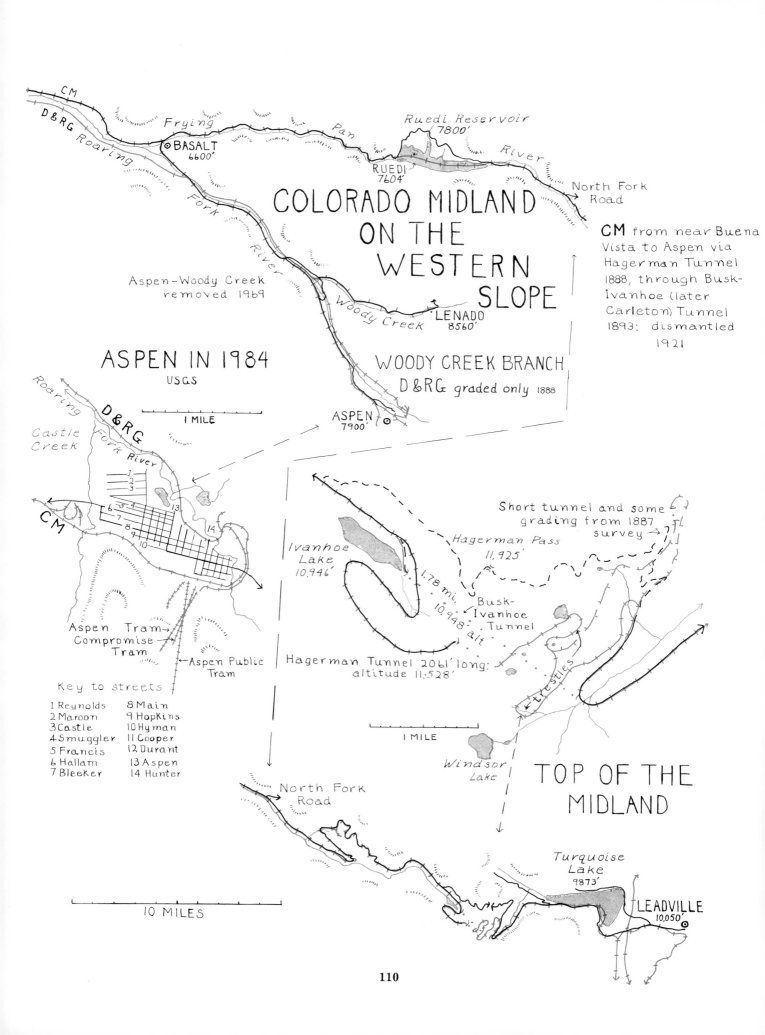

COLORADO MIDLAND
ON THE
WESTERN SLOPE

CM from near Buena Vista to Aspen via Hagerman Tunnel 1888, through Busk-Ivanhoe (later Carleton) Tunnel 1893: dismantled 1921

Ruedi Reservoir 7800'

RUEDI 7604'

North Fork Road

CM

D&RG

Frying Pan River

Roaring Fork River

BASALT 6600'

Aspen-Woody Creek removed 1969

Woody Creek

LENADO 8560'

WOODY CREEK BRANCH
D&RG graded only 1888

ASPEN IN 1984
USGS

1 MILE

Roaring Fork River

Castle Creek

D&RG

CM

ASPEN 7900'

Aspen Tram
Compromise Tram

Aspen Public Tram

Key to streets

1 Reynolds 8 Main
2 Maroon   9 Hopkins
3 Castle   10 Hyman
4 Smuggler 11 Cooper
5 Francis   12 Durant
6 Hallam   13 Aspen
7 Bleeker   14 Hunter

Short tunnel and some grading from 1887 survey

Hagerman Pass 11,925'

Ivanhoe Lake 10,946'

1.78 mi. 10,948 alt

Busk-Ivanhoe Tunnel

Hagerman Tunnel 2061' long: altitude 11,528'

trestles

1 MILE

Windsor Lake

TOP OF THE MIDLAND

North Fork Road

Turquoise Lake 9873'

LEADVILLE 10,050'

10 MILES

Colorado River USI 70

D&RGW realigned 1967 on CM roadbed

GLENWOOD TO MARBLE

CARDIFF, JEROME or SPRING GULCH BRANCH COLORADO MIDLAND

1889 - 1921

GLENWOOD SPRINGS 5760'

CARDIFF Coke ovens

Roaring Fork

10 MILES

CARDIFF 6000'

Black Diamond Mine Tram 7680'- 6730'

Sunlight Mine 7831'

Mine 8200'

Marion Mine 8300'

Union Mine 8500'

Coke ovens

GULCH 8200'

Thompson Creek Coal Mines

Abandoned 1892, removed 1899

5 MILES

Crystal River

SANDS

CARBONDALE 6170'

ASPEN & WESTERN
N Gauge 13 mi Carbondale to Th. Creek Mines 1888-92

ELK MOUNTAIN RAILWAY
1892 - graded only

A & W succeed by

CRYSTAL RIVER RY

1892, SGauged 1896 and extended to Hot Springs; to Redstone 1898, Placita 1899; 4 more miles graded for and whole line leased to CR&SJ 1906; operated with CR&SJ 1906-19 and when reopened 1922-1941 for Colo Fuel & Iron Co and Vermont Marble Company

SANDS

CARBONDALE

COLORADO MIDLAND
1888 - 1921

Colo 82

D&RG To Aspen

A&W

Crystal River

HOT SPRINGS

MARBLE AREA

1 MILE

MARBLE

REDSTONE

Colo 133

To Paonia

McClure Pass

PLACITA 7442'

TREASURY MTN RAILWAY
N Gauge 1905-15 Grade 7½ %

YULE CRK RY
Electric 1905-41

Prevailing grade 8%, max 17%

MARBLE 7950'

To Crystal

Strauss Quarry 8650'

9750

9200'

Yule Quarry

COAL CREEK BRANCH
N Gauge 1900 - c 1910

To Coal Basin

Coal Creek 8043'

REDSTONE 7200'

HOT SPRINGS

CRYSTAL RIVER & SAN JUAN RY
S Gauge Placita - Marble 1906-41.

Two grades run parallel east of the Crystal River for a stretch.

in 1917, two years before the Crystal River Railroad stopped running, but in 1922 reopened under CF&I control and operated the Crystal River Railroad as well as its own trackage. Control passed in the Thirties to the Vermont Marble Company.

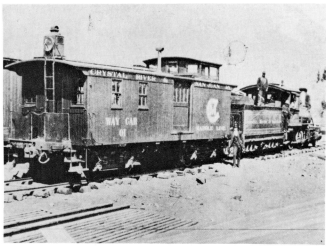

CR&SJ two-unit train. (Denver Public Library)

intended to run from the Roaring Fork 20 miles up Rock Creek to the Tuscarora Coal Bank (west of Marble), with branches up Rock Creek, Coal Creek, and the forks of Avalanche Creek to their sources. The Mineral Belt Railway was formed in 1897 to take it over and extend it.

One travels on the Elk Mountain grade much of the way from Carbondale up the valley, but it is only visible where it can be seen paralleling the Crystal River grade on the east side of the river.

The CRYSTAL RIVER RAILWAY COMPANY was formed in August of 1892 to take over the Aspen and Western, a road originally part-financed by the Colorado Coal and Iron Company and then in receivership. The CRRy fell heir to a 3 1/2-mile start up the Crystal River on its main line and from the end the Thompson Creek Branch up to CF&I mines in Willow Park, 6 1/2 more miles. The branch was left narrow gauge; the main line standard-gauged and extended 8 1/2 miles to Hot Springs.

The CRYSTAL RIVER RAILROAD COMPANY was a reorganization of the Crystal River Railway Company, q.v., which had been foreclosed in 1896 and bought in through the same controlling group — J.C. Osgood, J.A. Kebler, John L. Jerome, A.C. Cass, and others — for the CF&I.

The reorganization plan had been to run a side line to CF&I mining operations in Coal Basin, 12 miles west up Coal Creek from Redstone. This was accomplished about 1900 with narrow-gauge track and remained in operation through most of the next decade. The other extension intended by this railroad toward Crystal was carried out by another company, the Crystal River and San Juan, which however went only to Marble, 7 1/2 miles, the first four miles of it over grade built by the Crystal River Railroad and leased to the CR&SJ.

The CRYSTAL RIVER AND SAN JUAN RAILWAY COMPANY was chartered in 1906 and opened in June, 1907. It ran on standard gauge track from Placita to Marble, 7 1/2 miles along the Crystal River. The road rented 4 miles of grade from the Crystal River Railroad Company at $1800 a year. C.F. Meek, who had gone to the Colorado Coal and Iron Company from the UPD&Gulf road, was the president and resided in Marble, where the office was. Others involved were Charles Bates of New York, and a Denver group including some directors of the Crystal River Railroad. This road ceased to operate

The Crystal River grade becomes visible from Colorado 133 about 8 1/2 miles south of Highway 82. This is where the valley narrows. About mile 13 from 133, both grades are east of the river and make a pretty sight. There is some use of the CR grade for secondary road, and much of the Elk Mountain is covered by the main road.

At Marble you used to drive right along grade into the town between blocks of snow-white stone; now you are shunted a block north but can still see the ruins on foot.

The YULE CREEK RAILWAY COMPANY was formed July 18, 1905, by men of Denver and Redstone to build a narrow- or standard-gauge or tramway from Bryant on the Colorado Midland up Crystal Creek to Crystal and to Yule Creek, with a branch up Yule Creek to its source and such other branch lines to quarries and mines as were expedient. Either this company or the Colorado Yule Marble Company built the electric railroad whose road bed runs up the north side of Yule Creek from Marble to the quarry.

Bryant is a later name for Sands, the Colorado Midland junction point. The Yule Company was ready to take over the Crystal River and San Juan Railway if need arose.

From Marble you can drive across the Crystal River and up the steep grade used by the electric line to the quarry area. It is a road for trucks which some years ago were hauling out marble chips to use in wall construction, or perhaps in some cases to be degraded to the status of mere limestone. (Yule Marble was used for the Lincoln Memorial.) When I walked up the line in 1958 it was just a grassy roadbed with no sign of use. In 1973 it was easily driveable. The upper part of the tram route is quite spectacular. You can see the Treasury Mountain line across the valley and the tram up to the Strauss Quarry.

The TREASURY MOUNTAIN RAILROAD COMPANY was to have connected Redstone, on the Crystal River, with Anthracite, at the junction of Oh Be Joyful Creek and Slate River, 4 or 5 miles northwest of Crested Butte. The Pass near Treasury

Louisa Arps photographed this artifact maybe 40 years ago. It had been the proud servant of the Treasury Mountain Railroad.

Mountain would have been 11,750 feet above sea level, whereas Schofield Pass, about 3 miles farther east, would have been 1000 feet lower but far less direct. An incorporator of this 1909 plan was I.A. Strauss, who had quarry property up the east side of the Crystal River from Redstone. Louisa Ward Arps found a stretch of finished grade on Slate Creek.

Like the Yule Creek this road was ready to acquire the CR&SJ's line or build another down to Redstone to get marble out. I had no map but took this way back to Marble after the ascent on the Yule line. The grade is gentler and the road longer, through cool mountain forest country. I was on posted land part of the way so was glad I had started down instead of up. After all they would have to let me get out.

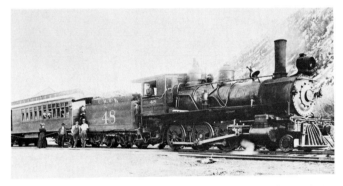

A brief Midland train at Aspen. (Colorado State Historical Society)

The WOODY CREEK BRANCH of the D&RG, though only graded, became the basis for the present road as far as the silver mining area of Lenado. The road diverges from it only slightly. The continuation that climbs out of the canyon on shelf road is something else. I have been up there to photograph the Elk Range, but always with the profound hope I would not meet a load of logs coming down it. Sullivan Vagneur, an elderly resident of Woody Creek, says there was an operating mill at Lenado, and the road on grade became a toll road. There are exits from Colorado 82 at both 6 and 9 miles from Aspen for Woody Creek, and the Lenado road takes off to the north from this about midway between the two exits.

The SOUTH CANYON COAL RAILROAD was an electric

Crossing the Maroon Creek bridge at Aspen. (Abby Kernochan Collection - Rudy photo)

line three miles long serving a mine between about 1905, when the South Canyon Coal Company bought holdings of a previous Boston Colorado Coal Company and raised the capital necessary for construction, and 1913 or 1914, when a mine fire caused cessation of operations. Lena U. Doose of Glenwood Springs, who is my only informant about the railroad, writes me that Mrs. Andy Zemlock, widow of a mine foreman there, told her that the power came from a steam plant in the present Whitehouse Dump area in a side canyon. There was a camp of some 20 houses near the mine, and at South Canyon, loading point on the Colorado Midland, there was a depot, a loading dock, a school, the superintendant's house, and a ferry. The camp was a polyglot of Welch, Austrian, German, Swedish and Irish, and Mrs. Zemlock could not speak English with them nor any of them Slovene with her. Mrs. Doose says that a history of the venture is in preparation by Charlotte Miklish.

To see what remains there takes little time. You leave I-70 at the South Canyon exit 5 miles west of Glenwood Springs and follow the road up to where it splits. Keep right at first to see where it came off the hillside and looped to lose altitude, then retreat and follow the left branch to where you come to the mine; total with detour, 3 miles. The trackage on the hillside west of the main draw should make a pleasant walk on a cool day, and should turn up an artifact or two.

A stretch of the South Canyon Coal line.

END OF THE MIDLAND

|————————————————————————|
7 MILES
D&RGW realignment on CM grade
Glenwood to 7.5 miles west 1967

NEW CASTLE

USI-70

D&RG
1889-1967

GLENWOOD
SPRINGS

Old bridge abutments

← COLORADO MIDLAND
Glenwood Springs to New Castle
1889-1921

5930'

SOUTH CANYON
COAL CO RAILWAY
Electric 20" gauge
1905-18

South Canyon → Creek

Canyon Mine 6400'

Helper engine wye on the Colorado Springs and Cripple Creek District Railroad.

114

PART V
SOUTHWEST

MAPS

Rio Grande Tank at bridge at Monero.

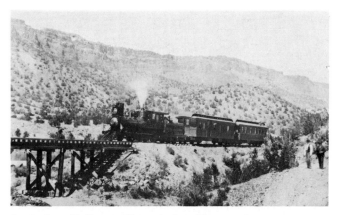

On the Santa Fe Branch. (Colorado State Historical Society)

The SANTA FE BRANCH of the D&RG, nicknamed the Chili line, represents General Palmer's refusal to drop his earlier ambition for a north-south railroad through New Mexico to Mexico City. His first incorporations had described a Merino Valley, a Galisteo and other lines in New Mexico, and a main line through El Paso to the Mexican capitol. These intentions were reiterated in a San Juan and Pacific of 1878 while the D&RG was in lease to the Santa Fe. The two roads had ended the Raton Pass and Royal Gorge war by signing an agreement to keep out of each other's territory for ten years, but the resourceful Palmer planned to be ready. He set up the Texas Santa Fe and Northern to complete the Santa Fe Branch and other companies to acquire that for the D&RG and extend it farther south. In the later eighties, when he was out of the D&RG and building a continuing empire for its line in Utah, he found the time and energy to help build on contract the narrow gauge Mexican National Railway from Mexico City north to the border. No true connections ever materialized, however, and the Santa Fe Branch did a rather meager business except for some lumbering along the way.

On the plateau south from Antonito to Taos Junction the grade is generally near the road and tends to be visible because the land is in grass and sage. You can drive on down the plateau on grade most of the way to the drop-off into Rio Grande Canyon. In the canyon you see parts of it first from the highway and then from side roads. There is a stretch of grade just west of San Juan and you can follow it along to where it crossed the Rio Grande, but below there agriculture has done for the most of it until you have to leave the river and go east from San Ildefonso to US 64. The canyon part from there to Buckman would be good exploring but the land is posted. I have not tried this, but have driven up from the Santa Fe end. To get on the Buckman Road takes some wandering in a new housing development in the northwest part of Santa Fe. Once you reach the city dump area you can catch up with the Buckman Road for sure. There are side roads north from that to the grade in a place or two in undisturbed dry hill country. Later as the Buckman turns north you run along the grade. When I went there in 1971 John Wayne was making a movie along the rough river section farther north. The road would be very bad in wet weather.

LUMBERING for ties had to precede and accompany the building of the railroad, particularly in the D&RG's broad expansion of 1881, but the building of spurs seems to have waited till 1888. Gordon S. Chappell's 1971 book *Logging along the*

Rio Grande gives both the corporate and the railroad history of the widespread harvesting of pine forests all the way from the Santa Fe Branch west to the Rio Grande Southern, together with maps which have been extremely useful for my exploratory efforts. His book has been the main source also for my summarizing remarks.

In 1888 R.W. Stewart negotiated with the D&RG for the first of three Tres Piedras spurs and a locomotive to operate on it. In the same year the railroad built the first of three Sullenberger spurs between Chama and Monero, and likewise sold him a locomotive. And in the same year John D. Biggs and Son negotiated for the first of another set of spurs - this to a mill southwest of Chama built by one George Laws with whom they had a partnership and who later negotiated for a D&RG locomotive.

Sullenberger lumbered the longest and westernmost of his spurs - to Spring Creek Pass and the Val Diamante - until 1897, and then joined the partnership with a Pueblo Thatcher and the Denver Newtons to form the Pagosa Lumber Company and built the Rio Grande Pagosa and Northern Railroad.

George Laws dropped out of the picture and more of the Biggs family became involved. The first Biggs and Son had been John D. and Clinton; there was a second Biggs and Son composed of John D. and Edgar; then there was Biggs Lumber Company including John's brother Samuel. Edgar M. Biggs remained a figure in lumbering till near the end of the era. The Chama's Spur grew into the Tierra Amarilla Southern, with operations to Brazos and east up the Rio Brazos and to the south past Tierra Amarilla, accomplished by Biggs Lumber Company, then with additional spurring to the west under a new company called Burns Biggs Lumber. All were related to the mill on the Brazos (close to Encenada north of the Rio Brazos), which remained busy until 1903.

Edgar Biggs sold out his part of the Brazos lumbering business in 1892 and bought, Chappell thinks with backing from McPhee and McGinnity of Denver, the first and easternmost of the Sullenberger mills - near Azotea - and operated it for five years. At the same time he joined McPhee and McGinnity in a new corporation called the New Mexico Lumber Company which was to lumber northward with the Rio Grande and Pagosa Springs Railway in the decade starting 1895. Though president of this McPhee and McGinnity company he is said by Chappell to have re-entered the management of the family organization at Brazos in 1897, the year it became the Burns Biggs Company. Strange as it may seem this is not altogether inconsistent with events. There were intimations of a rivalry when the Biggs Lumber Company started to put up a mill in Chromo, a town through which the New Mexico Lumber Company was about to build their RG&PS line, but the Biggs Company sold this mill to the New Mexico Company, and bought the latter's Lumberton Mill in a north-south division of the forests to be timbered. Burns-Biggs proceded in 1903 to build south to El Vado. Then as the two railroads developed, Chappell shows that they were operated practically as one line. In 1907 Edgar Biggs sold out his interests in Burns Biggs and the New Mexico to McPhee and McGinnity, so that Burns Biggs and the Rio Grande Southwestern Railroad became the property of the New Mexico Lumber Company. He returned and operated the M&M interests for a period starting in 1912 during which they finished the harvest on the north line with a new spur of the Rio Grande and Pagosa Springs to Coyotte Park and on the south line with the removal of the mill from El Vado to the south and construction of spurs to the north south and west from Gallinas Mountain. About 11

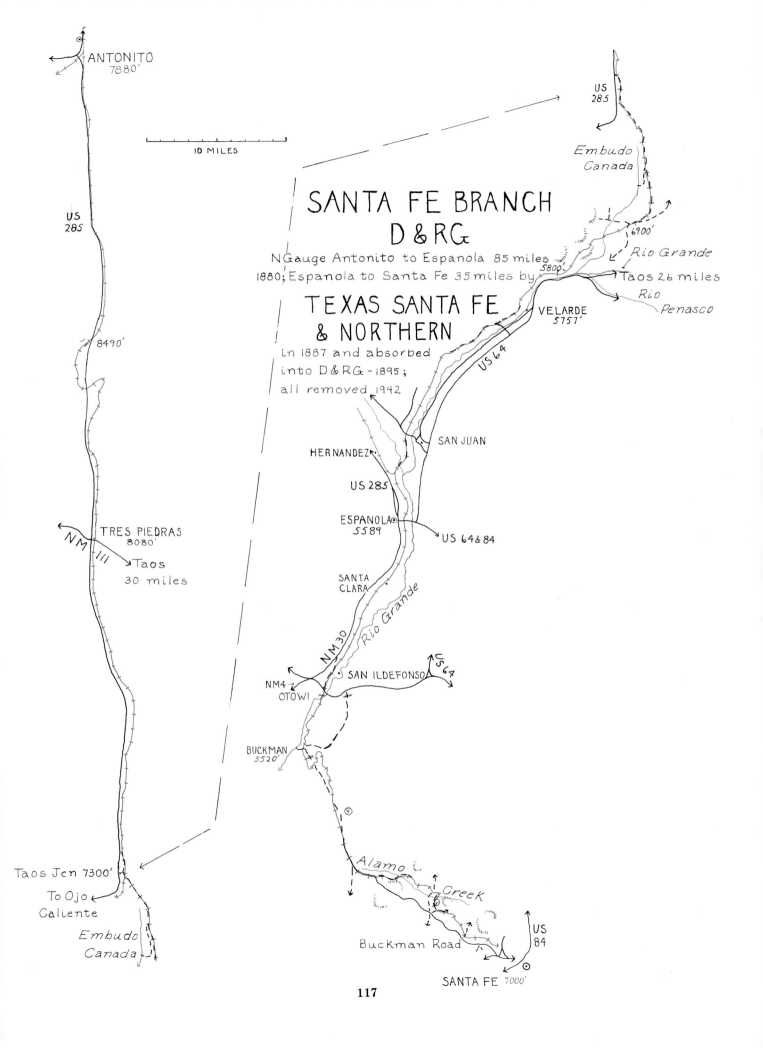

ANTONITO
7880'

10 MILES

US
285

8490'

US
285

*Embudo
Canada*

6900'

5800'

Rio Grande

Taos 26 miles

*Rio
Penasco*

VELARDE
5757'

SANTA FE BRANCH
D & RG
N Gauge Antonito to Espanola 85 miles
1880; Espanola to Santa Fe 35 miles by

TEXAS SANTA FE
& NORTHERN
in 1887 and absorbed
into D & RG - 1895;
all removed 1942

US 64

SAN JUAN

HERNANDEZ

US 285

ESPANOLA
5589

US 64 & 84

TRES PIEDRAS
8080'

NM 111

→ Taos
30 miles

SANTA
CLARA

Rio Grande

NM 30

SAN ILDEFONSO

US 64

NM 4

OTOWI

BUCKMAN
5520'

Taos Jcn 7300'

To Ojo
Caliente

*Embudo
Canada*

Alamo

Creek

Buckman Road

US
84

SANTA FE 7000'

years later the movable part of this business was taken to Dolores by McPhee and McGinnity, but E.M. Biggs, who had started the Dolores Paradox and Grand Junction and the acquisition of timber northeast of Dolores, had already left the firm. A nephew, son of Clinton Biggs, returned to lumbering there after the failure of McPhee and McGinnity, and still later - in 1942 - Edgar H. Biggs, son of Edgar M. Biggs, came to the management of the lumber milling and the 5-mile remnant of Montozuma Lumber Company Railroad track between McPhee and Dolores.

The Sullenberger-Newton-Thatcher corporation — the Pagosa Lumber Company and the Rio Grande Pagosa Springs and Northern — were in some respects rivals of the New Mexico Lumber people. They were lumbering not very far apart and both had railroads aimed toward connecting Pagosa Springs with the D&RG. But the areas were after all distinct, and it seems the McIrishmen did not take much interest in Pagosa Springs; the major area of rivalry was perhaps in the marketing outlets both had for their products, notably in Denver, where the New Mexico Lumber suffered more heavily in the depression. The Pagosa Lumber Company moved south of the D&RG much later than the New Mexico Company and stayed there only briefly. In fact they sold out a year or so after the move to a partnership of a T.A. Schomberg and none other than Edgar M. Biggs. Biggs became ill and left the country in 1928; Schomberg continued lumbering from Dulce three more years.

Chappell's book presents a very considerable list of men and firms that lumbered along the Rio Grande Southern during and after its construction.

Many of these presumably had sidings from which to load their lumber, but the earliest separate railroad was that of A.A. Rust, financed by some of the Newton family, F.F. Sayre and others in the Sayre-Newton Lumber Company. Some of the same people had been partners in an earlier Hallack Lumber and Manufacturing Company with E.F. Hallack. Meanwhile Hallack and a brother formed, with two of a Howard family, the Hallack and Howard Lumber Company. In 1906, the same year that Rust's railroad was dismantled, Hallack and Howard financed the first of two Montezuma Lumber Companies in the expansion of lumbering out of Glencoe. The Montezuma had reached the point where they needed a railroad, and they built the line up on to the Haycamp Mesa from the south.

The New Mexico Lumber Company of McPhee and McGinnity was not to move to Dolores until 1924, but they had already sewed up the lumber rights in the large forested mesa north of Dolores, and when the Haycamp Mesa harvesting was finished, Hallack and Howard could find no timber to work and so they picked up their rails and saws and went to La Madera, farther east in New Mexico than either the New Mexico Lumber's operations or the earlier ones along the Chama River.

The TRES PIEDRAS SPURS of the D&RG were early and shortlived and proved hard to find. I had made two previous trips to Tres Piedras - one in 1961 when a cafe owner there conducted me up a draw directly west from the town to find a very few old ties, a second after I had heard vaguely of other canyons where there were spurs. Palmer Canyon suggested a likelihood, but I floundered about there through a crusted snow over a foot deep. Chappell's book confirmed this as the northern spur, and I returned to find a good stretch of the old grade in 1971, confirmed by a few ties and a precious spike. You take the sketchy road marked Esquibel Canyon from about 3 miles north of Tres Piedras, and very soon find the grade on your right. To go on to

Remnants of the Palmer Canyon lumber in Tres Piedras.

the end in Palmer Canyon would require a rough-country car.

Chappel says that R.W. Stewart operated a lumber mill at the town from 1886 to 1892, when it caught fire. The mill track included a quarter-mile spur that switchbacked south up a hill from 500 feet west of the mill. A 2-mile spur next went west from 3.6 miles south of the station but after a year was pulled up and then laid down for the north spur in 1890.

On my fourth visit in 1972, Sr. Esteban Gurule took me from his farm west to the USFS boundary fence, showing me where there had been grade when he came there 27 years ago. We found one or two tie fragments identifiable only by their spike holes, and I could not find any of the branch that went in farther south.

Juniper, pinon and sage are the rule on the La Madera Branch.

The LA MADERA BRANCH of the D&RG had little or no lumber along the way as it came west down the hill from south of Taos Junction. You can drive south off 285 near the top of the hill and use the grade until it first comes back to cross the highway, but lower down it is washed badly. Soon after you turn north toward La Madera from 285 you are on and beside it again to La Madera.

The HALLACK AND HOWARD LUMBER COMPANY
RAILROAD was not separately incorporated and had no other
name. As on Haycamp Mesa near Dolores, where they had lumbered before moving here, they made different railroad grades
for the same trackage. Consequently though they had perhaps
25-30 miles of track, there is considerably more railroad than
that for the explorer to exhaust his energies on. However ruthless
the cutting may have been, what I have seen of this area has not
suffered the kind of erosional and chemical ruin described by
Chappell in some of the lumbered country. In fact it is very
pleasant driving and walking, with a second growth forest af-
fording ample shade and cover.

I paid it my first visit in 1970, tracing out the D&RG section
and then late in the day driving a perfectly good but narrow
grade - road up La Madera Canyon most of the way to Valle
Grande. I returned after dark, with one spike for proof. The next
day I went up the road to Vallecitos (superimposed on grade).
There I picked up one Martinez, who took me to another Martinez at Canon Plaza and interpreted for me the second Martinez's locating information from Spanish. This covered only the
third and easternmost of the northern branches - one which went
up the Canada Alamosa. The forest was closed to any exploration off the highway because of a fire hazard, but I went in
again in 1972 to see a little of this branch. One drives west 1/2
mile from 1 mile south of Canon Plaza. The grade, visible as a
mound west of the rio, would presumably be a pleasant grassy
walk.

In the spring of 1972 two lads from a seminar of mine drove
the full length of the Valle Grande Truck Trail, which was
Hallack and Howard's first and westernmost route north. It is
marked "Primitive Road, not maintained, hazardous to Public
Travel," but they had no difficulty with it. They found and
followed most of the laterals off the line and its switchbacked extension north of the Canjilon Road, walking up the latter. In the
fall I went in, after seeing the start of the Alamosa Branch, to
the curly middle branch. From 4 miles west of Vallecito on 100-
106 - the latter the Canjilon Road - one can drive south on one
of these "primitive, not maintained" roads to the Valle de
CaBallos for .8 mile before encountering a fence with locked
gate and posted land. I didn't take time to walk farther south as
I wanted to see how the north end looked. About .3 mile west of
this Valle de CaBallos road, just short of "Jacques Canon Tank
No. 1" a road leaves 106 and runs north more or less parallel to
the grade and east of it. This becomes rougher and less
navigable as it goes on, but would save some mileage even if
used only part way. I left it quite soon and walked about two
very pleasant miles of the grade - first well up a canyon to the
west, then around one after another of the little ridges and into
the succession of vallecitos they separate, including the one
labeled Jacques Tank No. 2. It is a delightful forest trip on an
almost level route, free of other tourists and of litter.

The TOLTEC SCENIC RAILWAY is both a ghost railroad
and a very live one. It owed its now assured success to a large
number of devoted volunteers and a few equally devoted paid
employees who run it. My explorations were made while the
D&RG people were in business there. They permitted me to ride
with a section crew to the Toltec Gorge. While Joe Rail, the
diminutive Mexican foreman, and his crew were at work I took
two cameras and two tripods down from the tunnel to the gorge
bottom and up the other side to make pictures of an Illinois
Railroad Club excursion train. The train didn't come till the
following day because the excursion had been brought all the
way from Chicago to Antonito behind a steam locomotive that
couldn't find any of the required water tanks. On the next trip

The last of the D&RG's extensive three-rail system went from Alamosa to Antonito.

The viewing stop for Toltec Gorge is just west of the tunnel mouth. (State Historical Society)

119

WEST FROM SANTA FE BRANCH

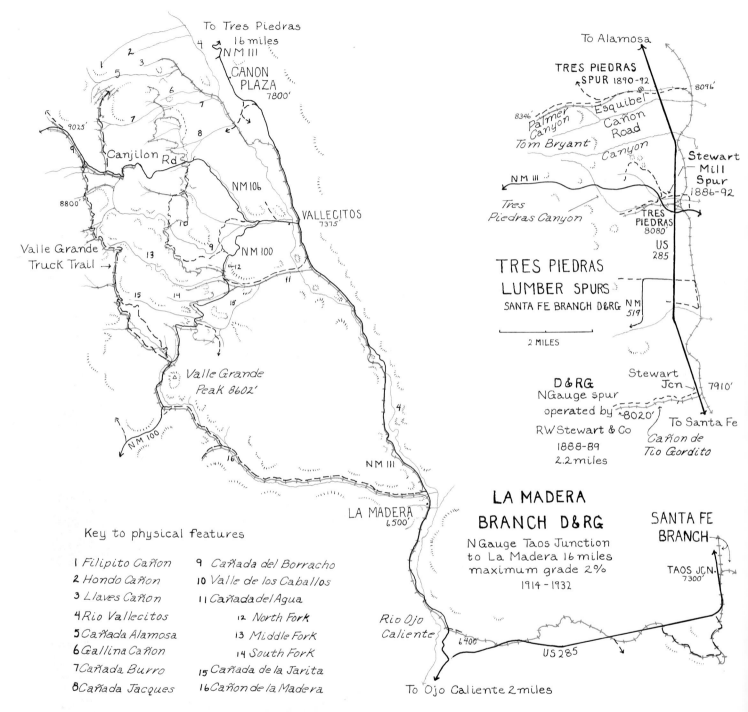

To Tres Piedras 16 miles
NM 111
CAÑON PLAZA 7800'

Canjilon Rd

9025'

8800'

Valle Grande Truck Trail

VALLECITOS 7375'

NM 106

NM 100

NM 111

Valle Grande Peak 8602'

NM 100

NM 111

LA MADERA 6500'

To Alamosa

TRES PIEDRAS SPUR 1890-92

8096'

Palmer Canyon
8346'
Esquibel
Tom Bryant
Cañon Road
Cañon
Stewart Mill Spur 1886-92

NM 111
Tres Piedras Canyon
TRES PIEDRAS 8080'

US 285

TRES PIEDRAS LUMBER SPURS
SANTA FE BRANCH D&RG
NM 519

2 MILES

Stewart Jcn 7910'

D&RG
N Gauge spur operated by R W Stewart & Co 1888-89 2.2 miles
8020'

To Santa Fe
Cañon de Tio Gordito

LA MADERA BRANCH D&RG
N Gauge Taos Junction to La Madera 16 miles maximum grade 2% 1914-1932

SANTA FE BRANCH

TAOS JCN 7300'

Rio Ojo Caliente
6400'

US 285

To Ojo Caliente 2 miles

Key to physical features

1 Filipito Cañon
2 Hondo Cañon
3 Llaves Cañon
4 Rio Vallecitos
5 Cañada Alamosa
6 Gallina Cañon
7 Cañada Burro
8 Cañada Jacques

9 Cañada del Borracho
10 Valle de los Caballos
11 Cañada del Agua
12 North Fork
13 Middle Fork
14 South Fork
15 Cañada de la Jarita
16 Cañon de la Madera

HALLACK & HOWARD LUMBER CO RR

5 MILES

H & H L Company moved here from near Dolores, where they operated the earlier of two Montezuma Lumber Companies; Madera Cañon line constructed 30 miles 1916-17; track rotated to east lines by 1922, abandoned in 1926 when the company moved to Idaho

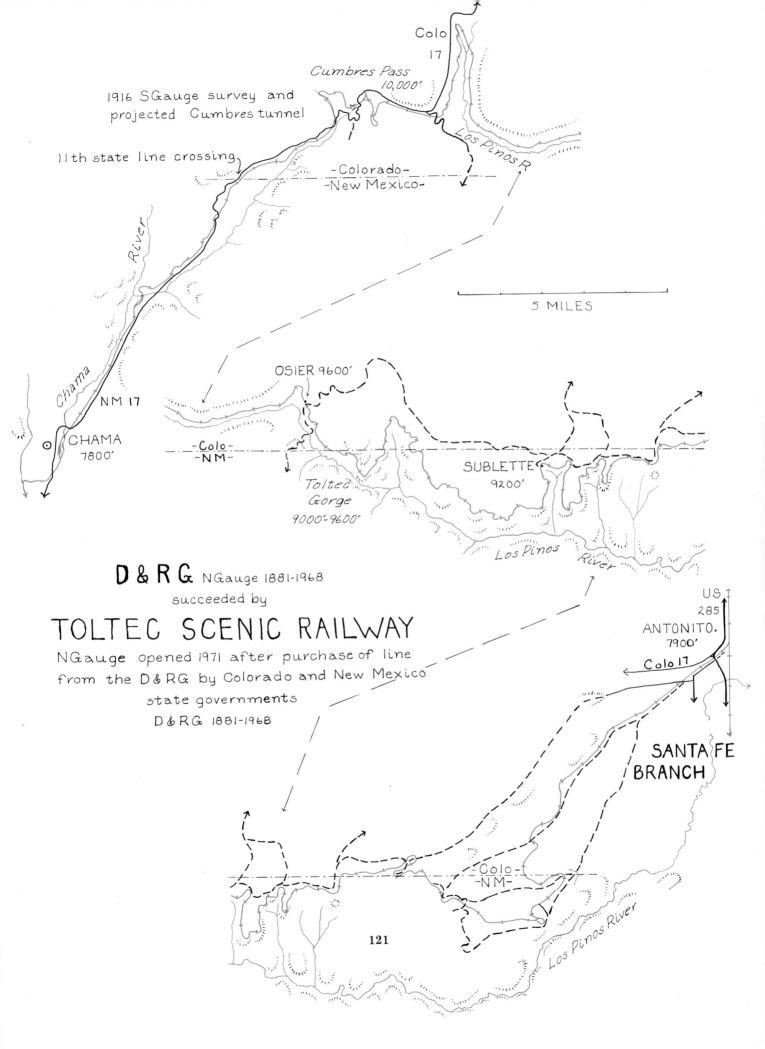

Colo
17

Cumbres Pass
10,000'

1916 SGauge survey and
projected Cumbres tunnel

11th state line crossing

Los Pinos R

-Colorado-
-New Mexico-

River

5 MILES

OSIER 9600'

Chama

NM 17

-Colo-
-NM-

CHAMA
7800'

Toltec
Gorge
9000'-9600'

SUBLETTE
9200'

Los Pinos River

D & R G NGauge 1881-1968
succeeded by

TOLTEC SCENIC RAILWAY

NGauge opened 1971 after purchase of line
from the D & R G by Colorado and New Mexico
state governments
D & R G 1881-1968

US
285

ANTONITO.
7900'

Colo 17

SANTA FE
BRANCH

-Colo-
-NM-

Los Pinos River

121

we drove in from Osier and walked to the photo spot at the gorge. That's the way it is - you seldom finish finding what you're after the first time in, and pretty often not the second time either.

The DENVER AND RIO GRANDE line from Alamosa to Durango was part of the extraordinary expansion that Palmer engineered right after the signing of the treaty with the Santa Fe. For several reasons it outlasted the rest of the narrow gauge lines. Supposedly the flourishing community of Durango and the lumber of those southern forests were the most important factors, along with the slow emergence of good trucking routes.

The roadbed gets less interesting west of Chama, but it is nevertheless in quiet country, pleasant to drive through. The line of the railroad is very much in evidence where you can see it from a car but hardly worth walking where you can't. It hasn't been gone long enough to acquire the petina of age, with grass and flowers on the gently mounded fills, bridges washed away, landslides interrupting your walk, and trees growing up between the ties. There is a nice stretch in pinon country south and east of Durango where the grade runs along the hillside north of US 160.

The grade of the Tierra Amarilla Southern is a heavy ridge of sage just north of T.A.

The TIERRA AMARILLA SOUTHERN RAILROAD grew out of the heavy demands of booming Creede and other places and of the railroads themselves for lumber. The owners built the line with D&RG cooperation. There was much talk (by others than its owners) of linking it with the Santa Fe Branch, and 40 miles of grading was done toward Tierra Amarilla from Espanola by the D&RG, but the lumber men could not be tempted to go into general railroading to the south.

The Tierra Amarilla Branch succeeded the TASouthern as per agreement when the D&RG rebates had repaid the lumber company for construction, but the new name and the line lasted only another year. The remains of this railroad have all been wiped out in the cultivated section along the Chama Valley. It took me a third visit to the area to find out that if you turn off US 84 to go through Brazos on New Mexico 162, you will come to the grade 1.5 miles to the east of US 84. It is a fill, visible on your right about 50 yards to the south. You can walk down there and proceed eastward a little way to find that the grade splits, one branch running off to the right through a meadow where the sawmill was, the other keeping left to higher ground, presumably

to become the branch up the Brazos River. A little east of this point Road 162 runs into and joins a better road, NM 512, and then goes off it again to ford the Brazos and go south through Ensenada toward Tierra Amarilla. About .2 mile short of that town 192 splits off to the west to return to US 84. If you take this right turn and follow it for .1 mile to the third house, and from there walk north, you will soon find yourself on what looks like a dam overgrown with sage brush. This proves to be a fill of the railroad. It takes you on to a cut and then soon blends itself into the road you just took south from Ensenada.

A brief search along the Brazos River on 512 and also on sketchy roads parallel to it on the south side of the river failed to turn up any grade. I wanted to find the long spur which ran west across the Chama from the mill and on up to Sawmill Mesa, but the roads are rough and the gates locked. George Schous, who owns a spread all the way from the Chama to Monero would probably authorize a visit by someone with good credentials and a 4-wheel drive vehicle. He can be reached by telephone, or you can drive the 2 miles in to his house by turning right of NM 95 on the hill just west of where it crosses the Chama.

Above and below

Lumbering activity along the Rio Grande and Pagosa Springs Railroad. (Photos courtesy of Mrs. Tabolita Young and Mrs. Fitzhugh Havens)

The RIO GRANDE AND PAGOSA SPRINGS RAILROAD was started in February of 1895 by McGinnity, McPhee and others to run from the D&RG line at Lumberton to Pagosa Springs. Successive milling points as the operations moved NNE were Lumberton, Edith, Chromo, perhaps others, and then Flaugh. The road had its own rolling stock; according to *Poor's Manual* this included two Shays of different sizes, three other locomotives and 29 assorted cars including one for passenger service. There was no incentive for this road to finish building to Pagosa Springs as the RGP&N had reached the town on a 31-mile line from Pagosa Junction.

Above and below
Lumbering activity along the Rio Grande and Pagosa Springs Railroad.
(Photos courtesy of Mrs. Tabolita Young and Mrs. Fitzhugh Havens)

Locomotive 32

I have found only bits and pieces of this railroad at different times. The first was a hunt for the Navajo River section on the road leading north into the Hughes Ranch from the Chromo-Chama shortcut road. There is grading close to where the end of the track was in a grassy meadow east of the Hughes road. The second was in the adobe flats about 1.7 miles north of Lumberton, where 80 yards east of the Lumberton-Edith road there were some tie fragments and a spike in the dried mud. The third was close to the U-bend on the south side of Echo Creek, near the north end of the line. Part of this stretch was used for the out-wall of an irrigation ditch but a tie and a spike clued us in. The grade shows too in the circuitous section north of Price, where it did some well-preserved side-hill climbing. It used to be evident also where it crosses US 84 about 2 miles south of US 160. I have not found grade along the Rio Blanco or any other side canyon spurs. It seems likely that McPhee and McInnity re-used ties as well as rails from this line in some of their New Mexico Lumber operations south of the Rio Grande and perhaps too when they moved to Dolores.

A beautiful curve on the Rio Grande and Southwestern north of Rio de las Yeguas.

The RIO GRANDE SOUTHWESTERN was the narrow gauge lumber railroad running from Lumberton, New Mexico, south through timber lands of the New Mexico Lumber Company. In 1903 the D&RG arranged to furnish equipment for the railroad — secondhand rails and other material — and the lumber interests did the necessary bridging, grading, and tracklaying under the agreement that after they received full reimbursement for their expenses out of the line's proceeds it would become D&RG property. Capital stock of the RG&SW amounted to $150,000. The expected length of the line in 1903 was 42 miles, of which 33 miles were in operation in 1904. This railroad was built by the same Biggs, McGinnity, and McPhee who built for their New Mexico Lumber Company the Rio Grande & Pagosa Springs Railroad north from Lumberton to Edith and eventually to within about 5¹⁄₂ miles of Pagosa Springs starting in 1895. Their RG&Sw went down as far as El Vado. At Duke City, 2 miles out of Pagosa and a mile up the Piedra Road, I found one Tom Darnell scaling logs as the trucks brought them in from the big woods up north somewhere. He had done various jobs for the outfits working both ways from Lumberton, and told us that after the line was built more or less straight to El Vado, he and Ed Pound, now in Albuquerque, engineered a line called the El Vado Log Camp Spur to reach operations on Thompson Mesa. This was a 7-mile line, very steep, with 3 safety switches on the lower part and a pair of switchbacks to reach the high ground above. The shays, which had been bought new by the company, could take 5 to 7 empties up the hill and could hold 5 on the descent. Except one day when they hung the larger shay in the trees 30 feet in the air. This railroad ended with departure of McGinnity and McPhee and their railroad equipment to greener forests north of Dolores. Darnell helped them move the houses to McPhee in 1924. Arrangements to turn the RG&Southwestern into D&RG side line did not materialize.

Driving SSE from Dulce you can keep track of the railroad until it departs eastward at Boulder Lake (Stone Lake now). A later branch which went west from near the lake can be found if you take the paved road west toward Lake La Jara. A mile or so short of where the road crosses the Continental Divide, about 8 miles west of Stone Lake, the grade appears south of the highway and parallel to it. A little farther up you can find it close to the highway on the north side, and you can follow it among the trees to what looks like a dead end spur, and on the west side of the pass you find it again for a short stretch a mile off the crest.

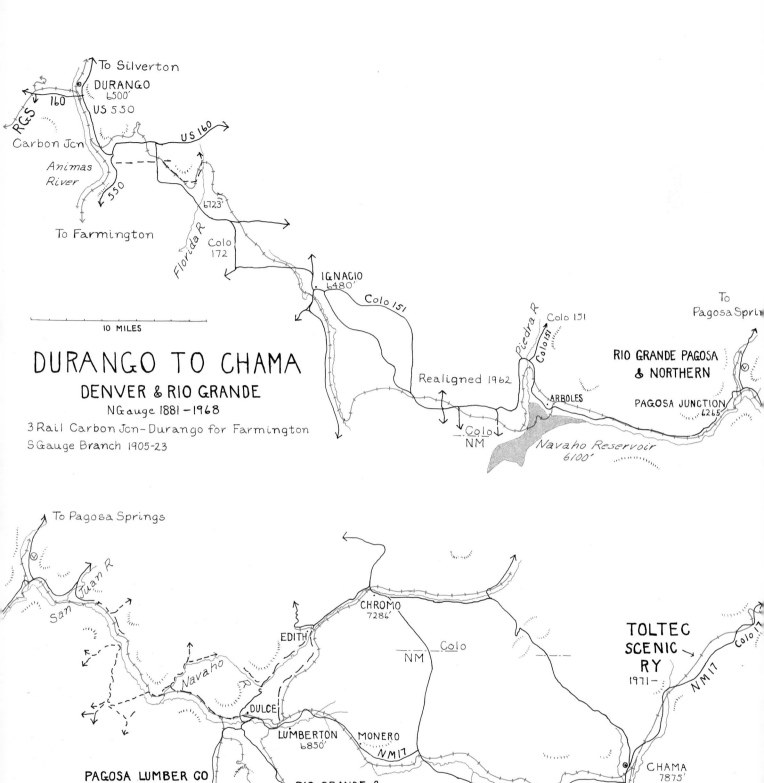

To Silverton

DURANGO
6500'

US 550

RGS

160

Carbon Jcn

US 160

Animas
River

550

6123'

To Farmington

Florida R

Colo
172

IGNACIO
6480'

Colo 151

Piedra R

Colo 151

Colo 151

To
Pagosa Spri

RIO GRANDE PAGOSA
& NORTHERN

Realigned 1962

ARBOLES

PAGOSA JUNCTION
6265'

Colo
NM

Navaho Reservoir
6100'

10 MILES

DURANGO TO CHAMA
DENVER & RIO GRANDE
N Gauge 1881 – 1968
3 Rail Carbon Jcn - Durango for Farmington
S Gauge Branch 1905-23

To Pagosa Springs

San Juan R

Navaho R

CHROMO
7286'

EDITH

NM   Colo

NM   Colo

TOLTEC
SCENIC
RY
1971–

Colo 1

NM 17

DULCE

LUMBERTON
6850'

MONERO

NM 17

PAGOSA LUMBER CO
moved from Pagosa Springs
N Gauge 1916-26

Dulce
Lake

NM 17

NM 537

John Mills Lake

RIO GRANDE &
S·WESTERN
To El Vado

US 84

CHAMA
7875'

To Tierra
Amarilla

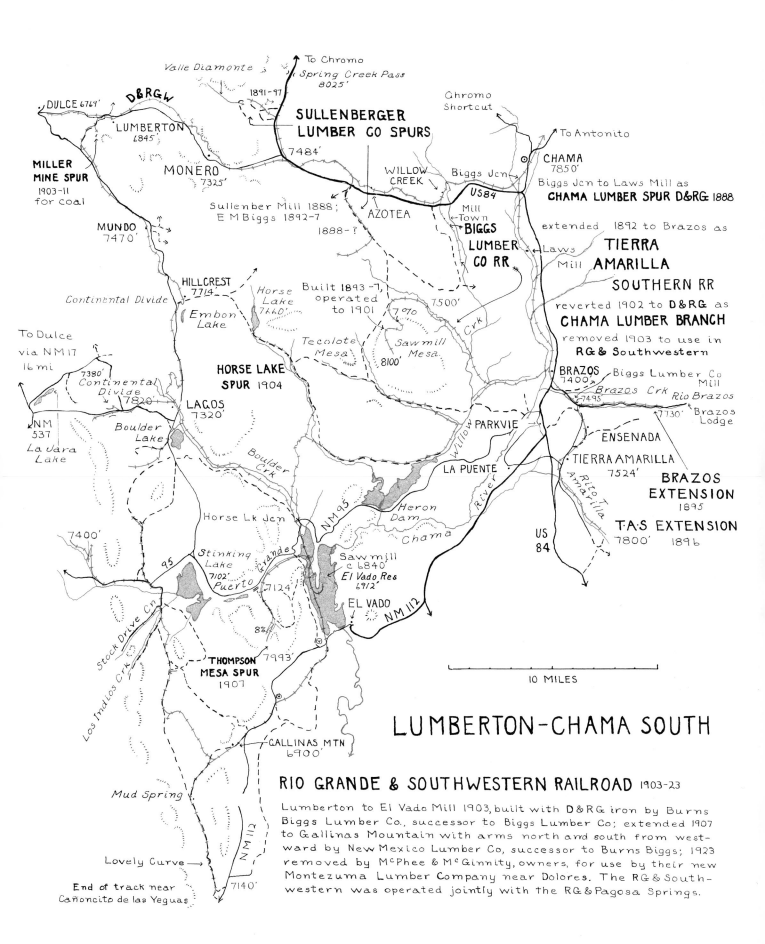

To Chromo

Valle Diamonte

Spring Creek Pass
8025'

1891-97

Chromo
Shortcut

DULCE 6769'

D&RGW

LUMBERTON
6845'

SULLENBERGER
LUMBER CO SPURS

7484'

To Antonito

**MILLER
MINE SPUR**
1903-11
for coal

MONERO
7325'

WILLOW
CREEK

Biggs Jcn

CHAMA
7850'

US84

Biggs Jcn to Laws Mill as
CHAMA LUMBER SPUR D&RG 1888

Sullenber Mill 1888;
E M Biggs 1892-7

AZOTEA

Mill
Town

extended 1892 to Brazos as

MUNDO
7470'

1888-?

BIGGS
LUMBER
CO RR

Laws
Mill

**TIERRA
AMARILLA
SOUTHERN RR**

HILLCREST
7714'

Horse
Lake
7660'

Built 1893-7,
operated
to 1901

7970

7500'

Crk

reverted 1902 to D&RG as
CHAMA LUMBER BRANCH

Continental Divide

*Embon
Lake*

*Tecolote
Mesa*

*Sawmill
Mesa*
8100'

removed 1903 to use in
RG & Southwestern

To Dulce
via NM17
16 mi

7380'
*Continental
Divide* 7820'

**HORSE LAKE
SPUR** 1904

LAGOS
7320'

BRAZOS
7400'

Biggs Lumber Co
Mill

Brazos Crk
7495'

Rio Brazos

Brazos
Lodge
7730'

NM
537

*La Vara
Lake*

*Boulder
Lake*

*Boulder
Crk*

PARKVIE

ENSENADA

**BRAZOS
EXTENSION**
1895

La PUENTE

•TIERRA AMARILLA
7524'

7400'

Horse Lk Jcn

Willow

River

Heron
Dam

Chama

US
84

*Rito T
Amarilla*

T·A·S EXTENSION
7800' 1896

95

*Stinking
Lake
7102'*

Grandes

Puerto 7124'

Sawmill
c 6840
El Vado Res
6912'

Stock Drive Cn

8%

7993

**THOMPSON
MESA SPUR**
1907

EL VADO

NM 112

NM95

Los Indios Crk

GALLINAS MTN
6900'

10 MILES

LUMBERTON–CHAMA SOUTH

Mud Spring

Lovely Curve →

End of track near
Cañoncito de las Yeguas

NM112

7140'

RIO GRANDE & SOUTHWESTERN RAILROAD 1903-23

Lumberton to El Vado Mill 1903, built with D&RG iron by Burns
Biggs Lumber Co., successor to Biggs Lumber Co; extended 1907
to Gallinas Mountain with arms north and south from westward by New Mexico Lumber Co, successor to Burns Biggs; 1923
removed by McPhee & McGinnity, owners, for use by their new
Montezuma Lumber Company near Dolores. The RG & Southwestern was operated jointly with the RG & Pagosa Springs.

A much longer line went north from northeast of Mud Springs on the extension south from El Vado Reservoir through Gallinas Mountain to Canoncito de las Yeguas. It is in sketchy road country, some of it blocked by Indian prohibitions between Mud Springs and Stinking or Buford Lake (now dry), but from the J8 - New Mexico 95 junction north of Buford Lake you can go west 3.8 miles to a point where the railroad crosses 95 from south to northwest. Following 95 in the opposite direction - eastward 4 miles from the same junction you come to the liveliest of all the branches, the line south to the top of Thompson Mesa. It started up Railroad Canyon .2 mile east of the Jicarilla Boundary fence. There you can find what is left of the 7% switchbacks, and the 10% safety switches.

On my second visit to El Vado I went south from there and followed the railroad line where it intersects the roadway a little west of the dam. I was told it went all the way to Gallinas Mountain and I wasted a lot of time trying to find where it climbed to the top of that eminence before I learned that Gallinas Mountain was a station on the line south to Canoncito de las Yeguas. The line between there and Mud Springs is a delightful forest road on the grade. One comes away from the Rio Grande Southwestern with always more to go back for. There is for instance all that grade from El Vado Dam up to Horse Lake and beyond, which would probably have to be done with Indian permission and on foot.

The D&RG tank at Pagosa Junction served the Rio Grande Pagosa and Northern as well.

The RIO GRANDE PAGOSA AND NORTHERN RAILWAY COMPANY was the 31-mile lumber railroad which became the Pagosa Springs Branch of the D&RG narrow-gauge line running west from Alamosa to Durango. The intention to build this line north from Gato (later Pagosa Junction) up Gato or Cat Creek was filed in 1889 by D&RG men Gilluly, Vaile, and others, but the builders of the road were the partners in the Pagosa Lumber Company, formed 10 years later (May 27, 1899) — two of the Newton family and two Sullenburgers. They built north as far as Dyke the first year, and after a period of some months resumed construction west of Pagosa, which they reached in September of 1900 with a train consisting of locomotive 42, two passenger cars, and a flat with rocks on it. The company had bought this locomotive and Number 70 from the D&RG, and it also owned a caboose, an old coach which was refurbished, and numerous freight cars used for lumbering. The locomotives were occasionally sent to the Rio Grande's shops at Alamosa to be re-tired.

The partners enjoyed their property; they used their RGP&N stationery to collect themselves passes on every railroad in the United States. Newton tells me he was simultaneously the president, the track boss, and the conductor. When the D&RG took over, it was stipulated that Schonifielt, who had pulled throttle on the first train to Pagosa Springs, should continue as engineer on this run.

Besides lumber trains there was a scheduled mixed daily which went down to Pagosa Junction and back except on Sundays, meeting there a D&RG mail and passenger train out from Alamosa. There were 28-degree curves needed to make the grade, and these were planked to let the flat wheels swing off and on the track. Trains often jumped the 30-pound rails for this and other reasons, and when they did the passengers all got out and helped.

Whitney Newton, an original partner in the lumber operation, told of the policy of building spurs into the timber areas both before and after the D&RG took over the main line. He penciled these spurs as he remembered them on an old advance sheet Pagosa Springs Quadrangle I had along.

Whitney Newton died recently and the beautiful ranch where this conference took place - between Wolf Creek and Pagosa Springs - is now occupied by someone else.

The Pagosa Lumber Company financed their railroad with a stock issue which the D&RG bought by rebating 25 percent of shipping charges until the line was purchased. It became D&RG property about 1903 through ownership of around $170,000 common stock. The spurs, however, were company property; they were very informally surveyed — often by Newton carrying a spirit level on horseback — and the track and the good ties were moved from place to place as the lumbering operation moved. After transfer of the railroad to the D&RG, the lumber company paid that railroad a trackage fee. After removal of the mill from Pagosa Junction to South Pagosa, there were no lateral spurs except down the San Juan River, but lumbering continued along the main line.

The PAGOSA LUMBER COMPANY RAILROAD began to be a fact when the Rio Grande Pagosa and Northern became the Pagosa Branch of the D&RG, because the lumber spurs which remained and the new ones which were built were not taken over as D&RG trackage. After closing operations in the Pagosa Springs area, the Pagosa Lumber Company moved to the south and southwest of Dulce and operated there for another decade.

The Pagosa Lumber Company's railroad south from Dulce approaches Burns Hill. (Photo by Alvin Warner)

I have twice driven from Dyke to Pagosa Junction without taking out much time to look. Sometimes the grade is one side or other of the road, sometimes the road uses it. The old Dyke station is still in place near the north end, and at the south one still sees (1972) the Rio Grande tank at Pagosa Junction. The bridge abutment a little short of the south end is one of the more conspicuous grade features.

Spurs between Dyke and Pagosa Junction are not in evidence as you drive the road, and most of them are on Indian land marked no-trespass. Of the side line down the San Juan River there is little to be seen except near the north end, where the road climbs a hillside on old grade two or three miles south of Pagosa Springs and a little farther down parallels the road to the east of it on a conspicuous hillside. One can drive up Burns Canyon on a road that seems to be partly on old grade.

The branch directly north of Pagosa Springs does its earlier windings on private land, most of it farmed. You can find unmolested grade by driving north on Second Street to the end of the good road at 5.5 miles, and with permission from the Hershey's home there you can drop to Snowball Creek on the right. It is possible to drive the sketchy road north from there as it parallels Snowball Creek and look for further railroad. Mr. Ray Mott, who lives south of the Hersheys on the road, knows the area well. The northeast part of this branch can be seen and in dry weather visited by taking the Turkey Creek Road, which starts west about 8 miles north of Pagosa Springs on 160. Walter Thomas, who also knows something of the country, lives on a short road spur .7 mile farther south than the Turkey Creek Road.

Another north branch - the middle of three - can be found if you take the Piedra Road north from 160 about 4 miles west of Pagosa Springs. Vague traces of the upper end near Hatcher Reservoir can be found if you walk south along Martinez Creek from where the Piedra Road crosses it, 4.5 miles north of 160, but the more distinct part of this grade is only 2.4 miles from 160; it runs down the draw which you cross there and can be followed a considerable distance on foot. Where the grade crosses the draw and heads NW below the road level it has been used as a ditch and obliterated.

The third branch northward had two branches - one running north toward Chris Mountain, the other dropping west into Devil Creek. The road to take - and it won't go in wet weather and can be rough even when dry - goes north from US 160 one mile east of the Pagosa Junction exit and follows the grade west as it flanks the lower slopes of Chris Mountain. You can drive into Devil Creek part way (1.6 miles) on a game and fish road running north from .2 mile east of the Chimney Rock Cafe, and may be able to take a car 2 miles farther if it is dry.

In 1915 Newton went south into New Mexico and carried out surveys on horseback which resulted in two lines of railroad from Dulce. The earlier one, which went generally SSW, is most clearly in evidence .2 mile north of Burns Hill where you can see ties on the grade above and west of the road (NM 17) and a little farther north where you can walk in and find more grade on the ground. The second branch went a little east of south from Dulce and perhaps used rails from the first. At the end, 4.5 miles down, it comes close to convergence with the RG&Sw's line to El Vado. Three boys from a railroad seminar found this one with the help of a Jicarilla farmer and walked it out in September of 1972. Parts of it were being used as a trail, and it was generally easy to trace.

The SAN JUAN REGION of southwest Colorado is the roughest imaginable terrain for railroading. The peaks, instead of forming neat rows with parks or long valleys between, are in such a jumble that even trying to group them is artificial. There are valleys to be sure, but as they approach the mountain concentration they become short, steep and rocky. There are predictable slide courses where the snow crashes down every spring and in years of heavy precipitation, new avalanches are tripped and carry down with them trees that have stood for a century. With a few hot days in June, the streambeds, along with the railroads had to be built, are roaring with muddy water and rolling rocks.

Gold and silver were being discovered in various places during the 60's, and in the next decade a competition developed among railroads to reach the "San Juan" as the region was called. Many of these were merely the hopeful incorporations called paper roads, but the Denver South Park and Pacific, the Santa Fe, and the Rio Grande were serious contenders. Before the Santa Fe had agreed to trade their claim to western Colorado for Palmer's claim to New Mexico, the General had crossed to the Rio Grande at Alamosa. With the end of the war between these roads and the prosperity of 1881, he hustled a line to Durango on the south of the San Juan, and to Montrose on the north. Both these served other functions as well - the south one as a preparation to penetrating New Mexico and the north one as extended to connect with the railroad empire building in Utah. Together they pincered the mining region of southwest Colorado for the Rio Grande.

When the D&RG reached Silverton, the field was ripe for Otto Mears. A Russian Jewish boy, he had emigrated to the United States to an uncle in Calfornia. He enlisted in an army unit which walked from the west coast to El Paso. Not caring for some more of this, he drifted to Colorado and worked his way to a partnership with a San Luis Valley merchant named Gottlieb. When Leadville was being discovered and he was hauling wheat to the young camp, a wagon load spilled off the sketchy road on the hillside near Poncha Pass. William Gilpin, the territorial governor, rode up on a horse and in the ensuing conversation urged the young man to go into the toll road business. Mears' road over Marshall Pass became the base route for the Denver and Rio Grande and useful to them for construction.

Mears moved with the miners and built the main toll roads that opened up the rugged valleys of the San Juan, and then as

127

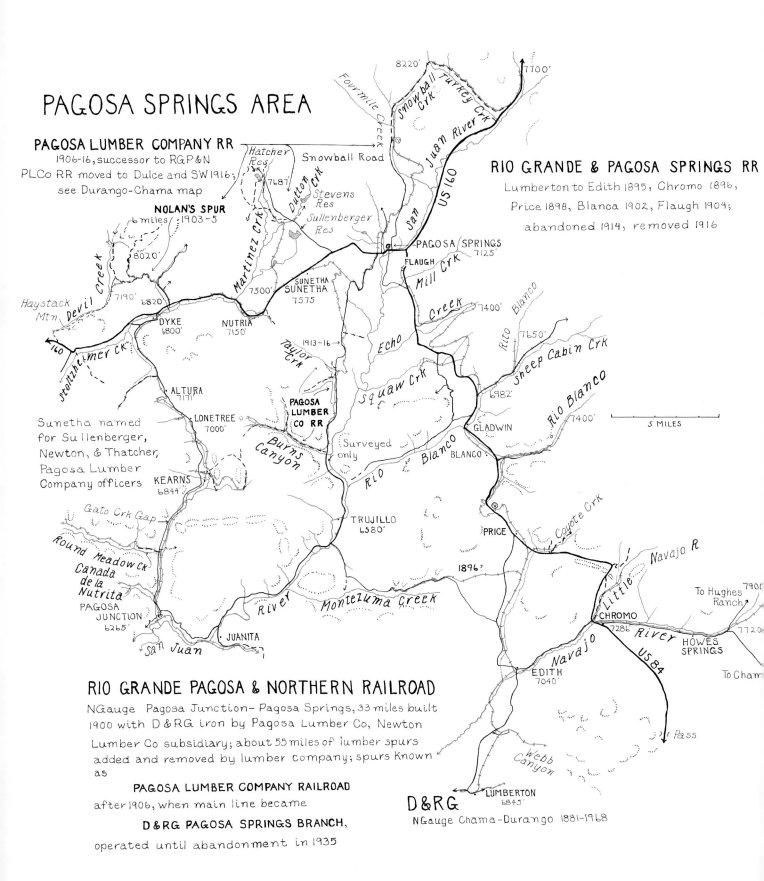

PAGOSA SPRINGS AREA

PAGOSA LUMBER COMPANY RR

1906-16, successor to RGP&N
PLCo RR moved to Dulce and SW 1916;
see Durango-Chama map

NOLAN'S SPUR 6 miles · 1903-5

Hatcher Res
7687'

Snowball Road

Stevens Res

Sullenberger Res

8220'

7700'

Snowball - Turkey Crk

San Juan River Crk

US 160

Fourmile Creek

Dutton Crk

Martinez Crk

PAGOSA SPRINGS 7125'

FLAUGH

Mill Crk

RIO GRANDE & PAGOSA SPRINGS RR

Lumberton to Edith 1895, Chromo 1896,
Price 1898, Blanca 1902, Flaugh 1904;
abandoned 1914, removed 1916

8020'

7190'

6820'

7500'

SUNETHA
SUNETHA 7575

1913-16

Echo Creek

7400'

Rito Blanco

7650'

Sheep Cabin Crk

Haystack Mtn

Devil Creek

160

Stollzhelmer Crk

DYKE 6800'

NUTRIA 7150'

Taylor Crk

Squaw Crk

Rio Blanco

7400'

5 MILES

Sunetha named
for Sullenberger,
Newton, & Thatcher,
Pagosa Lumber
Company officers

ALTURA 7171'

LONETREE 7000'

PAGOSA LUMBER CO RR

Burns Canyon

Surveyed only

Rio Blanco

BLANCO

GLADWIN

6982'

KEARNS 6844'

TRUJILLO 6580'

PRICE

Coyote Crk

Navajo R

Gato Crk Gap

1896?

To Hughes Ranch 7900'

Round Meadow Crk

Canada de la Nutrita

PAGOSA JUNCTION 6265'

River

Montezuma Creek

Little

Navajo

River

CHROMO 7286'

HOWES SPRINGS 7720'

To Cham

San Juan

JUANITA

US 84

Pass

Navajo

EDITH 7040'

Webb Canyon

RIO GRANDE PAGOSA & NORTHERN RAILROAD

N Gauge Pagosa Junction - Pagosa Springs, 33 miles built
1900 with D&RG iron by Pagosa Lumber Co, Newton
Lumber Co subsidiary; about 55 miles of lumber spurs
added and removed by lumber company; spurs known
as

PAGOSA LUMBER COMPANY RAILROAD

after 1906, when main line became

D&RG PAGOSA SPRINGS BRANCH,

operated until abandonment in 1935

D&RG
N Gauge Chama-Durango 1881-1968

LUMBERTON 6845'

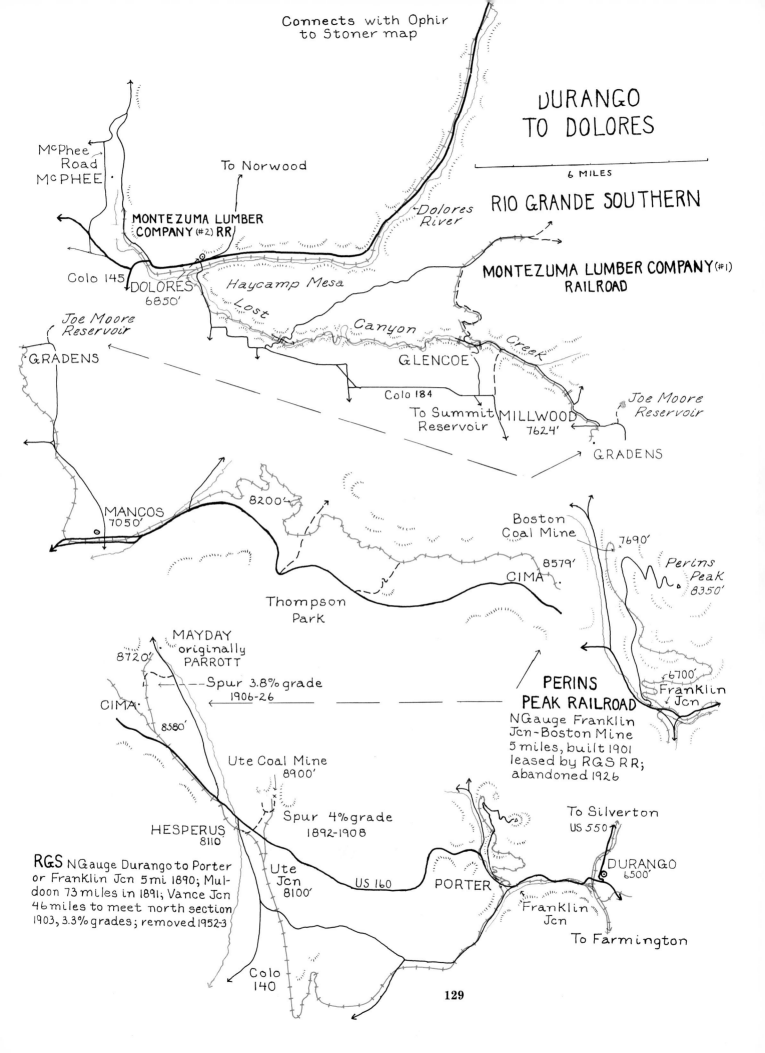

Connects with Ophir
to Stoner map

DURANGO
TO DOLORES

6 MILES

RIO GRANDE SOUTHERN

McPhee
Road
McPHEE

To Norwood

MONTEZUMA LUMBER
COMPANY (#2) RR

Dolores
River

MONTEZUMA LUMBER COMPANY (#1)
RAILROAD

Colo 145

DOLORES
6850'

Haycamp Mesa

Lost

Canyon

Creek

Joe Moore
Reservoir

GRADENS

GLENCOE

Colo 184

To Summit
Reservoir

MILLWOOD
7624'

Joe Moore
Reservoir

GRADENS

MANCOS
7050'

8200'

Boston
Coal Mine

7690'

Perins
Peak
8350'

8579'

CIMA

Thompson
Park

MAYDAY
originally
PARROTT

8720'

Spur 3.8% grade
1906-26

6700'
Franklin
Jcn

PERINS
PEAK RAILROAD
NGauge Franklin
Jcn-Boston Mine
5 miles, built 1901
leased by RGS RR;
abandoned 1926

CIMA

8580'

Ute Coal Mine
8900'

Spur 4% grade
1892-1908

To Silverton
US 550

HESPERUS
8110

Ute
Jcn
8100'

US 160

PORTER

DURANGO
6500'

Franklin
Jcn

RGS NGauge Durango to Porter
or Franklin Jcn 5mi 1890; Muldoon 73 miles in 1891; Vance Jcn
46 miles to meet north section
1903, 3.3% grades; removed 1952-3

Colo
140

To Farmington

mining communities developed he built three of the independent railroads in the region and afterward acquired the fourth. The "pathfinder of the San Juan" was versatile as well as energetic. As a legislator he sold the idea of a gold plated dome for the state capitol, and as a linguist he learned enough Ute to become the chief interpreter and bargainer in the treaties by which the Indians were induced to move out of the way of the straining prospectors.

Rounding a curve above Rico. (State Historical Society)

The RIO GRANDE SOUTHERN RAILROAD never paid its stockholders a dividend, but it was the richest of all the railroads in the ruggedness of its mountain setting and in the feats of engineering required to build it. Operations began in 1890 and lasted until 1960. When the north and south segments were joined in 1903, it connected the two Denver and Rio Grande lines across the state, and formed the major part of a curious 236-mile narrow gauge rail link between Albany, at the north end of the Silverton Railroad in Red Mountain Park, and Ouray. Albany and Ouray are about 6 miles apart. Its 168 miles of main line and 12 of spurs, cutting through the west flank of the San Juan region, served the towns of Dolores, Rico and Telluride, and other outlets for ore, coal, timber, and livestock. Mrs. Josie Moore Crum's *The Rio Grande Story,* published in 1957, has many absorbing details about happenings and people on the line, and we hear that a new volume is to come out soon.

Crum tells us that R.M. Ridgway, father of the long-time chief Engineer of the D&RG, was the superintendent, his brother, J.H. Ridgway, the assistant superintendent, and T.J. Guinn

the road-master and train dispatcher. The general office was in Denver, and the local one in Ridgway. A profile study of the road shows high points at Cima (8600 feet), Milwood (7652 feet), Lizard Head (10,250 feet), Pandora (end of the spur in to Telluride, 9007 feet), and Dallas Divide (8989 feet). A train from Ridgway to Durango via Pando, above Telluride, made a total clumb of 8576 feet and descended 8093 feet to average nearly 100 feet to the mile of climb or descent through the entire length of the line. Branches included the one to Telluride and Pando, just under 10 miles long; the Enterprise, close to 5 miles long, climbing switchbacks to mine operations 400 feet higher, with one prong running northeast up Silver Creek and other southeast around Newman Hill; a 2-mile line from Mayday, near Hesperus, through Parrott City to the Mayday Mine and a turning loop. This, built in 1906 and operated until 1926, in effect replaced the earlier Ute Coal Mine Branch operated from 1892 until 1898 and occasionally thereafter until 1907 or so. Mrs. Crum indicates the Enterprize Branch was built in 1892 and abandoned because of difficulties with snow in 1900. Mrs. Crum's book lists spurs and passing tracks all along the line. The mill at Vanadium and some other places supplied or worked carnotite ores. Many points loaded lumber, notably Glencoe, about halfway between Mancos and Dolores, where there was a Halleck and Howard Mill and lumber camp; and at Gradens' mill, east of the high point and 5 miles nearer Mancos.

East of Trout Lake - driving a car across a trestle got more and more sporting as car hoods got higher, wider and longer.

The Lizard Head, volcanic neck in the background, gave its name to this highest pass on the RGS. (State Historical Society)

38½-mile run to Vance Junction; No. 5, December 28, shows a 45-mile run to Telluride; No. 10, October 19, 1891, shows a 66-mile run to Rico; No. 11, January 31, 1892, shows a 162 mile run to Durango, with an overnight stop at Durango. Mrs. Crum states that there was a period during the '90's when through trains with sleepers made the whole run at once, and that up to 6 daily freights ran over the line. Mine shipments fell off, however, and the sheep, cattle, and lumber shipments of later years were an inadequate substitute. Under the Miller and White management, expensive passenger serive was replaced in 1931 by a fleet of 7 automobile rail busses, some of them with Pierce Arrow engines, two with Buicks and one with a Ford. The first of these plied the track between Dolores and Telluride, the second from Dolores to Telluride, and the third from Durango to Dolores. The last was discontinued in 1942, the north ones in 1950, and replaced by highway bus service. Track was not removed until 1952.

The north end crosses cultivated fields and turns west to make it climb along the side of a dry ridge. Some of this lower part is posted but I was able to drive in north from Colorado 62 about 8 miles west of Ridgway and run far enough on the grade to see the place where it jumped the Pleasant Valley Creek. This piece is not for limousines.

On Dallas Divide you can see it coming in to cross the road, and you can follow it much of the way down to Placerville - particularly the parts that are above you on the hillside, in a couple of places with ex-trestles. As you go up the river you see a stretch of it on the far side, but most of it under you, where it serves much of the way as a fishing road. There are signs of two dif-

The last fine trestle of the RGS - a telephoto from north of Ophir in 1973.

Feeder railroads included those of the three lumbering operations near Dolores and the coal line to Perins Peak near Durango. The panic of 1893, which broke many silver mines, brought about a receivership from which the RGS emerged as a dependent of the D&RGW.

A second receivership began in the wet year of 1929 when the Ames Slide carried a considerable length of track down the hillside and cut off through traffic — mainly 40 cars a week of Farmington crude oil that went to Salt Lake and daily 10-car ore shipments from Rico to Utah smelters. J.S. Pyeatt, president of the D&RG, was the RGS president as well, and under his management there was little disposition to restore the track. Hence the petition for a receiver and the appointment of Victor Miller. Miller named Forest White superintendent and the Ames slide was cleared. The road did not get on its feet financially, and remained under receivership until 1942, when the government's Defense Supplies Corporation bought it to keep a line open to the zinc and lead mines it served. Of the $65,000,000 paid for the road, $50,000,000 was reserved for rehabilitation and $15,000,000 to pay off outstanding vouchers. No bond interest was paid after 1922, and no taxes after 1928.

Passenger service has had an interesting history on the RGS. Timetable No. 1, dated October 1, 1890, shows a 27-mile run from Ridgway to Placerville; No. 2, November 16, shows a

A trainload of Illinois buffs tops the cliffs of Toltec Gorge.

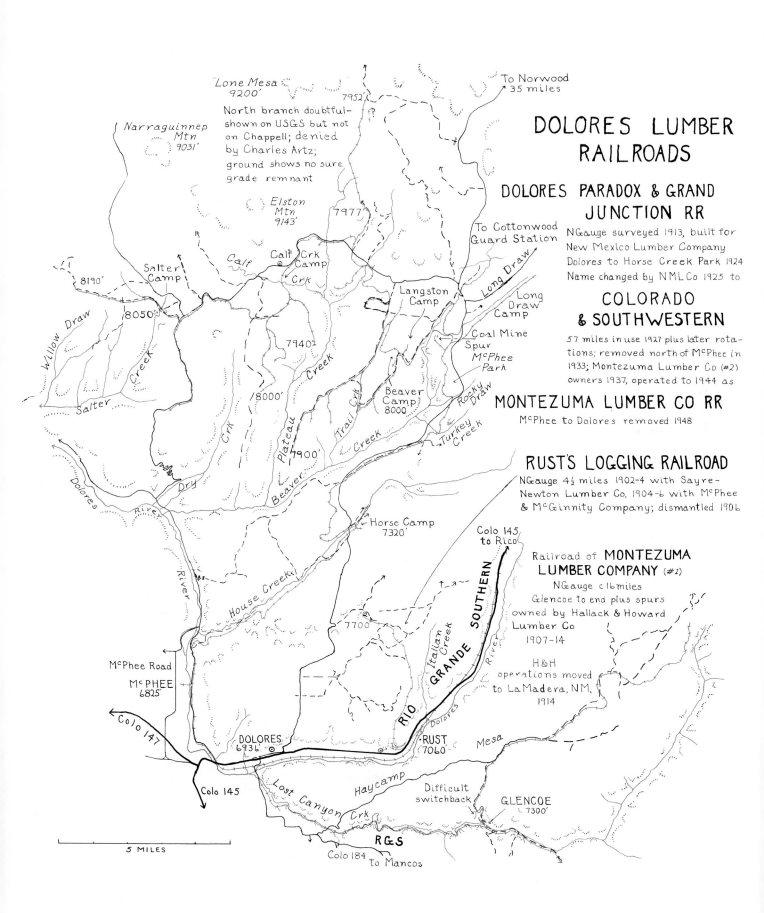

DOLORES LUMBER RAILROADS

DOLORES PARADOX & GRAND JUNCTION RR

N Gauge surveyed 1913, built for New Mexico Lumber Company Dolores to Horse Creek Park 1924 Name changed by NML Co 1925 to

COLORADO & SOUTHWESTERN

57 miles in use 1927 plus later rotations; removed north of McPhee in 1933; Montezuma Lumber Co (#2) owners 1937, operated to 1944 as

MONTEZUMA LUMBER CO RR

McPhee to Dolores removed 1948

RUST'S LOGGING RAILROAD

N Gauge 4½ miles 1902-4 with Sayre-Newton Lumber Co, 1904-6 with McPhee & McGinnity Company; dismantled 1906

Railroad of **MONTEZUMA LUMBER COMPANY** (#1)
N Gauge c 16 miles Glencoe to end plus spurs owned by Hallack & Howard Lumber Co 1907-14

H&H operations moved to La Madera, NM, 1914

Lone Mesa 9200'

North branch doubtful- shown on USGS but not on Chappell; denied by Charles Artz; ground shows no sure grade remnant

Narraguinnep Mtn 9031'

7952

To Norwood 35 miles

7977

Elston Mtn 9143'

To Cottonwood Guard Station

Salter Camp

8190'

8050'

Calf Crk Camp

Calf Crk

Langston Camp

Long Draw

Long Draw Camp

Coal Mine Spur McPhee Park

Willow Draw

Salter Creek

Salter

7940'

8000'

Beaver Creek

Plateau Creek

7900'

Trail Crk

Beaver Camp 8000

Rocky Draw

Creek

Turkey Creek

Dolores River

Dry

Horse Camp 7320'

Colo 145 to Rico

River

House Creek

7700

RIO GRANDE SOUTHERN

Italian Creek

Dolores River

McPhee Road

McPHEE 6825'

Mesa

Colo 147

DOLORES 6936'

RUST 7060

Colo 145

Lost Canyon Crk

Haycamp

Difficult switchback

GLENCOE 7300'

5 MILES

RGS

Colo 184 To Mancos

132

ferent bridges where it crossed to the south side of the San Miguel, and if you turn off the highway to the secondary road up to Ilium and Ames, there are grades above you on both sides, the one high on the left swinging around east into Telluride, the other approaching the stream level, where it makes its not very conspicuous U-turn from Vance Junction toward Telluride. Of the high trestles farther along only one was left in 1971. The grand one which starts the Ophir Loop by crossing the precipitous canyon to head east for Ophir was a delapidated pile of splintered timbers - enough to make a body cry.

When you climb again to the highway just north of Ophir you can see the upper and lower lines opposite you, converging for the Loop, and if you want a touch of rough grade you can try the little side road down from Ophir to Ames along the lower grade. You get very close to the broken trestle that way. But inquire first: it's no place to back out of.

When you come to where the grade crosses the road below Trout Lake, you can drive down the railroad a little way but it dead-ends. Going the other way you have one of the fine railroad drives - left around the lake and up to the pass, no longer, of course, including the trestle as it did a few years ago, but connecting at the upper end with 550 on Lizard Head Pass. A good deal less of the railroad down the Dolores is visible now than was the case a decade ago.

In Lost Canyon Creek you are generally only allowed to see what you can from the roads that cross the valley. You can come in a short distance from the Millwood area to a gate prohibiting entrance to Indian lands there. Some grade can be found north of Mancos, and from east of Mancos to southeast of Cima would make a good hillside walk in cool weather. The line runs through scrub oak with obstacles and is unspectacular enough not to have attracted much traffic. Between Hesperus and Porter the grade is visible wherever you are close enough to see it. At the entrance to Wildcat Creek you can see where it came around to lose altitude, cross US 160, and turn east for Durango. If you take the La Plata Canyon road north from .3 mile west of Hesperus to where the canyon narrows and at 4.4 miles from 160 you can drive to Mayday Mine, visible across the canyon to the east.

This piece of rolling stock rests peacefully in dried mud at the terminus of the Boston Coal Mine, Perins Peak terminus.

The PERINS PEAK RAILWAY was the name used for the branch line from Franklin Junction, two miles west of Durango on the Rio Grande Southern, to the Boston Coal Mine, two

miles to the north and 800 feet higher. To make this climb in its 5.2 miles, the road ascends the right side of Lightner Creek on a small triple horseshoe, then takes a big horseshoe to the east, flanks Twin Buttes on the west, and runs north. Perins, the 7650-foot terminus where the mine is, takes its name from the surveyor who laid out the town of Durango for Gov. Hunt of the D&RG. This road was in operation for the quarter-century ending in 1926, when the mine closed down. George Cory Franklin, who built the road, got his start when he carried his landlady out of her burning home in the night and took her to safety at her son's house. She knew of this coal deposit, and when her son took no interest in developing it, she told the young assayer to make what he could of it. The line was laid out by William Wigglesworth, son of the Thomas Wigglesworth who had surveyed for parts of the D&RG and for the south half of the Rio Grande Southern. Josie Moore Crum tells me that Franklin sold his Boston Coal and Fuel Company and the Railroad with it to the Utah Coal and Fuel Company, which was owned by the Calumet Fuel Company, a property of D&RG. The latter leased it to the Rio Grande Southern. Franklin had fun being a railroader. There was a golden spike ceremony, with Senator Chase Newman's pretty daughter Edna driving the silver spike, and three years later found himself one of the figures in the Arizona and Colorado Railroad, a plan to link Durango with the mountain-free exit to the south.

An early cut on the Perins Peak Railroad in 1961.

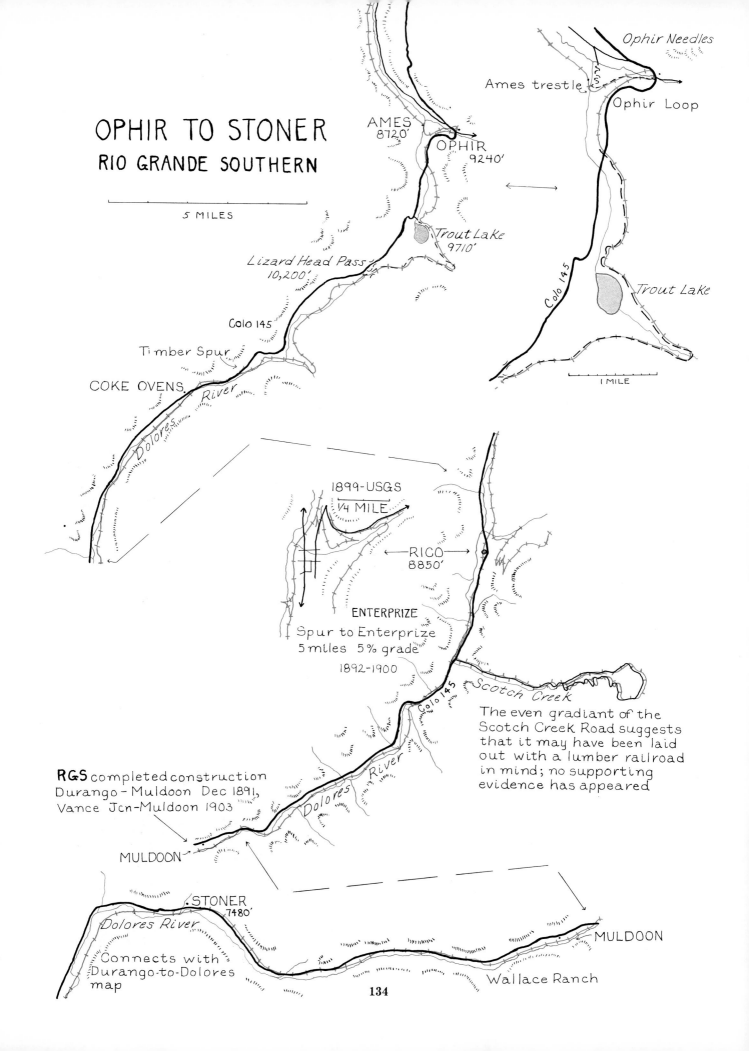

OPHIR TO STONER
RIO GRANDE SOUTHERN

5 MILES

Ophir Needles

Ames trestle

Ophir Loop

AMES
8720'

OPHIR
9240'

Colo 145

Trout Lake

Trout Lake
9710'

Lizard Head Pass
10,200'

Colo 145

1 MILE

Timber Spur

COKE OVENS

Dolores River

1899-USGS
1/4 MILE

←→ RICO →
8850'

ENTERPRIZE

Spur to Enterprize
5 miles 5% grade
1892-1900

Colo 145   *Scotch Creek*

The even gradient of the
Scotch Creek Road suggests
that it may have been laid
out with a lumber railroad
in mind; no supporting
evidence has appeared

RGS completed construction
Durango - Muldoon Dec 1891,
Vance Jcn-Muldoon 1903

Dolores River

MULDOON

. STONER
7480'

Dolores River

Connects with
Durango-to-Dolores
map

MULDOON

Wallace Ranch

134

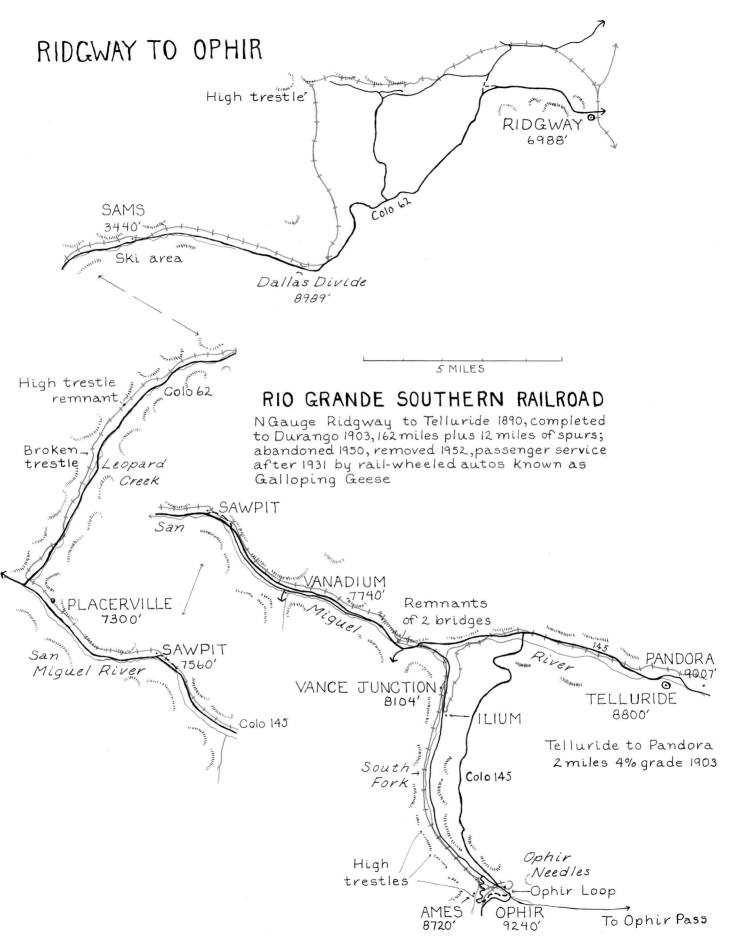

RIDGWAY TO OPHIR

High trestle

RIDGWAY
6988'

SAMS
3440'

Ski area

Colo 62

Dallas Divide
8989'

5 MILES

High trestle
remnant

Colo 62

Broken
trestle

Leopard
Creek

RIO GRANDE SOUTHERN RAILROAD

N Gauge Ridgway to Telluride 1890, completed
to Durango 1903, 162 miles plus 12 miles of spurs;
abandoned 1950, removed 1952, passenger service
after 1931 by rail-wheeled autos known as
Galloping Geese

SAWPIT

San

VANADIUM
7740'

Remnants
of 2 bridges

PLACERVILLE
7300'

Miguel

145

PANDORA
9007'

SAWPIT
7560'

San
Miguel River

Colo 145

VANCE JUNCTION
8104'

ILIUM

River

TELLURIDE
8800'

South
Fork

Colo 145

Telluride to Pandora
2 miles 4% grade 1903

High
trestles

Ophir
Needles

Ophir Loop

AMES
8720'

OPHIR
9240'

To Ophir Pass

Evidence remains, very close to US 160 on its north side, of a coal-weighing platform about 2½ miles west of the Durango Animas River bridge. The road up Perins Peak, which would take you to the higher part of the railroad grade, is firmly closed. To see it you can drive to mile 4 west of Durango and keep right up the Lightner Creek road for .8 mile. Climb the steep hill to the east with a powerline until you intercept the grade. The mine is a half-mile walk to the left and has the skeleton and tank remains of a three-fourths buried locomotive for you to carry off. The shelf road, which you can see from down on the highway, begins after a mile walking in the opposite direction. In 1971 there were still plenty of souvenir spikes. For one who doesn't mind a short but rough scramble this is an altogether satisfying trip of half a day or less.

The MONTEZUMA LUMBER COMPANY (NO. 1) RAILROAD, which crossed Lost Canyon Creek from Arloa or Glencoe, climbed north to the Haycamp Mesa and wandered off east and northeast for what Chappell estimates was 25 miles or so plus movable spurs. This fed lumber into the Rio Grande Southern, sometimes with the help of RGS crews and a locomotive or two. I came near to making an end of my affairs one afternoon when I was racing across the mesa from a more westerly starting point than Glencoe to see what I could see of the railroad line before dark. There had been no stir of life along the road until suddenly I rounded into a corner charging into a huge truck full of logs that loomed like the prow of an ocean liner. When we stopped I was midway along the side of the truck with my little car tilted up as high as it would go on the bank of the road but not quite touching the truck. My lumbering friend checked the situation out with his mirror and drove on. A mile or two farther along, the ex-railroad appeared. I followed it until it merged with the road, then retraced it to where it turned off southward and went down the switchback route to Lost Creek. Only the upper half of the switchback is left; the rest you wouldn't know about without a map.

The RUST LOGGING RAILROAD is visible from the highway about 3.5 miles up the river from Dolores. You see two levels of a switchback high on the hillside north of the road. The upper one is working its way up a draw to the mesa. You can climb the bushy hillside to the grade from near the mouth of the draw, walk east up the lower arm of the switchback and west on the upper. The easier way to reach the sawmill area is to take the Dolores Road north from Norwood and turn east. We found this road blocked short of the sawdust pile which marks the mill site, but the walk in was quite short and rewarding. Mr. Charles Artz describes Rust as a rough tough customer. He was the first of the Dolores lumbermen to build a separate railroad for his operations.

The DOLORES PARADOX AND GRAND JUNCTION RAILROAD COMPANY was formed in 1913 to send out three lines from Dolores: (1) northeast to Horse Creek Divide, (2) to Grand Junction, (3) to New Mexico. When the name was changed in the summer of 1925 to the Colorado and Southwestern Railroad, the purpose was restated.

The COLORADO AND SOUTHWESTERN RAILROAD COMPANY inherited as grade the above DP&GJ line from Dolores to Horse Creek Divide and the rails from the New Mexico Lumber Company's line south of Lumberton, and constructed perhaps the most extensive of Colorado's lumber railroads. If any of the trackage was lifted and moved as was usual in logging the total C&Sw was considerably over 60 miles. A source says there were 57 miles of track by the fall of 1926. Horse Creek Camp was center of operations in 1924-25, Beaver Creek from late 1925 to 1927, when Langston's Camp, 2½

Colorado & Southwestern - it starts out from McPhee in the most promising sage and pinion country.

miles north of Beaver, was established. The next center was Long Draw, and then Calf Creek 6 miles to the west. The first reduction was a removal of less than .5 mile of track for a spur off the Rio Grande Southern at Timber.

McPhee in full blast - Superintendent Artz' home in foreground, planing mill right, sawmill under water tower, stacking area and kilns above house chimney. (Courtesy Charles Artz)

The full exploration of this railroad would take a lot of time. From Horse Creek Camp to near where it turns west into the Beaver Creek drainage one can keep track of it pretty well. My last trip was with Mr. Charles Artz, who at 87 was full of life and interest. He showed where there was a short spur to load

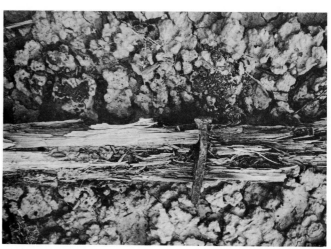

Discovery - proof of an indistinct grade south of El Vado - and one for the spike collection.

136

and carry out logs from the mesa to the south at the Horse Camp switching place and we walked the next section of the main line going west after it made the turn there - this after a visit to the house where he had lived in McPhee as superintendent of the milling operations. On an earlier occasion I had gone south along Beaver Creek as far as fences would permit, and much farther south on the mesa to the west of there. One group of students have gone down two other spurs southward from the main line that worked its way west across Plateau Creek and beyond; another explored Long Draw, another the west end of the line and still another looked much farther north for grade as represented on a USGS Quadrangle. They found nothing, and Chappell's map shows nothing, so I assume the quad is in error. One finds anyway that there was an astonshing quantity of railroad on this quiet mesa.

The MONTEZUMA LOGGING RAILROAD (NO. 2) succeeded to the Colorado and Southwestern when the latter was reorgainzed to continue operations on the southern part of the mesa northeast of Dolores with the help of trucks instead of spurs. This went on until after World War I.

The SILVERTON BRANCH of the D&RG includes a stretch of over 25 miles of the Animas Canyon which is remote from the nearest highway and generally without any road at all. Some mining still goes on in Silverton and the line has at least until recently carried freight, but its main business is to serve throngs of passengers who want to ride on a genuine narrow gauge railroad line such as ran through the same mountains 90 years ago. To take the trip you must make reservations well in advance with the D&RG at Durango.

After one of the line's worst floods, Otto Mears, whose feeder lines depended on this railroad, was called into service to make the needed repairs. The story goes his Indian crew were so busy hunting the fat marmots or "whistle-pigs" that he could not get anything out of them until he hired a second crew of young marksmen to shoot the marmots ahead of his Utes.

A Silverton Northern bridge in 1961.

The SILVERTON NORTHERN RAILROAD COMPANY, easternmost of the three railroads built north out of Silverton, ran up the Animas 14 miles to Animas Forks. The charter date was November 4, 1895, and the instrument was signed by Otto Mears, Fred Walsen, Alexander Anderson, Jerome B. Frank, Wiswell, and Moses Liverman. According to Poor's Manual the 9-mile stretch to Eureka was completed in June, 1896, at which

time the first locomotive and 10 cars started turning their wheels on the line.

The 1.3 mile Green Mountain spur to the Old Hundred Mines was laid out by Arthur Ridgway in 1905 and operated at least through 1910. In 1903 Thomas Wigglesworth extended the easier main line from Eureka to Animas Forks on grade that averaged almost 7%. The locomotive could pull one coal car and one empty up, and never took more than three cars of ore down. The four miles of descent required one hour. Surveys were made both for going to the pass top and down Poughkeepsie Gulch and over Cinnamon Pass to Lake City. Here as on Cement Creek one sees evidences of snowslides.

The drive to Animas Forks is perhaps too rough and steep for a very ladylike automobile, but it affords a fine way to see what a mountain railroad could do. Just beyond Eureka it is above you on the timbered mountainside until you come into it, and after that pretty much with your road. When the locator told Mears that his toll road occupied the best part of the canyon, Mears told him to go ahead and take it; he'd built it.

Looking west into the Chattanooga curve from the climb toward Red Mountain Pass. (State Historical Society)

The grade come down off Red Mountain Pass to a maze of hillside spurs and mine wreckage.

137

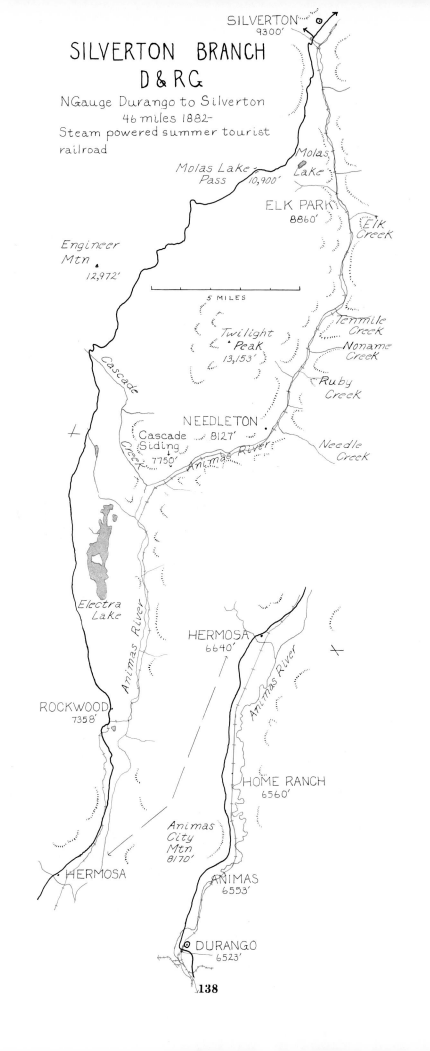

SILVERTON BRANCH
D&RG

NGauge Durango to Silverton
46 miles 1882-
Steam powered summer tourist
railroad

SILVERTON
9300'

Molas Lake -
Pass   10,900'

Molas
Lake

ELK PARK
8860'

Elk
Creek

Engineer
Mtn
12,972'

5 MILES

Tenmile
Creek

Noname
Creek

Twilight
Peak
13,153'

Ruby
Creek

NEEDLETON
8127'

Cascade
Siding
7750'

Cascade Creek

Animas River

Needle
Creek

Electra
Lake

Animas River

HERMOSA
6640'

Animas River

ROCKWOOD
7358'

HOME RANCH
6560'

Animas
City
Mtn
8170'

HERMOSA

ANIMAS
6553'

DURANGO
6523'

SILVERTON

To Ouray 6 miles;
by rail 223 miles

US 550
•ALBANY
9605'

ANIMAS
FORKS
11,120'

IRONTON

Red Mtn
Pass 11,080'

SILVERTON GLADSTONE
& NORTHERLY RR

GLADSTONE
10,950'

N Gauge 7½ miles
Leased by Silverton
Northern after 1910

CHATANOOGA

Cement Creek

EUREKA
9850'

4 MILES

Mineral

HOWARDSVILLE
9650'

River

GREEN MOUNTAIN
9840'

Animas

Crk 550

SILVERTON
NORTHERN
RAILROAD

SILVERTON
9300'

N Gauge 9 miles to Eureka 1896,
4 miles of 6.9% average grade
to Animas Forks 1903, 1.3 mile
Green Mountain Branch 1905;
removed above Eureka by 1920;
ceased operation 1939, removed 1942

To Durango D&RG

SILVERTON RAILROAD

N Gauge 18 miles plus 4 miles in
spurs 1887-89; dismantled 1924
Maximum grade 5%

DURANGO

⊙ DURANGO
6400'

US 160

LODO

Indian land
and roads

POSTA

US
550

BONDAD
6060'

Colorado
New Mexico

Animas

River

FARMINGTON
BRANCH D&RG

S Gauge 1905 N Gauge 1923 Carbon
Junction to Farmington;
removed 1968

AZTEC
5650'

10 MILES

FARMINGTON
5300' ⊙

Otto Mears in front of one of his locomotives on the descent to Red Mountain Park in 1888. (Abby Kernochan Collection)

The SILVERTON RAILROAD COMPANY built the earliest and longest and westernmost prong of the trident of railroads from Silverton northward. The corporation was set up on July 11, 1887, by Otto Mears and John Wingate of San Juan County, Fred Walsen, Sam Wood, John Porter, George Crawford, and O.P. Posey, the last two of Pennsylvania and Wisconsin. Their plan was to go to Red Mountain Park by way of Mineral Creek, Chatanooga, Red Mountain (Red Mountain Pass), Red Mountain (town)), and Ironton. The first 5-mile stretch was built in 1887, 11 more miles to the Yankee Girl Mine the next year, and in 1889 the road went to Albany, in about the middle of Red Mountain Park, 18 miles from Silverton. During 1888 the purpose was very considerably enlarged: (1) a separate line was to run up Canyon Creek from Ouray to

Yankee Girl Mines. (Jackson Collection - Colorado Historical Society)

the Virginius Mine. (2) A line was to go to Howardsville, Eureka, Animas Forks, and Mineral Point where it would cross west into the main line in Red Mountain Park. (This is essentially the Silverton Northern which was started on its own steam in 1895-96). (3) A line was to run north from Silverton up Cement Creek to the divide and down Poughkeepsie Gulch to a connection with the main line. (This was what became the Silverton Gladstone and Northerly, built as far as Gladstone by other interests in 1899). (4) The line up the Animas was to cross to the east and run down to Lake City, a plan which the Silverton Northern fell heir to and went so far as to survey to the ridge crest in 1903. *Poor's Manual* reported in 1889 that the railroad was to go to Ouray and that work was in progress on the 19-mile Mineral Point Branch (No. 2 above); in 1895 that there were 3 locomotives, 50 freight cars, and 2 passenger cars in operation; in 1898 that the road was completed to Albany, which with 4 miles of spurs meant 22 miles of track in operation; in 1899, that there were 31 freight cars and 1 locomotive and the road had gone into receivership in July; in 1900, that 7 1/2 miles were no longer in operation; in 1910, that with 4 miles of spurs and 17 miles to the Joker Tunnel from Silverton, the road was 21 miles long; and in 1924, that the road was dismantled.

M.S. Wolle reports that stage coaches from Ouray met the trains in Red Mountain Park, and that in 1889 there was considerable excitement over a Mears project to replace the carriage road down the Uncompahgre with a cog railroad like the one up Pikes Peak. Arthur Ridgway has stated that in 1892 Mears had a survey completed for an electric line from the D&RG station at Ouray to Red Mountain Park. This involved sharp curves and a 7-percent grade. The wish to build to Ouray seemes to have died out with the panic of 1893.

The receivership lasted until 1904, when a reorganization produced the new Silverton Railway Company. Mears is given the chief credit for raising the $725,000 which the Silverton Railroad cost; he regained control at the end of the receivership. The road had periods of making money — mainly in the early 1890's. Passengers paid $.20 a mile fares that were about 20 percent short, according to one source. Branches or switchbacks served the Yankee Girl, the Silver Belle, the Guston, the Vanderbilt, and other mines. The maximum grades ran generally at 4 percent but there were 5-percent grades north of Sheridan or Red Mountain Pass.

In driving US 550 from Ouray to Silverton one presumably follows almost exactly the route on which Mears' survey would have taken his electric line up the Uncompahgre from Ouray to Albany except for some excessive curvature near the top. The north terminus at Albany is obliterated by a settling pond. There is little in evidence until you begin to climb from Ironton to Red Mountain Pass. This part is on sidehill and the switchbacks and side spurs to mines are visible across the valley from the highway and also drivable. It is a good prowling area, and can be approached in a car from a road directly through the Idarado Mining operation below the main milling ducts. The covered turntable, which has long interested visitors, is in Corkscrew Gulch north of most of the mining and I am told still visible though not still covered. The area has considerably more grade than my map indicates; the map is merely a copy of what shows on the 1902 Silverton Quadrangle. The top of the switchback system is not in sight from US 550, but you can either climb to it on the grade from below, or drive into it from a little N of Red Mountain Pass crest on the highway, where a steep little side road goes down. This side road shortcuts east across the U-bend the railroad made just after it overpassed the present highway. As you go on down 550 south of the pass toward Chatanooga you can still see ties protruding into the air from the grade above the road. The grade and road appear to have coincided for some distance down Mineral Creek until after awhile the railroad veers off left to run parallel on the side hill. This is a pleasant walking stretch, but you needn't expect to find any spikes to speak of. They've been pulled out. The only place I could find one in 1970 was down in the rock slide 100 feet below the grade.

The SILVERTON GLADSTONE AND NORTHERLY RAILROAD ran on narrow-gauge track from Silverton north up Cement Creek to Gladstone from a few months after its incorporation in April of 1899 to about 1915. Mears was not in this railroad until later. His Silverton Northern leased it in 1910, bought it in 1915, and apparently junked it a few years later. The road was started by a group from Silverton, Maine, and New Brunswick as an outlet for their Gold King Mine at Gladstone, and to make a railroad out of it they planned to go all the way to Lake City for a total length of about 30 miles. The U.S.G.S. 1902 Silverton Quadrangle, listing the road as the Gladstone and Northern, shows a 3/4-mile double track where Cement Creek debouches into the Silverton meadow, a .1-mile spur reversing across Illinois Gulch, and a Y where the various forks of Cement Creek come together at Gladstone. A Silverton newspaper item quoted by Muriel Wolle in her book states that Cyrus Davis, president of the new railroad, brought engineers from Boston to lay it out. The map indicates there were several stream crossings and a total rise of over 1200 feet in the 7 1/2-mile length — from about 9275 to 10,510 feet.

The Cement Creek road turns off the Animas Canyon road a little east of Silverton, and keeps high on the hillside for a while before you begin to see the grade below you. Much of the line was still in evidence in 1970 in this middle and lower part of the

canyon, but after the road crosses to the west of the stream it appears to have covered much of the grade. The mine at Gladstone is still - or again - in operation. The canyon usually has considerable remnants of snowslides well into the summer.

The Corkscrew Gulch turntable near Ironton. (Denver Public Library)

The FARMINGTON BRANCH of the D&RG has a curious story told by Earl H. Ellis titled "Broad Gauge Trail on a Narrow Gauge Dog," showing why the Denver and Rio Grande company built standard gauge track to stave off threats of more than one competitive railroad to link the Durango coal area with their mining and transportation networks. This appeared in the Westerners Brand Book for 1954 (Volume 10). The D&RG plan included standard gauging the full line from Alamosa to Durango, and in a conversation with Colorado's long time Coal Inspector Tom Allen, I learned that he had conducted the survey for the realignment which would take the railroad through a Cumbres Pass tunnel.

One can find the separation of the branch line from the main one about 3 miles south of Durango and much of it is in evidence between where you drop off the mesa, and the town of Aztec. The best place to have a look, however, is where you are still on top of the mesa and can get a bird's eye view to the north. The reconstructed ruins at Aztec are a fringe benefit of this expedition.

The BOOK CLIFF RAILWAY. This company was organized

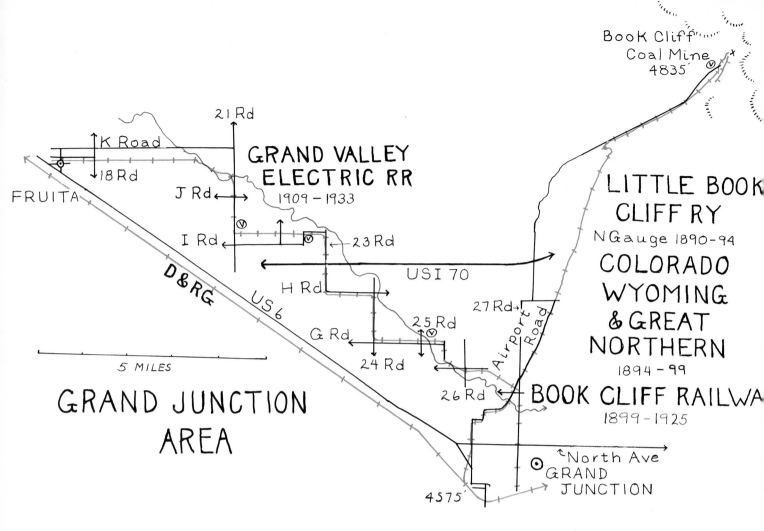

GRAND VALLEY ELECTRIC RR
1909-1933

LITTLE BOOK CLIFF RY
N Gauge 1890-94

COLORADO WYOMING & GREAT NORTHERN
1894-99

BOOK CLIFF RAILWAY
1899-1925

Book Cliff Coal Mine 4835'

21 Rd

K Road

18 Rd

FRUITA

J Rd

I Rd

23 Rd

D&RG

US 6

US I 70

H Rd

27 Rd

Airport Road

25 Rd

G Rd

24 Rd

26 Rd

North Ave

GRAND JUNCTION

4575'

5 MILES

GRAND JUNCTION AREA

The RGS, which never made money, drove past more picture country than any other in America - here the last train runs down past the Sneffels Range to its Ridgway home. (Abby Kernochan Collection)

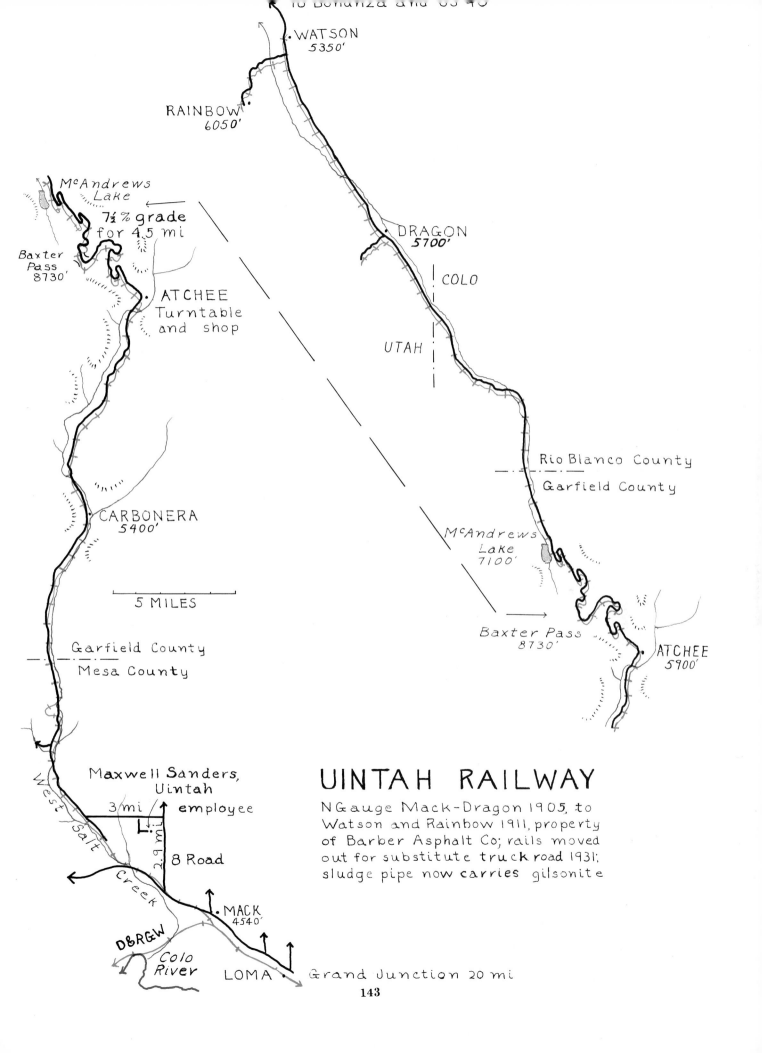

To Bonanza and US 40

WATSON
5350'

RAINBOW
6050'

DRAGON
5700'

COLO

UTAH

McAndrews
Lake
7100'

Baxter Pass
8730'

Rio Blanco County
Garfield County

ATCHEE
5900'

McAndrews
Lake

7½% grade
for 4.5 mi

Baxter
Pass
8730'

ATCHEE
Turntable
and shop

CARBONERA
5400'

5 MILES

Garfield County
Mesa County

Maxwell Sanders,
Uintah

3 mi employee

2.9 mi

8 Road

West Salt Creek

DBRGW

Colo
River

MACK
4540'

LOMA

Grand Junction 20 mi

UINTAH RAILWAY

N Gauge Mack-Dragon 1905, to
Watson and Rainbow 1911, property
of Barber Asphalt Co; rails moved
out for substitute truck road 1931;
sludge pipe now carries gilsonite

A Silverton train stops at Red Mountain. (Denver Public Library)

The railroad up Cement Creek. (State Historical Society)

in 1899 to acquire the property of the narrow-gauge Little Book Cliff Railway, which had spent second half of its ten years' existence as the running part of a more ambitious scheme called the Colorado Wyoming and Great Northern. The Book Cliff road was 11 or 12 miles long, and ran out from D&RG tracks in Grand Junction north and northeast to the Book Cliff Coal Mine, in the foothills under Book Cliff. The roadbed can still be seen as a low but perceptible ridge of the adobe where it crosses the west approach to Grand Junction's airport. Except for a kink about two-thirds of the way out it consists of tangents and very slight curves. The 1920 *Poor's Manual* reports it was not operated as a common carrier. The Book Cliff incorporation showed an intention to branch off from the existing Little Book Cliff Railroad and go to Douglass Creek Summit in Garfield County. This was considerably less of a scheme than the plan of the Colorado Wyoming and Great Northern, though it would have meant a line of some 50 miles. Purpose must have been tapping coal seams northwest of the Book Cliff Mine. A 1912 Grand Valley Project Map of the Reclamation Service shows the railroad's route over the glaring flats.

A load of coal from the Book Cliff. (Denver Public Library)

The mine area, which was situated in a gully on the sweeping skirt of the Book Cliffs, was a scene of frequent picnics. To return to town without the locomotive, both picnickers and miners made use of a monstrosity of unsafe travel known as the Go-Devil. This car consisted mainly of two coal car trucks and a connecting plank which served as the seat. My reporter tells me twelve people could straddle it at the beginning of a run, but braking on the line packed them so close there was soon room for four or five more at the back end. The kink on the line, which they called the Horseshoe, had a long history of pile-ups for these thrill riders, but no serious accidents seem to have happened. Once they made the Horseshoe they would cut loose and let the thing build up speed to fifty-five or sixty. There were two bona fide passenger cars for more staid affairs. The line may have owned up to four locomotives, but only two were in action most of the time — geared Shays with a vertical piston on one side. These had ample power for the hill. In its peak period the railroad had 50 odd cars. Mr. H. Hrika, who had retired to a peach and chicken farm not far from where the railroad goes

north out of Grand Junction, was an employee of the company. He was usually busy mining coal, but one time after a series of derailments the boss told him, :"Take a sack of fishplates and a wrench and put that railroad together again."

Mr. W.C. Kurtz, whose Kurtz-Biggs Hardware store is on the site of the Book Cliff station in Grand Junction, tells me that he and his partner bought the railroad in April, 1925, and dismantled it shortly afterward. They stored 30 cars and 600 tons of 30-pound rails at Grand Junction and afterward sold them to customers all over the country. The ties were given away for the hauling. One of the two passenger cars was open, with seats clear across, a favorite type for picnickers. Dismantling was done with a D&RG locomotive and a former D&RG engineer who had lost his job on account of a wreck. The crew were a group of ex-penitentiary convicts whose genius for destruction was a cause of rejoicing to the owners.

The road never paid; there was much better coal close to the tracks of the D&RG near Palisade. The Mr. Philips, who owned this property and a whole lot more that was better, left it to Princeton University. Occasion for closing the railroad was a fire which broke out in the mine. Princeton agents spent considerable sums trying to seal off the fire and still preserve the coal, but were not successful. The whole mine was sealed later and has remained so. The Kurtz-Biggs purchase was made to obtain downtown real estate which the partners had leased from Mr. Philips.

There is a write-up of the road in Volume 39, No. 4 of the *Colorado Magazine.* The number of things in Grand Junction named Book Cliff so and so attest to the affection the town had for their little railroad. To find the interesting upper end, drive to the airport and take H Road west until you come to 27¼ Road (road numbers are distances from the Utah line) and go generally north on a dust-or-mud road with a couple of short-wheel-base only ravine crossings. An openable fence gate at mile 5 from H Road will let you down right (east) into some of the upper end of the grade, but the main road you are on continues north another mile. There you meet the grade and walk it the last tenth of a mile. The mine itself goes through tilted layers of buff colored sandstone to meet the coal seam within.

The GRAND VALLEY ELECTRIC began operations in 1909 in Grand Junction as the Grand Junction and Grand River Valley Railway, and completed the line to Fruita the following year. It was renamed the Grand River Railway in 1914, and in a second reorganization in 1926 it was officially named the Grand River Valley Railroad Company, but called the Grand Valley Electric. It was owned before 1926 by Spencer Penrose and associates with the general office in Colorado Springs. As these owners also had an interest in the Uintah it would seem that despite the Grand Valley's right angle turns on or parallel to section lines, they thought of putting together a longer railroad system. The road was operated until 1933 and removed by 1935.

A curious experience of the hunt for this railroad was running into a truss bridge on I Road that looked as though it must have been moved there from the nearby track line. The grade is usually evident where it does not coincide with presently used roads.

The UINTAH RAILWAY COMPANY ran from Mack, Colorado to Waston, Utah, 68 miles, over narrow-gauge track. It was incorporated by William N. Vaile and others November 4, 1903, to be operated from a Denver office. Its primary function was to bring gilsonite from around Watson to the D&RG. It was finished as far as Dragon on February, 1905, and the last 15 miles added in 1911, all as originally described: from two miles west of Crevasse (Mack is 2 miles northwest of Crevasse) north up West Salt Creek Wash to its source; thence over the Book Cliffs to the west fork of Evacuation Creek and down it through the west Colorado line in Rio Blanco County to Watson. Control was in the hands of the Barber Asphalt Paving Company. Other shippers from mines at Dragon, Watson and Rainbow were the American and the Utah Asphalt companies.

A firm ruin at Atchee.

Fourth of July on the Uintah. (Courtesy Ben O'Dell)

Mr. Mack, for whom the Uintah's terminus of Mack on the D&RG was named, was president of the Barber Asphalt Company. Gilsonite was named for a Barber Company engineer, and Baxter Pass for an engineer who came to this project from a tour at the Panama Canal.

The 30-pound rail used at first was replaced by 40-pound and later by 60-pound on the mountain. A Major Hood was killed a little way out of Mack when a rail crystalized and broke. The line which runs generally through rimrock canons can be driven in a car. It is a dusty trip and would be impossible in wet weather. Points of interest are Lake McAndrews on the Utah side — in early days a picnic excursion spot — and the locomotive shop, roofless but still standing, at Atchee on the Colorado side. Baldwin engineers designed special locomotives to wrap around the sharp curves like the one which surprises motorists at Moro Castle, a rock outcrop a little above Atchee.

Curves went up to 67% (later slightly reduced) and grades to 7% on the Colorado side. The largest locomotive, a side-rod numbered 30, which was designed for hauling gilsonite up the west side, had to be brought up the east side as freight in order to negotiate the curves. The 1970 book *The Uintah Railroad* by

Harry E. Bender covers the story of the line. The Barber Asphalt describe other phases of their operation in a 1957 book *The Story of Gilsonite*. This product is so flammable that the least sort of spark can ignite it. We are told of an explosion in the Dragon Mine which blew heavy timbers a distance of 3 miles. Explosions have been eliminated: gilsonite is now mined by high pressure hoses which enter the seams and crack it, and it is piped over Baxter Pass in a slurry (crumbs and water).

Carbonera, where twenty coal miners worked and lived with their families, has nothing to see, but at Atchee the sturdy walls were still standing around a roofless shop. The drive follows the railroad most of the way.

Oh, for the good old days.

146

PART VI
ADDITIONS AND CORRECTIONS

MAPS

FOREWARD FOR THE AFTERWARD

A second printing of this book called for (1) correction and expansion of the Index, (2) inclusion of some material which had not found its way into the first printing, and (3) the addition of some material suggested or brought to light by readers. I am grateful to these last. Some of their queries and comments have sent me back to explore and inquire further - in the books, among fellow railroaders, and best of all in the field.

Jackson Thode, long time member of the Rio Grande family and their historian, has given me a great deal of help in all Rio Grande matters.

ERRATA

The first printing refers to the Rocky Mountain Railroad Club as the Colorado Railroad Club. My apologies: the latter does not exist; the former has a long record of progress in preserving railroadiana, in sponsoring and aiding publication, and in scheduling informative programs and trips.

Properly the name of Toltec Scenic Railroad used in maps and script of this book is the Cumbres and Toltec Scenic Railroad.

Page 12, column 1 line 6 should read late '20's

Page 90, key in upper left corner - last item: Graded only

Page 95 map of Golden Circle S-Gauge 1917-1919 instead of - 1949

The Silverton Northern clears track after a spring snow. [Photo courtesy of H.H. Burt].

Slides and fires played havoc on the Cunningham Gulch Branch of the Silverton Northern [Photo courtesy of H.H. Burt].

The SANTA FE abandoned and removed its trackage through Colorado Springs in 1975 in agreements with that city and with the Rio Grande. The Santa Fe now shares the Rio Grande trackage between Crews, 13½ miles south of the city, and Palmer Lake. The two roads are continuing the paired track operations north and south of this section. Joint operation began in 1918 with the elimination of four crossovers between the two roads - Sedalia, Spruce (northeast of Palmer Lake), Fountain, and Bragdon, (north of Pueblo.) This is a verbal revision of the maps on page 18 and 90.

The DENVER AND RIO GRANDE has left ghost railroad stretches on its present main line through realignments, some of which did not show in our first printing. These include some along the upper Arkansas, two along the Colorado, and one on the Gunnison.

The top map on page 102 does show the main change on the upper Arkansas - from the present route of U.S. 285 west of the river to an east side tangent. Lesser changes seem to have been made farther up the river: at Harvard, where Highway 82 leaves U.S. 24 for Twin Lakes, the railroad moved its east to west (northbound) crossing to a point about half a mile south of where it had crossed formerly. There is a place where the D&RG line seems to have been superimposed on the Midland grade - this 3½ miles farther north, where an abutment shows the Midland crossed to the west side. These changes were made in 1922.

Four D&RG abandonments for realignment have been added to the book in this edition. One is the long, curvaceous mileage between Mack, near the Utah line, and Cisco, Utah. Another is the segment between Pueblo and Swallows, which is being slowly inundated as the water in Pueblo Reservoir rises. The dam, 200 feet high and two miles long, will impound 357,000 acre feet of water. The new track is slightly shorter than that along the river. Virtually the whole line between Canon City and Pueblo - 41 miles - was washed out and rebuilt in 1921.

The remnant of the river grade is reached from the start of Colorado 96, and when the reservoir is not full you can get in to some of the parts between Swallows and Pueblo on secondary roads, some serving ditches. Though I have not been over all this ground I understand the river is more accessible from this south side than from the north.

I learn from Mr. Ed Haley, railroad cartographer extraordinary, that the maximum height of the water will be 4893 feet above sea level, which would make it 129 feet deep in the deepest place.

The third addition is a short one but long discussed by the Rio Grande officials. A sharply bending track west of Rifle is replaced by the Webster Hill realignment. This involved a cut up to 120 feet deep and 4000 feet long, and 800,000 cubic feet of fill. New track, 4.02 miles long replaces 5.35 miles of old, and the staightening increases permissible speed from 35 to 75 miles per hour in an otherwise high speed part of the railroad. As both highway and railroad are on the same side of the river it should be possible to get a look into the new line and perhaps to walk the old one.

Fourth, the D&RG tunneled a cutoff near Bridgeport, between Delta and Grand Junction. To see the place you go down to the Gunnison River from US 50 on the Dominguez Canyon road. A slight change, not mapped, also came in the same year - 1884 - at Roubideau, where a new bridge was put in. To have a look, drive out of Delta on 5th Street, keeping straight west. About 4 miles from the main street - US 50 - where your road turns south to leave the tracks, you have a walk of ¾ mile west to the replacement bridge.

The CALUMET BRANCH of the D&RG was revisited, this time for a full-length walk. Some pictures, a few spikes and a fine day, ending with a wet raft-crossing of the swollen Arkansas to repossess the car we had left there. The grade reached 7.7%, which meant that the crown sheet, between fire and boiler, would be dry and burn out unless it was tilted and the locomotive kept facing the same direction both climbing and descending.

The BLUE RIVER BRANCH of the D&RG, graded somewhat intermittently between old Dillon and Kremmling, has been included with the help of some knowledgeable ranchers - the Yusts at the north end and the two Knorr brothers in the upper part. There is more than one grade in two or three places, indicating that the Union Pacific, through the Denver South Park and Pacific, was playing the same game. Some of the grade climbing toward Green Mountain Divide is visible in the spring when the reservoir level drops; more can be seen - in disconnected spots - looking east from the highway, beginning a half mile north of the same divide, and running intermittently down to near Harsh Creek. Down near the Colorado River the Yust Ranch has some in a meadow not far from the house, and Mr. Yust tells me some more can be seen along the Colorado.

The CREEDE BRANCH of the D&RG, according to Mr. Westcott, extended farther up the right or east fork of Willow Creek than the map indicates.

The TAYLOR PARK RAILROAD, discovered only as a tunnel mouth by Francis Rizzari some years ago, is the subject of a researched article in Volume 45 of the *Colorado Magazine*. Along with it is a map of the founders' fullsome intentions.

The SILVERTON NORTHERN BRANCH in Cunningham Gulch, Mr. H.H. Burt tells me, ran along close to the stream and is probably washed out of existence. If so, too bad, for that was another place where the Jeffery spike was used.

The BROADMOOR MOUNTAINEER was moved, bodily to Telluride in 1974. It had to be moved out of the way of the growing hotel complex, but the grade is still visible as it moves up Cheyenne Mountain slopes toward the zoo.

The DENVER SOUTH PARK AND PACIFIC, Mr. Westcott reminds us, had an earlier grade down Trout Creek than the one shown - in practically the same place as the one shown but buried in the mud and sand beneath. Perhaps there are no remnants of that, but anyone can enjoy a short but sweet trip through the gorge which ends Trout Creek's descent to the Arkansas. A dirt road, very sketchy, takes you down hill from pretty near the same place where the signed road for the Midland Scenic Drive goes north off U.S. 24 (in the opposite direction). Leaving the car near the stream bed you walk down between rock walls where remanants of the old grade seem to hang in the air above you.

For the MANITOU PARK LOGGING RAILROAD there is an additional item of interest - a page in Volume II of the La Massena *Colorado's Mountain Railroads*. Page 13 will tell you how the locomotive was hauled up Ute Pass in wagons to serve in the isolated lumber operation.

The DENVER AND SALT LAKE climb over Rollins Pass now starts directly on grade from Tolland in the valley instead of by a short cut, and Mr. Linn Westcott tells me there is the "beginning of tunnel construction at Yankee Doodle Lake running at right angles to the D&SL grade."

The BALD MOUNTAIN RAILROAD is perhaps my favorite piece of new business. Linn Westcott, editor of *Modern Railroader* and the cartographer for the invaluable old Kalmbach map of **Colorado's Railroads**, wrote in his letter "...when I rode over the line about 10 years ago in the La Veta Pass area, I think I recall seeing what I then assumed was the narrow gauge line at a somewhat lower level than the present main line somewhere near Oakview and doubling back in the canyon of Middle Creek..." This was not, he found the old line which was much further north than Middle Creek.

Drive into the town of La Veta, 16 miles west of Walsenburg via US 160. From a north end street drive west past the post office. Leave the hardtop to go straight west at mile 2, the Middle Creek Road. The present D&RG line, which you have crossed, and lost, will reappear on your left. About mile 4½ a branch-off grade, not in use, comes toward the creek between you and the main line. Around mile 5 it jumps the creek bed where there was a trestle, and heads off up the flat valley toward your right, gently S-curving around northwest to the Oakview Mine. On the far side of this Oakview valley you come to Robert Andreoli's house. You should ask permission to go on if he is there; if he isn't, proceed a mile farther west to the other house, where Gino Andreoli and their sister Mrs. Andrietta live. At this point, with permission, you can drive directly north .4 mile on a sketchy road until you come to the grade near the mines in an open grass clearing, or you can drive directly west up Middle Creek Canyon and see the middle part of the grade.

Two visits - one to each end of the line - gave me some pictures, enough information for a correct map, and some trophies - spikes of three lengths but all extra stocky, a rail joint, a washer, and a tie plate helpfully dated 1901. Much of the grade is on steep hilside and supported by dry-wall; there had been several trestles curving across ravines and the main canyon, and perhaps most surprising of all, the first grade I had seen in the mountain country that stayed on the same contour almost all the distance between the mines and the transfer point on the D&RG.

On the KANSAS-COLORADO RAILROAD map on page 21, Myrtle belongs where you see Stone City, and Stone City about where the northbound road from U.S. 50 reaches Booth Creek. In the second paragraph on this railroad, page 17, Beaver Creek Ranch and Beaver Creek should both read Turkey Creek.

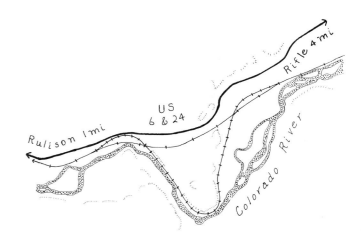

D&RG WEBSTER HILL
REALIGNMENT 1969

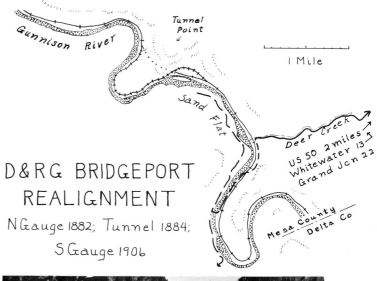

D&RG BRIDGEPORT
REALIGNMENT
N Gauge 1882; Tunnel 1884;
S Gauge 1906

This guard house dates back to the strike associated with the Ludlow Massacre. It commands a view of the Oakview Mine.

This bridge, at the confluence of the old narrow gauge La Veta Pass line and the present route, is almost the only visible remnant of the former.

Mr. Westcott remembers the Creede Branch extended farther up the right fork of the stream above town than the map indicates. Our photograph shows a road wye on that of the grade.

149

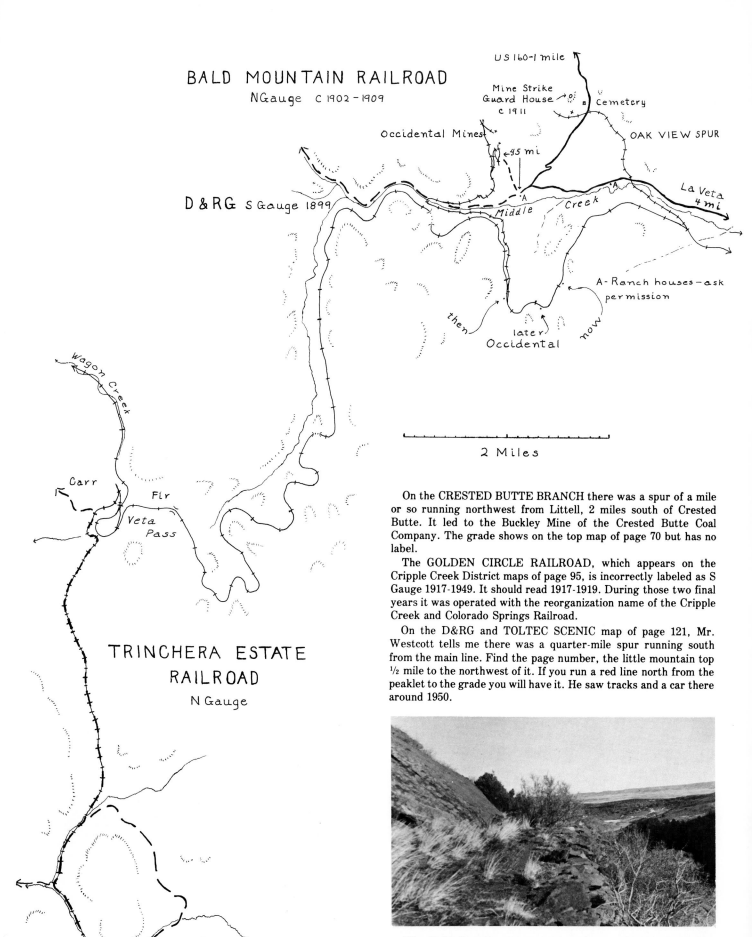

BALD MOUNTAIN RAILROAD
N Gauge C 1902-1909

US 160-1 mile

Mine Strike
Guard House
c 1911

Cemetery

Occidental Mines

OAK VIEW SPUR

←45 mi

D & RG S Gauge 1899

"A"

La Veta
4 mi

Middle   Creek

A-Ranch houses—ask
permission

then

later
Occidental

now

2 Miles

Wagon Creek

Carr

Fir

Veta
Pass

TRINCHERA ESTATE
RAILROAD
N Gauge

Saw mill

On the CRESTED BUTTE BRANCH there was a spur of a mile or so running northwest from Littell, 2 miles south of Crested Butte. It led to the Buckley Mine of the Crested Butte Coal Company. The grade shows on the top map of page 70 but has no label.

The GOLDEN CIRCLE RAILROAD, which appears on the Cripple Creek District maps of page 95, is incorrectly labeled as S Gauge 1917-1949. It should read 1917-1919. During those two final years it was operated with the reorganization name of the Cripple Creek and Colorado Springs Railroad.

On the D&RG and TOLTEC SCENIC map of page 121, Mr. Westcott tells me there was a quarter-mile spur running south from the main line. Find the page number, the little mountain top ½ mile to the northwest of it. If you run a red line north from the peaklet to the grade you will have it. He saw tracks and a car there around 1950.

The Bald Mountain had a comfortable roadbed on a steep mountainside.

150

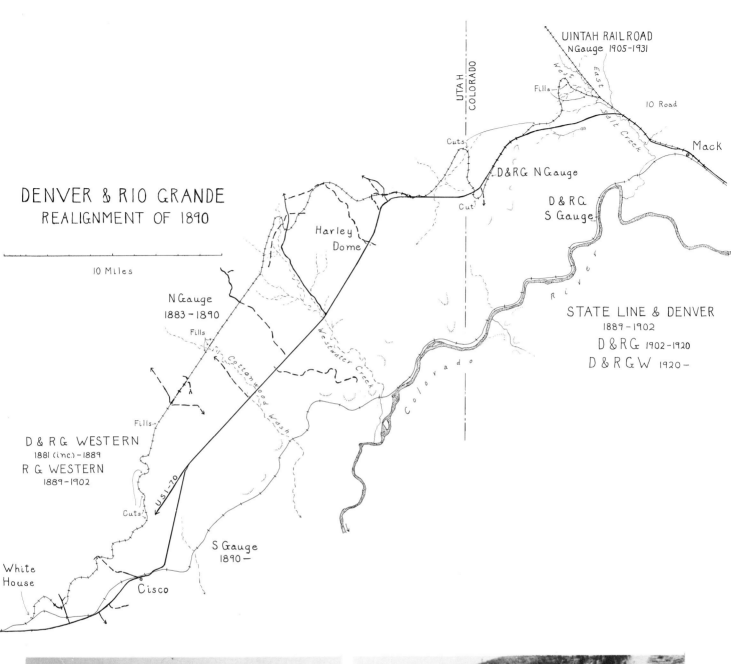

DENVER & RIO GRANDE
REALIGNMENT OF 1890

10 Miles

UINTAH RAILROAD
N Gauge 1905-1931

Fills

10 Road

Mack

UTAH
COLORADO

Cuts

D&RG N Gauge

Cut

D & RG
S Gauge

Harley
Dome

N Gauge
1883-1890

Fills

River

Westwater Creek

Cottonwood Wash

Colorado

STATE LINE & DENVER
1889-1902
D & RG 1902-1920
D & R G W 1920-

D & R G WESTERN
1881 (inc.) -1889
R G WESTERN
1889-1902

Fills

U.S.1-70

Cuts

S Gauge
1890 -

White
House

Cisco

The Bald Mountain leaves Middle Creek through a handsome cut.

Bald Mountain trackage edges slowly toward the higher Rio Grande. The gap in the former was trestled.

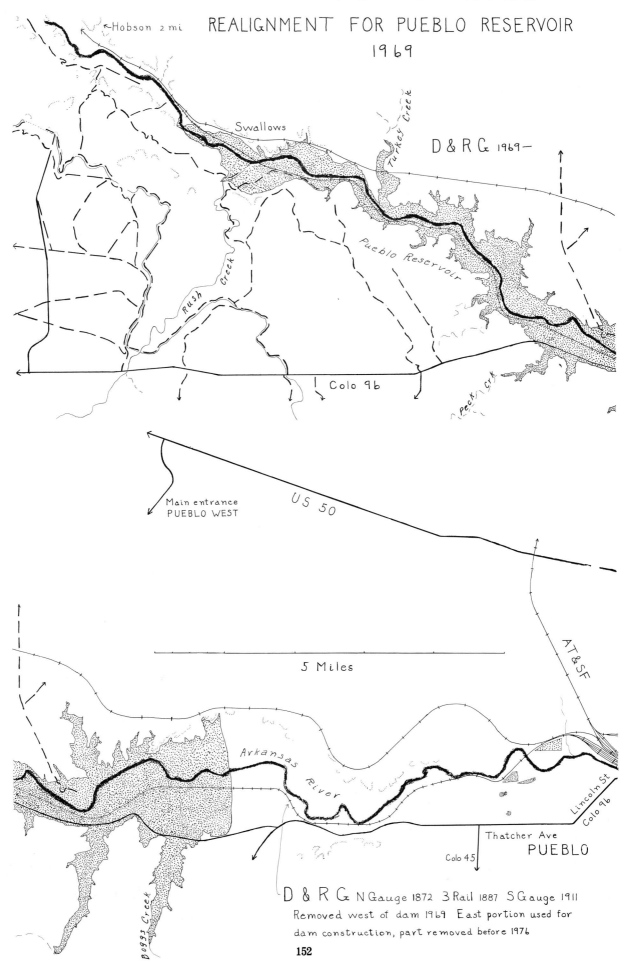

DENVER & RIO GRANDE
REALIGNMENT FOR PUEBLO RESERVOIR
1969

← Hobson 2 mi

Swallows

Turkey Creek

D & R G 1969 —

Pueblo Reservoir

Rush Creek

Colo 96

Peck's Crk

Main entrance
PUEBLO WEST

US 50

AT&SF

5 Miles

Arkansas River

Lincoln St
Colo 96

Thatcher Ave
PUEBLO

Colo 45

Boggs Creek

D & R G N Gauge 1872 3 Rail 1887 S Gauge 1911
Removed west of dam 1969 East portion used for
dam construction, part removed before 1976

152

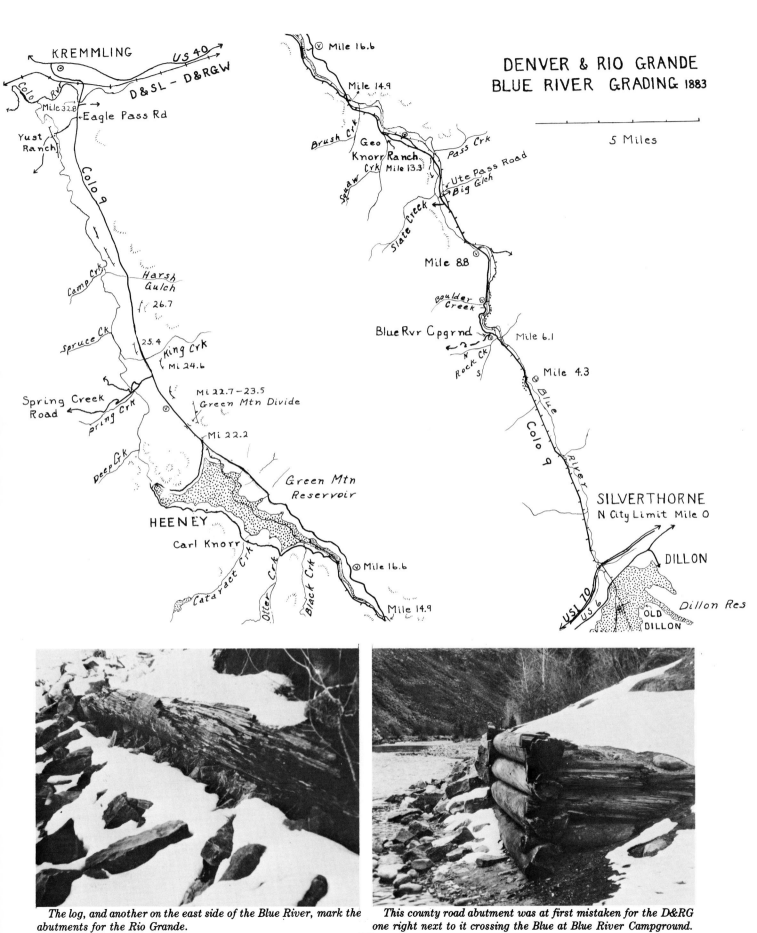

KREMMLING

US 40

D&SL – D&RGW

Mile 32.8

Eagle Pass Rd

Colo Rvr

Colo

Yust Ranch

Colo 9

Camp Crk

Harsh Gulch

Spruce Ck

26.7

25.4

King Crk
Mi 24.6

Spring Creek Road

Spring Crk

Deep Crk

Mi 22.7 – 23.5
Green Mtn Divide

Mi 22.2

HEENEY

Carl Knorr

Cataract Crk

Otter Crk

Black Crk

Green Mtn Reservoir

Mile 16.6

Mile 14.9

Mile 16.6

Mile 14.9

Brush Crk

Geo Knorr Ranch

Squaw Crk

Mile 13.3

Pass Crk

Ute Pass Road

Big Glch

Slate Creek

Mile 8.8

Boulder Creek

Blue Rvr Cpgrnd

N Rock Ck S

Mile 6.1

Mile 4.3

Blue River

Colo 9

DENVER & RIO GRANDE
BLUE RIVER GRADING 1883

5 Miles

SILVERTHORNE
N City Limit Mile 0

DILLON

Dillon Res

US 70   US 6

OLD DILLON

The log, and another on the east side of the Blue River, mark the abutments for the Rio Grande.

This county road abutment was at first mistaken for the D&RG one right next to it crossing the Blue at Blue River Campground.

153

This bridge belongs about 60 yards upstream, on the Calumet Branch.

Through the narrows with a passenger load (from the collection of Dr. Lester Williams).

The grade kept to river level; the old county road climbed over the humps: this is the scene from near the mouth of Boulder Creek.

George Knorr, long time Blue River rancher, stands on the fill where the D&RG would have crossed the stream at Blue River Campground.

INDEX
Boldfaced Numbers Refer to Maps

MAP REVISION SECTION

Most of the revisions below were made with the help of Tom Daniels of the Colorado Midland Chapter of the Railway Locomotive and Historical Society. The page number refers to that of the map being revised or complemented.

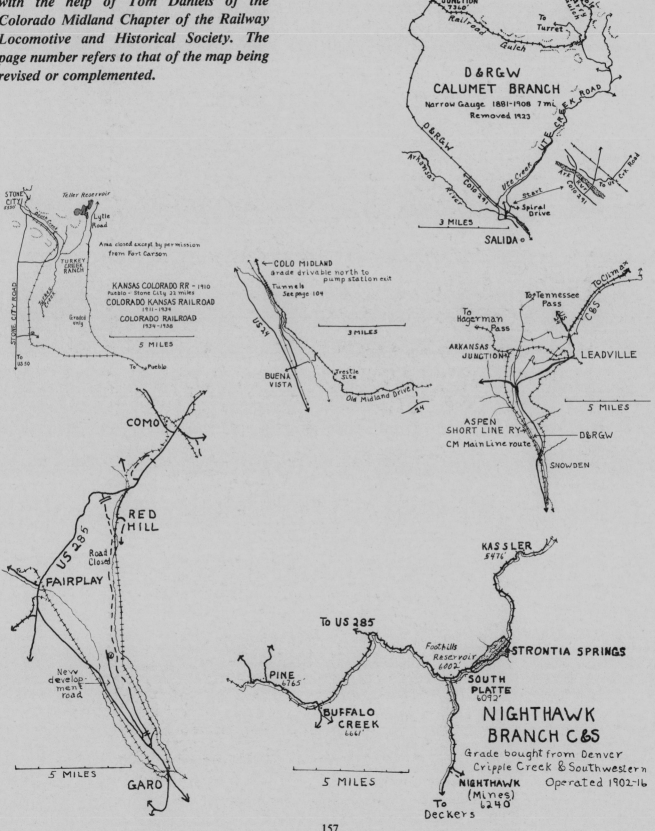

D & RGW CALUMET BRANCH
Narrow Gauge 1881-1908 7 mi.
Removed 1923

KANSAS COLORADO RR - 1910
Pueblo - Stone City 22 miles
COLORADO KANSAS RAILROAD
1911-1934
COLORADO RAILROAD
1934-1938

NIGHTHAWK BRANCH C&S
Grade bought from Denver
Cripple Creek & Southwestern
Operated 1902-16

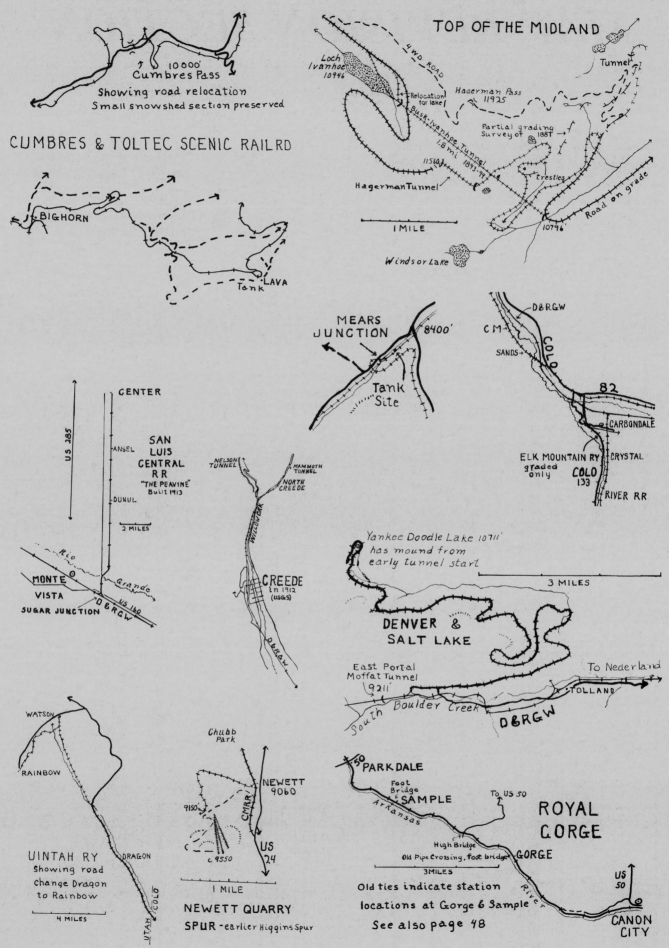

CUMBRES & TOLTEC SCENIC RAILRD

10000'
Cumbres Pass
Showing road relocation
Small snowshed section preserved

BIGHORN

Tank LAVA

TOP OF THE MIDLAND

4 WD ROAD

Loch Ivanhoe 10946
Relocation for lake
Hagerman Pass 11925
Busk-Ivanhoe Tunnel 1.8 mi 1893-94
Partial grading Survey of 1887
Tunnel
11500
Hagerman Tunnel
Trestles
Road on grade
1 MILE
10796'
Windsor Lake

MEARS JUNCTION
8400'
Tank Site

D&RGW
CM
COLO
SANDS
82
CARBONDALE
ELK MOUNTAIN RY graded only
CRYSTAL
COLO 133
RIVER RR

CENTER

US 285

ANSEL

SAN LUIS CENTRAL RR
"THE PEAVINE"
Built 1913

DUNUL

2 MILES

NELSON TUNNEL
MAMMOTH TUNNEL
NORTH CREEDE
WILLOW CR
CREEDE in 1912 (USGS)
D&RGW

RIO
MONTE VISTA
SUGAR JUNCTION
Grande
D&RGW
US 160

Yankee Doodle Lake 10711'
has mound from
early tunnel start
3 MILES

DENVER & SALT LAKE

East Portal Moffat Tunnel 9211'
To Nederland
TOLLAND
South Boulder Creek
D&RGW

WATSON

RAINBOW

UINTAH RY
Showing road
change Dragon
to Rainbow

4 MILES

DRAGON
UTAH COLO

Chubb Park

9150'
NEWETT 9060
CM RR
US 24
c 9550
1 MILE

NEWETT QUARRY
SPUR - earlier Higgins Spur

50 PARK DALE
Foot Bridge
SAMPLE
To US 50
Arkansas
ROYAL GORGE
High Bridge
Old Pipe Crossing, foot bridge
GORGE
3 MILES
US 50
River
Old ties indicate station
locations at Gorge & Sample
See also page 48
CANON CITY

158

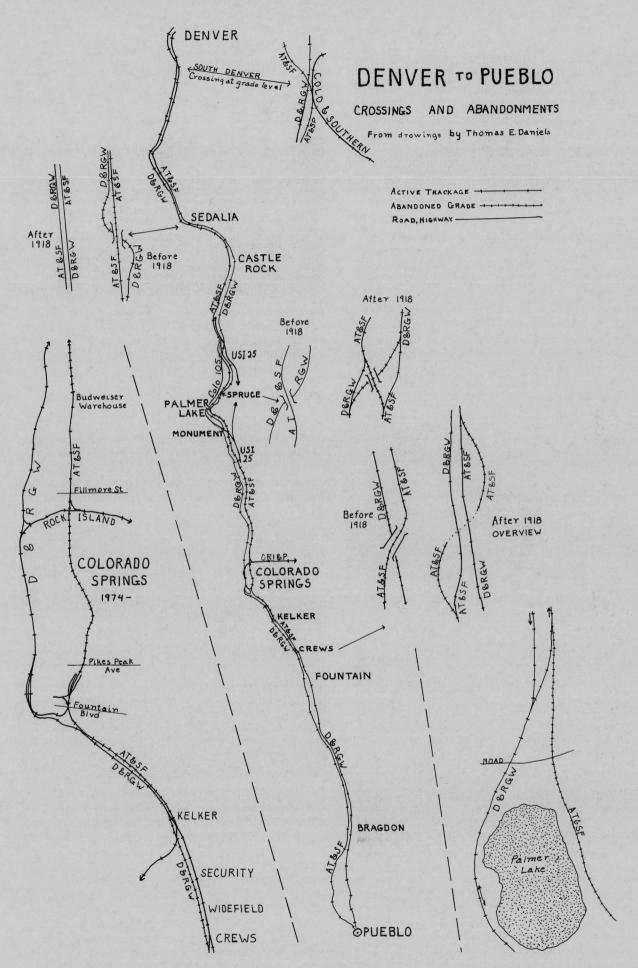

DENVER TO PUEBLO
CROSSINGS AND ABANDONMENTS
From drawings by Thomas E. Daniels

ACTIVE TRACKAGE
ABANDONED GRADE
ROAD, HIGHWAY

DENVER

SOUTH DENVER
Crossing at grade level

AT&SF
D&RGW
COLO & SOUTHERN

D&RGW AT&SF
After 1918
AT&SF D&RGW

D&RGW AT&SF
Before 1918
AT&SF D&RGW

AT&SF
D&RGW

SEDALIA

CASTLE ROCK

AT&SF
D&RGW

USI 25

Colo. 105

SPRUCE

PALMER LAKE

MONUMENT

USI 25

D&RGW AT&SF

Before 1918
D&E&SF
AT&RGW

After 1918
AT&SF D&RGW
D&RGW AT&SF

Budweiser Warehouse

D&RGW
AT&SF

Fillmore St.

ROCK ISLAND

COLORADO SPRINGS
1974-

Pikes Peak Ave

Fountain Blvd

AT&SF
D&RGW

KELKER

SECURITY

D&RGW

WIDEFIELD

CREWS

CRI&P

COLORADO SPRINGS

KELKER
AT&SF
D&RGW
CREWS

FOUNTAIN

D&RGW

AT&SF

BRAGDON

PUEBLO

Before 1918
D&RGW AT&SF
AT&SF D&RGW

After 1918
D&RGW AT&SF
AT&SF D&RGW

After 1918
OVERVIEW

ROAD
D&RGW
AT&SF

Palmer Lake

The station at Monument was for a time that of the D&RG. An Otto Perry photo in the Denver Public Library Western History Department collection. Rivalry with the Santa Fe people caused the D&RG to fence off its Palmer Lake Depot and the complementary in-the-lake dance floor from the view of Santa Fe passengers, who could only hear the music and wonder what was going on.

The Colorado Midland Station in Manitou Springs was built to stay. The purchaser remodeled and enlarged it in similar style and of late years its occupants have been Nelson Hunt and his western history writer wife, Inez Hunt. Many a station has had a second existence as a well-built home.

Leadville's Union Pacific Passenger Depot served under other corporate names as well. It was one time the Denver South Park and Pacific earlier, and the Colorado & Southern later. Photo of the Denver Public Library Western History Department.

Alpine, close to the Alpine tunnel's west portal, had a busy if lonely and wintry station, its short span of life enough to give gray hairs to those who maintained its activities. Denver Public Library Western History Department, collection of Harold Seely. To get the feel of life up there one should read the tunnel book by Dow Helmers.

The D&RGW station at Grand Junction, a white brick building with rounded second story windows, has been recently refurbished with a red rust trimmed in gold. While the second story is leased by the telephone company, the first is all used by the railroad for ticket office, freight office, baggage room and waiting space. The affection with which the railroad people regard their station is shown in a sign over the doorway labeling it as the Puffer-belly station — this from an old song of the steam locomotive days reading "See the little puffer-bellies all in a row." The south (right) end was once for Railway Express but now houses a store. McClure photo of the Denver Public Library Western History Department.

Denver's Union Station in 1881. This grand long pile had its shoulder pieces taken off and retains little of its fresh and spacious air. The Denver Chapter of the Rocky Mountain Railroad Club meets in the building. From the Harold Seely Collection.

The Union Station at Pueblo is one of those designated a historic landmark. Once a Harvey House combination, it now serves a mixture of railroad and non-railroad functions, being the center for the Western Weighing and Inspection Bureau, a housing place for railroad personnel, and the home of a school and a poetry establishment. Photo from Harold Seely Collection.

The large succesor Santa Fe station in Colorado Springs, showing exit for passenger to station subway. This building is in process of remodeling for a variety of business offices.

The station and Harvey House at La Junta was typical of the Santa Fe's system of running first class hostelries in connection with their depots. From a colored postcard dated Sept. 1, 1920, Collection of Harold Seely.

The 1888 Santa Fe Station in Colorado Springs was of stone — as attractive and permanent-looking a building as you could ask for. But as passenger traffic rose it had to give way. Harold Seely Photo from Western History Department, Penrose Public Library.

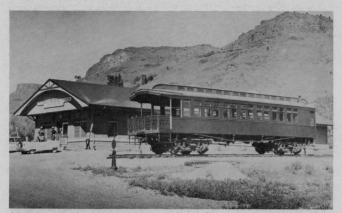

Museum and passenger car.

Locomotive 318 with tender and caboose.

Locomotive 346 with short freight train.

5629 a 4-8-8 built in 1940.

Ticket Office interior.

The COLORADO RAILROAD MUSEUM *began as a small collection of rolling stock and lesser items attached to a roadside motel in the San Luis Valley a few miles from Alamosa. Mr. Bob Richardson, one of the partners in this venture, bought out the railroad part and moved it to the present location, 17155 West 44th Avenue, Golden. The museum, suggesting in its architecture a typical town railroad station, houses a considerable library and research facility, all sorts of lamps, photographs, timetables and other small treasures and in the basement an elaborate operating model railroad which is turned on at announced times for visitors. The museum property of twelve acres has a diverse collection of large and small locomotives, trolley cars, freight and passenger cars, some of them famous, standing about to be studied and admired, along with such smaller items as baggage carts, benches, and switches.*

Mr. Richardson and his partner Cornelius W. Hauck started the Golden venture in 1958 and since 1967 it has been operated by a non-profit organization known as the Colorado Railroad Historical Foundation. An early publication of the Museum called The Iron Horse *was succeeded by* The Colorado Annual *1963, which has been followed by another each year since.*

The Antero, west of Nathrop on the Denver South Park and Pacific's Chalk Creek line leading to the Alpine Tunnel. From the George White Collection.

Cascade, a short way up Ute Pass from Colorado Springs, had its Cascade House just back of the train stop, and a short block west the more elegant Ramona Hotel of David N. Heizer, the town's main early day promoter. From the George White Collection.

Also in Ute Pass, about where Chipeta Park centers today, was the Ute, or Ute Pass Park Hotel. From the George White Collection.

No expense was spared in the building of Gunnison's famous railroad hotel, the La Veta. For so modest a town it was a princely mass of finery and hardwood. From the George White Collection the photo is dated July 1944.

Como, a round house town on the Denver South Park and Pacific, had its Pacific House for passengers who liked the open spaces of South Park. From the George White Collection.

The SILVERTON BRANCH of the D&RGW was detached from its Antonito to Durango connection with Denver in 1968. A narrow gauge, steam powered line since its completion in 1882, it continues in reasonable health as a scenic passenger railroad. Traffic figures for the decade 1970-79 show 948,101 passengers. Negotiations are presently going on related to a transfer of ownership to a company whose central interest is its preservation as a tourist and railroad buff attraction. We understand that the price of $2.2 million would be right if the railroad were not forced by its abandonment to provide a six-year severance payment to each of its employees.

Recent years have seen two fully packed trains a day, running an hour apart, on the Durango-Silverton round trip. For reservations write to the Ticket Agent, D&RG Railroad or successor, Durango, CO 81301.

Some of Colorado's steepest and roughest peaks line the route along the Animas Canyon. Climbers with their back packs and ice axes often fill the baggage car en route to Elk Creek or Needle Creek.

On this stretch the trains must take to the cliffs to get through the gorge.

The CUMBRES AND TOLTEC SCENIC RAILWAY, mentioned and mapped on pages 119, 121 and 122, celebrates in the 1980 season the 100th anniversary of track laying on the line. Regular passenger service was discontinued by the D&RGW about 1951 and all traffic ended in 1968. The scenic part of the line, included in the 46 miles between Antonito and Chama, was purchased by the states of New Mexico and Colorado. It has been run by Scenic Railways, Inc., a California Company, under the supervision of a two-state commission since 1971. Except for some snow clearance excursions with a rotary plough — open to a few hardy rail fans — operations are limited to the summer season from about mid-June to mid-October.

The 1980 season changes from a four to a five day schedule — Friday through Tuesday — with a train starting from each end. The New Mexico Express climbs the 4% grade from Chama to Cumbress Pass and on to Osier and return for a 52 mile round trip. The Colorado Limited climbs less steeply from Antonito past the Toltec Gorge to Osier for a 76 mile round trip. A full length one-way ride is open to those who have reserved transfer tickets and make use of both trains. For reservations and information address the railroad at Box 789, Chama, NM, 87520, or at Box 668, Antonito, CO 81120. You will receive a brochure in color that is itself a souvenir.

The management, housed at Chama, has a peak employment of about 40 persons. There have been grants to help the project survive heavy costs. The project has profited from the use of its trains in several movies and TV commercials.

The snow shed, vital in the days of year-round operations, has been reduced by decay to a fraction of the original length, but this remainder is due for some restorative attention. Each of the past two seasons has seen about 75 trains carry around 30,000 passengers.

Engine No. 483 is one of the 2-8-2 or Mikado type locomotives built by Baldwin in 1925. It weighs 143 tons loaded with coal and water. The passengers are comfortably fitted into nine converted box cars and a gondola.